faith and the Magic Kingdom

by Randy Crane

Leaving Conformity Coaching

To my mom, Kay, who saw this project begin while she was on this side of heaven, and completed while on the other side. Also to my dad, Rodney, my wife, Faye, and my cater-cousin, Andy. Without you, this journey would not have been possible.

Advance Praise for *Faith and the Magic Kingdom*

Randy's delightful (and insightful) book made me want to do two things: (1) Go back to Disneyland with new eyes, and (2) completely immerse myself in the wonder of being God's child, surrounded by His infinite care and incredible design. This is a new kind of Pilgrim's Progress—through the Magic Kingdom to the Eternal Kingdom.

  Larry Winger, CEO, Provision Ministry Group

Walt Disney created one of the most well-loved places in the world, a part of the fabric of society, when Disneyland opened in 1955. Throughout its history, though, most people have seen it as simply an impressive "amusement enterprise." In *Faith and the Magic Kingdom*, Randy does an exceptional job of taking this familiar and fanciful place and showing it to be so much more, drawing from it practical lessons and valuable reminders for a dynamic life of faith. If you're a fan of Disneyland and a Christian, this book is a must-read!

  Pat Williams, Orlando Magic cofounder and Senior Vice President, author of *How to Be Like Walt*

Randy Crane has masterly woven the story of Disney to the story of Scripture to our story. He presents unique perspectives of Disney's history to biblical application in today's world. You will find his writing engaging, educational, and encouraging as the Magic Kingdom connects our faith to the Kingdom of God.

  Dr. Joseph C. Grana II, Dean, Pacific Christian College of Ministry & Biblical Studies

Randy Crane ingeniously provides what amounts to a Disneyland Devotional, drawing spiritual lessons from life inside the Magic Kingdom to improve our walk with Christ. He uses the attractions, the architecture, the parades, the cast members, the characters, nearly everything about "The Happiest Place on Earth" as the springboard for solid, accessible biblical teaching.

David Koenig, author of *Mouse Tales: A Behind-the-Ears Look at Disneyland*

If Disneyland is just a fun place for you to go and nothing more, this book will inspire you to "look harder!" I love *Faith and the Magic Kingdom* because it ties in my faith and my passion for Disney. In fact, it gave me many great things to think about and reflect on. I thought I'd seen it all, but with this book, Randy has opened my eyes to a whole new way of thinking about one of my favorite places by connecting it to the most important thing in my life—my faith in Christ. Now, let it do the same for you!

Danielle Ernest, author/creator of *Tales of a Disneyland Cast Member*

To paraphrase a famous Christian hymn: in history Kingdoms rise and wane but God's Kingdom, with Jesus Christ as its King, shall remain. Author Randy Crane cleverly draws upon ideas in Disney's Magic Kingdom to illustrate and underscore historic Christian truths and principles. Crane knows both Kingdoms well and shows how Disney's magic is sometimes a useful metaphor for understanding God's historic and eternal Kingdom.

Kenneth Samples, author of *7 Truths That Changed the World*

Disneyland is one of the most exciting places on the planet. In fact, it IS the "Happiest Place on Earth!" Millions of people visit annually, many making return trips throughout the year. But few SEE the Park as Randy Crane does. In Randy's first book, *Once Upon YOUR Time*, Randy helped us to take control of one our most precious commodities—our time—by giving us key strategies through a unique tour of Disneyland. In *Faith and the Magic Kingdom*, Randy once again takes us on an inspiring and dynamic tour of the Happiest Place on Earth in a way only he could—by showing us that valuable lessons of faith, and "magical" examples of God's wonders CAN be found at Disneyland. By backing up biblical scripture with real-life examples that you CAN see while visiting the Resort, *Faith and the Magic Kingdom* is the perfect companion book to your next Disneyland Resort vacation. It will open your eyes to the wonders God has to offer in a way you never thought possible!

Al Kessel, host of the *Tales from the Mouse House* Disneyland podcast

No matter what your faith is, you will find *Faith and the Magic Kingdom* interesting, educational and inspirational.

Lee Cockerell, Executive Vice President (Retired & Inspired), Walt Disney World® Resort

Faith and the Magic Kingdom is a unique gift to Christians who desire to be more childlike in heart yet be deeply immersed in their identity in Christ. It is biblical, applicable, and helps you access the presence of God in a simple way. Start reading it before you vacation at Disneyland with your kids and you will have plenty of spiritual teaching moments to share.

Becky Harmon, Identity Expert and CEO of Successnotsabotage Coaching

Many people view a trip to Disneyland as a way to escape reality for awhile and enter a world of fantasy. But in *Faith and the Magic Kingdom*, Randy Crane flips that notion on its head. He uses a place that is known and loved for its escapism to teach and explain Christian doctrine, turning the Happiest Place on Earth into the ultimate picture illustration of Bible truths.

Sue Kisenwether, Disney runner and cohost of the *Anomaly Supplemental* podcast

Having grown up in Southern California, Disneyland has been a part of my existence: childhood memories, dates with my bride to be, annual passes with my children. I thought I knew a lot about Disneyland until I read Randy's book. *Faith and the Magic Kingdom* provides plenty of Disney secrets I never knew (and those are fun!), but more so, this book challenges you to think beyond the pixie dust and "hidden Mickeys" to the real purpose of life. Randy Crane takes you on a tour of "The Happiest Place on Earth," then brings insight to make you think about the things that bring true happiness.

Brad Dupray, President, Church Development Fund, Inc.

In the book *Faith and the Magic Kingdom*, author Randy Crane unites his deep faith in Christ with a love for all things Disney in an intriguingly creative way. While many would not initially see the connection between Disney and Christianity, through personal reflections, scripture and poignant questions, Crane manages to draw parallels that help the reader consider both subjects in a new and thoughtful way. Great for a daily devotional or an afternoon read, *Faith and the Magic Kingdom* speaks to both followers of Christ and fans of the Mouse.

Kristen Pfeifer, co-host of the *Mousetalgia* podcast

As Paul made God accessible to those gathered on Mars Hill (Acts 17), Randy, in a fresh and surprising way, has used the backstory of Disneyland to challenge seekers and Christ-followers to deepen their faith in God and more fully understand their place in His story. As a Christ-follower and Disneyland alumnus, I was especially encouraged by *Faith and the Magic Kingdom*!

Tom McGlinchey, Chief Financial Officer, Provision Ministry Group

I grew up playing in Disney World as if it were my backyard and performed in both Disney World and Disneyland. Now I view these oh so familiar places in such a differently enriching way since reading this book! Even though *Faith and the Magic Kingdom* is about Disneyland, I can see a lot of it in Disney World, too. I will never step inside again without being reminded of God's purposeful details in my own life, as well as the big picture!

Jennifer McGill, former Mouseketeer, recording artist, and vocal coach

Contents

Acknowledgments

Writing a book is a sizeable undertaking, and I would have been foolish to undertake it alone—at least if I expected a quality result. Without these people, that simply would not have been possible, so let me say a word of thanks to:

My wife, Faye ~ This has been a very long process, and your patience, encouragement, support, and love have been invaluable to me. You are among the most precious gifts God has given me.

My cater-cousin, Andy Brown ~ You've been behind me from the very start, always looking forward to my next step. Your confidence in me and in this project helped me to have confidence in it, too.

Joe Aguirre ~ I think this book was good before I put it in your capable hands. Thanks to your careful and skillful editing, it's now better than I could have made it on my own.

Jen Rhodes ~ A good cover can make all the difference, and the one you designed is fantastic! You perfectly captured my vision for the look and feel, then made it better. Many people will be blessed by this book because the cover you created caught their eye.

Rick Warren, Max Lucado, and Chip Ingram ~ I admire the way you enable your readers and listeners to connect God's truth. I have striven to do the same here, and you inspired and challenged me to do so.

Disney's Cast Members, especially those at Disneyland ~ You make the place what it is.

Al & Joyce Kessel ~ Your support, cheerleading, and constant encouragement helped me believe that God had given me a message worth sharing.

The many people who helped fund this book and make its publication possible:

~ Staci Abshire, Katie Bamford, Hank & Lynne Behrns, Tyson & Shelley Behrns, Andrew Brown, Andrew Burkum, Jim Collins, Denise Coy, Debra Crane, Mary Jane Crawford, Katy Daniel, Jason Domer, Faith Dority, Joann Fortier, Jeff Frankowski, Mike Grissom, Ken & Lisa Haas, Carolyn Hoagland, Jim & Jeanette Hocking, Sandra Karelius, Doug & Emily Kinnes, Brian Levine, Lee & Tricia Malchow, Dan Martin, Tonja McElroy, Rick & Amy Moyer, Rachel Neilson, Sonia Nelson, Rikki Niblett, Carlyn Obringer, James Ohnemus, Amber Palm, Camron Palm, Leslie Palm, John Primm, Melissa Quigley, Nancy Roettger, Betty Sue Sanders, Cindy Schultz, Carolyn Smuts, Nancy Tucker, Lesley Victorine, and some who wished to remain anonymous.

Of course, Walt Disney ~ Without the incredible Magic Kingdom you imagined and created, this book would certainly not exist.

And finally, you, the reader. My prayer is that God uses this book to minister to you. As I write these words, I'm praying for you, and ask that you would do the same for me as your read them. I'm honored that you would choose to read this book. Thank you.

Introduction

*D*isneyland is all about story. Every land in the park tells a story. Every attraction tells a story. Some of the stories are obvious. Some are hidden, but still there.

Walt Disney was among the best at making movies that tell stories, and Disneyland is the ultimate, immersive, interactive "movie." It is "Immersion Toward Interesting Illusion" (see chapter 1). The park is one huge narrative, and like all good narratives, it contains lessons, examples, reminders, and warnings.

God is also a God of story—and of visual aids—and He uses them to teach, encourage, and even rebuke. The apostle Paul says, referring to the events of Israel's history:

> Now these things occurred as examples to keep us from setting our hearts on evil things as they did....These things happened to them as examples and were written down as warnings for

us, on whom the fulfillment of the ages has come. (1 Corinthians 10:6–11)

When Jesus told people what God is like, or what heaven is like, He said things like, "Look at the birds…Look at the flowers…Let me tell you a story." Jesus spoke in parables, tying in what His audience saw and heard every day with spiritual truth that may have been difficult for them to grasp.

Jesus spoke all these things to the crowd in parables; He did not say anything to them without using a parable. So was fulfilled what was spoken through the prophet:
"I will open my mouth in parables,
I will utter things hidden since the creation of the world."
(Matthew 13:34–35)

With many similar parables Jesus spoke the word to them, as much as they could understand. (Mark 4:33)

Why this book?

First, as we will show, Disneyland can serve as an allegory for many aspects of the Christian life. Tens (if not hundreds) of millions of people are familiar with Disneyland to one degree or another. Childhood memories, special events, memories as parents, and more have been forged in this magical theme park. That familiarity will provide a hook on which to hang other ideas, so that they connect to you in a powerful way.

Second, this word-journey serves as a reminder that the Christian faith is not something we compartmentalize. It's not just a Sunday morning obligation, or even a Sunday morning and Wednesday night thing. It's all day, every day. Everywhere we go. Everything we do. If our faith can relate to Disneyland, it can relate anywhere, right?

Third, some of you who will read this book work at Disneyland, have worked there, or will work there someday. I pray that this excursion will help motivate you to work each day as though you are working for the Lord. And as you go about your work, I hope you'll be able to look around and remember that God is with you, and that your work there truly honors Him.

Finally, I hope this book will act as a springboard for conversations with your friends and family—such that the next time you go to Disneyland, or just drive by, or even see something about it, that the experience might trigger a reminder of what you've read here. That reminder can perhaps be used to start a nonthreatening conversation with a nonbelieving friend, or as a word of encouragement or challenge to a Christian friend—or to yourself. This effort is one way to make some of the truths of Scripture accessible, and maybe more understandable. Think of it, if you will, as one big parable.

As always, an illustration breaks down if pushed too far. So, we will do our best to not do that. If we venture off the "official" storyline (Disney or otherwise), it's OK. The illustrations I will create are in service to the Word of God and His purposes, not the other way around.

A couple of caveats: I am not saying that Walt Disney or the company intended to put into Disneyland the messages and lessons that I have drawn out of my experiences in the park. In fact, I know that promoting a Christian or even an explicitly religious message was not Walt's intention at all. His daughter, Diane Disney Miller, told one minister that there are no churches on Main Street at Disneyland because her father did not want to favor any particular denomination. On the other hand, he was a strongly religious man who truly believed that good would triumph over evil and that it was important to accept and help everyone, even if they were very different from you.

Nor am I saying Disney is not out to make money—on the contrary, most of what they do is for the dual purposes of entertainment and revenue-generation. After all, why do you think most of the locations on Main Street are shops, and that the largest one is on the right (the easiest to get to) as you're leaving? And why else would so many rides exit to merchandise locations?

Most movies, books, or even everyday life events do not deliberately contain the messages we sometimes draw from them for illustrations, and every for-profit corporation wants (and needs) to make money. But that doesn't mean that we can't draw lessons and parallels from them, and use them as illustrations and metaphors.

That's exactly what *Faith and the Magic Kingdom* hopes to accomplish. So, to all who come to this happy place, welcome.

Chapter 1: Lay of the Land

Enjoying Disneyland: Immersion Toward Interesting Illusion

*W*hat is it that makes Disneyland and the other Disney parks unique? What sets them apart from what so many of the "other guys" do? When I think of what Disney does better than just about anyone else, one word comes to mind: theme. So many of the rides, shows, and attractions work together in every aspect to create an overall theme, story, or feeling.

Kevin Yee, a writer for MiceAge.com has coined a term for this phenomenon. He calls it "Immersion Toward Interesting Illusion."

What has historically made Disney special is the ability to "transport" visitors somewhere else; the illusion is complete enough that we are able to "suspend disbelief" and get into the spirit of pretending that we are really there. How is the illusion created? Through total immersion. There are no distracters, and cost-cutting measures like painted bricks (rather than real bricks) are avoided in favor of something more authentic-looking.

But only experiences which grant immersion in service of an illusion come close. And I'd interject that the hoped-for illusion has to be an "interesting" one too....To qualify as "interesting," it should be exotic, or different in some fundamental way from the everyday reality people experience.

In short, truly enduring attractions—and even parks—in the Disney vein seem to have succeeded because they meet several unique criteria: they offer complete immersion in a fictional setting, the entire atmosphere is not just reality, but an illusion, and finally, the illusion itself must be deemed an "interesting" one by the viewer, most likely because it is exotic or different from his usual experience in life.[1]

Now, if Disney succeeds—at least most of the time—in producing experiences that so completely immerse people in interesting illusions, why don't some people like Disneyland?

They might say they don't like crowds or the prices are too high, but many of these same people will suffer big crowds for a sporting event or a conference. Or they'll accept the high prices for concert tickets or lift tickets at a ski resort.

Perhaps the real reason, though, when you really get down to the heart of it, is they don't allow themselves to be fully immersed in the illusion. Some people carry too much baggage into the park. They have too many worries. Or they try so hard to find the flaws

---

[1] Kevin Yee, "It's the Tourists," http://miceage.micechat.com/kevinyee/ky082307a.htm, accessed July 6, 2013.

and criticize that they don't have time to experience the magic. These people failed to heed the message on the plaque at the entrance tunnels: "Here you *leave* today...." They bring extra stuff with them.

Ron Schneider discusses a proper frame of mind in an article he wrote a few years ago about taking his daughter to Disneyland for the first time:

> Once inside Fantasyland I take her straight to my childhood favorite, Peter Pan's Flight. As we step up to the load area, Katie asks me, "Daddy, what happens in here?" What can I tell her? I don't want her to be nervous, but I also don't want to spoil anything. I decide to try this: "Honey, I have no idea." And that's what I do for the next two days. As a result, every attraction is a voyage of discovery that we make together....
>
> My wish for every father is to make this same "voyage of discovery" with your child. The world has enough commonplace thrills in it; they can be found at the side of any freeway in America. There are far too few flights of fancy.[2]

Ron decided, for the sake of his daughter, to approach Disneyland as a child himself, to completely immerse himself in the experience, in the illusion.

Consider your life as a Christian. You may be thinking, "Why do I struggle to believe? Why haven't I seen answered prayer? Where is that 'abundant life' Jesus talked about?"

At the risk of oversimplifying, I will suggest that what's missing much of the time is *total immersion*. I'm not talking about baptism. And I'm not talking about joining a monastery. I'm talking about complete, absorbing, all-encompassing daily commitment to Christ.

---

[2] As told to me in the *Stories of the Magic* podcast, Episode 006, http://storiesofthemagic.com/episode-006-ron-schneider-part-2/.

Or, as the apostle Paul said:

So here's what I want you to do, God helping you: Take your everyday, ordinary life—your sleeping, eating, going-to-work, and walking-around life—and place it before God as an offering. Embracing what God does for you is the best thing you can do for Him. Don't become so well-adjusted to your culture that you fit into it without even thinking. Instead, fix your attention on God. You'll be changed from the inside out. Readily recognize what He wants from you, and quickly respond to it. Unlike the culture around you, always dragging you down to its level of immaturity, God brings the best out of you, develops well-formed maturity in you.[3]

And from Jesus Himself:

What I'm trying to do here is to get you to relax, to not be so preoccupied with getting, so you can respond to God's giving. People who don't know God and the way He works fuss over these things, but you know both God and how He works. Steep your life in God-reality, God-initiative, God-provisions. Don't worry about missing out. You'll find all your everyday human concerns will be met.[4]

While Immersion Toward Interesting Illusion makes Disney's magic come to life, what we have in Jesus is something infinitely better: Immersion in Life in Christ. Not "interesting illusion" but ultimate reality.

But we must be truly, completely committed to Jesus—to following Him daily in every part of our lives. It's not enough to just pay Him lip service. It's not enough to just give Him a couple of hours once a week.

---

[3] Romans 12:1–2 (MSG)
[4] Matthew 6:31–33 (MSG)

As one of my former professors at Hope International University, David Timms, said,

> Christian "faith" that consistently fails to touch our anger, lust, despair, jealousy, fear, bitterness, mean-spiritedness, violence, and unrestraint is unworthy of Christ and dishonoring of the Holy Spirit. Unless we grow steadily and measurably in love, we discredit the "new creation" for which Christ died....
>
> All too often we affirm the foundational teaching of Jesus—"Love the Lord your God, and love your neighbor as yourself"—then permit all manner of disunity, gossip, division, conflict, and criticism to pour forth from us and around us. With disheartening regularity, we confuse transformation of the heart with modification of the lifestyle. We honor those who volunteer for service, regularly attend worship, and give generously, while failing to confront deep character flaws. A deacon in the church can be a dictator in the workplace with barely a raised eyebrow among us.[5]

Jesus put it simply:

> Just as no branch can bear fruit of itself without abiding in (being vitally united to) the vine, neither can you bear fruit unless you abide in Me.[6]

And Paul described his own transformation:

> What actually took place is this: I tried keeping rules and working my head off to please God, and it didn't work. So I quit being a "law man" so that I could be God's man. Christ's

---

[5] David Timms, In Hope, "For Him," http://www.hiu.edu/inhope/issue8_29.htm, accessed July 6, 2013.

[6] John 15:4 (AMP)

life showed me how, and enabled me to do it. I identified myself completely with Him. Indeed, I have been crucified with Christ. My ego is no longer central. It is no longer important that I appear righteous before you or have your good opinion, and I am no longer driven to impress God. Christ lives in me. The life you see me living is not "mine," but it is lived by faith in the Son of God, who loved me and gave Himself for me. I am not going to go back on that.[7]

That's living for Christ. It's not about rules and regulations. It's not about shoulds and should nots. Not teeth-gritting determination. Not extraordinary reserves of self-discipline. Not Type-A drivenness. Not overachieving. But death. Simply dead to ourselves and alive to Christ. I'm not there yet, and I probably never will be this side of heaven, but it's what I'm aiming for, a little more today than yesterday, and a little more tomorrow than today.

St. Augustine said, "Love God and do as you please." When we truly love God, our desires will align with His. But what about Jesus in Gethsemane? No one would argue that He didn't love God, but He did say, in His travail, "Take this cup from Me."[8]

So what held Jesus to the cross? Did God the Father force Him? No. It was His love. Because He was both fully God and fully man, He suffered the weight of atoning for humanity's sin. But in the end, He chose to do the Father's will. Through all of Jesus' life God the Father was at the center.

When we love God that passionately, that completely, our decisions will reflect that love. Our lives will be completely immersed in His love.

Professor Timms offers some wisdom:

---

[7] Galatians 2:19–20 (MSG)
[8] Luke 22:42

Living for Christ involves less straining and striving than we might imagine. It emerges from surrender and trust. The Kingdom of God is not advanced by the brilliant and the bold but by the broken—those whose own will, agenda, ambition, pride, and plans have been broken and are completely in the hands of God.[9]

We are still living life, pursuing our dreams, going to work, being with friends, maybe looking for that special someone, having fun. But doing all of it with God as the focus—pleasing Him, serving Him, honoring Him. Fully immersed in Him.

Kingdom Thinking: On a scale of 1–10, how fully immersed in Christ would you describe your life? What is one thing you can do (or avoid doing) to nudge that number higher today?

Attention to Detail: God Is in the Details

If you were to ask a Disney parks fan what it is that makes Disneyland (or Walt Disney World) unique and special, you may get several answers. World-class service. Fun for the whole family. Great storytelling. But one phrase that'll you'll hear more than almost any other is, "Their attention to detail is amazing."

It's true. Whether it's the details that support the story in a queue, or those that make what could be an ordinary play area exciting, or even the special touches in the landscapes and buildings that combine to tell a single story, Walt Disney Imagineering shows details that are unmatched in degree and scope.

[9] Timms, http://www.hiu.edu/inhope/issue8_29.htm.

For example, the Imagineers did not have to put a nametag on the "ticket seller" in front of the Main Street Cinema, and they certainly didn't have to give her the hometown of Marceline, Missouri—Walt's own boyhood hometown—but they did.

But why does this matter to park guests? One reason that comes to mind is our almost subconscious understanding that when the *little* details are right, we know the people behind them cared about and paid equal attention to the *big* picture too. They cared enough to craft a story for each balcony in New Orleans Square, to put many jokes and references in the Disneyland Cast Members' window on Main Street, and to use authentic props in the queue for the Indiana Jones Adventure, so when we board the attraction we will be confident that it will be good.

Architect Mies van der Rohe said, "God is in the details." He may not have meant it in a Disney context, but van der Rohe was absolutely right. As the Imagineers care about the design details of Disney parks, God cares about the everyday details in our lives.

> Are not two sparrows sold for a penny? Yet not one of them will fall to the ground apart from the will of your Father. And even the very hairs of your head are all numbered. So don't be afraid; you are worth more than many sparrows.[10]

Do you see what Jesus is saying? God cares for you so much that He's numbered the hairs on your head (which some people estimate at 100,000). God is involved when a single sparrow falls to the ground, and you are worth more than many sparrows.

If God is involved in the details of a sparrow's life, we can be assured that He's also got the "big stuff" of *our* lives covered. At Christmas, we celebrate His coming to "dwell among us" as a baby born in a feed trough to a poor family. He descended from the majesty of heaven, fully God, to the most humble of beginnings, fully man. Or as Paul said of Jesus:

---

[10] Matthew 10:29–31

Who, being in very nature God,
did not consider equality with God something to be grasped,
but made Himself nothing,
taking the very nature of a servant,
being made in human likeness.
And being found in appearance as a man,
He humbled Himself
and became obedient to death—
even death on a cross![11]

There is no detail too small for God. There is no problem too big for Him. Jesus has been as low as one can be, and above all there is. There is no concern so insignificant that He doesn't want you to tell Him about it. There is no triumph or success so enormous that it's bigger than He is.

Those little details found throughout Disneyland each stand as a reminder that *God is in the details*, thus we know He's also got "the big stuff" covered. He created the universe. He created all living things. He created you. He shaped and designed you uniquely for His purpose. He knows the number of hairs on your head and, for that matter, all the cells of your body and the 3 billion base pairs of your DNA. From the vastness of the universe to the microscopic genetic code, He's in it all.

Kingdom Thinking: What is one "little detail" in your life that reminds you of something big about God?

---

[11] Philippians 2:6–8

Disneyland and You: Both Still a Work in Progress

On the cusp of a new year, we reflect on the past and imagine what lies ahead. We've changed. We *will* change (intentionally or not).

Walt Disney captured this idea when he said, "Disneyland will never be completed. It will continue to grow as long as there is imagination left in the world." From the beginning, he planned for change. His overall goal and vision for the park didn't change, but over time he would mold it and reshape it so it came closer and closer to that vision.

In Philippians, Paul tells us that God takes the same approach to us. "In all my prayers for all of you, I always pray with joy because of your partnership in the gospel from the first day until now, being confident of this, that He who began a good work in you will carry it on to completion until the day of Christ Jesus."[12]

From the day you were born, God has been continually working to bring you closer and closer to that ideal, to being like His Son. That day *will* come. It won't be fully realized until the day believers are finally united with Him in person in heaven, but each day brings the potential for us to grow.

God is working on us, but we are also learning to see what God's vision is for our lives. The more we understand His vision, the better we will understand the intentional changes that He wants to make in us.

Change is inevitable, but people crave stability, too. In the case of Disneyland, that stability existed in the person of Walt Disney. As long as he was around guiding, making decisions, and leading, progress went in a single direction. Sure, there were differences in approach, and sometimes something he tried didn't work. But the specific project, attraction, or idea wasn't the point. The overall growth and identity of Disneyland was.

---

[12] Philippians 1:4–6

In the case of the Christian, that stability comes from God. "Jesus Christ is the same yesterday and today and forever."[13] Sometimes changes are difficult, and sometimes they don't work out as we'd originally hoped or planned. Unlike Disney, though, God is not surprised when something does not seem to work. He does not have to try something else because one idea went badly. He sees the whole picture.

And, like Disney, the specific activity or circumstance isn't the point. Your growth and your identity in Christ is. It's much more "big picture" than we're used to thinking, but it may help as you look ahead to a new year (though you may be reading this book at a different time) and look back at the previous one.

Consider each of your recent successes and failures, however you define each, and ask yourself this question:

Let's say that God custom-designed that situation for my growth—that this was exactly what I need to move to the next level, to become more like Christ and live my purpose more fully. If that is true, what was (or is) God doing through this?

The answer to that question will go a long way toward making this year your best ever. Not necessarily because you will make more money, get a better job, find the perfect mate, or travel somewhere you've always wanted to go—though any of those may happen. It will be your best year ever because you are more consciously aware of what God is doing in your life and that recognition enables you to work with Him—or, more accurately, allow *Him* to work in and through you. You'll be looking for what God is doing, and the more you look the more spiritual progress you'll see.

---

[13] Hebrews 13:8

> **Kingdom Thinking:** How have you seen God making you more like Jesus in the past year?

You Can't Force 'Em—For Disneyland or Faith

I've been to Disneyland with many different people, and most of *them* love Disney, too—or at least they enjoy it. However, as hard as it is for me to understand, I have been there a few times with people who don't think much of Disneyland, and I've talked to several more who will not go the park. In these visits and conversations, I have learned something very important: I can't force someone to like Disneyland.

There are certainly things I can do to make it more likely they will have a positive experience, and thus more likely to begin to like it. I can...

- Find out what they enjoy about other fun things they do (so I can try to find something similar);
- Ask them what interests them, and highlight those aspects of the park;
- Go during less crowded times;
- Go at their pace;
- Plan special "magical" moments tailored to them;
- And more.

The more they experience the park in the best possible way, the more likely they'll enjoy Disneyland, but only if they are open to it. Even under the most favorable circumstances, I can't force someone to enjoy themselves and begin to love Disney like I do.

Trying to "convince" an unwilling person to become a Christian is like trying to force someone who is indifferent about

Disneyland to enjoy the park. Exposure to the best face of the faith helps, as does honest discussion/recognition of the difficulties they see and questions they have. But even then, God does the convincing, and they still have the choice to accept or reject the truth (and the Truth).

In Acts 26:28, Paul "almost" persuaded King Agrippa to become a Christian, but the "convincing" came at Agrippa's invitation to speak. In the very next chapter (Acts 27), Paul shared his faith/conviction directly when there was a definite need to hear good news—people were struggling to survive a shipwreck. At that time of peril, the people were ready to listen!

People will enjoy Disneyland more if they come with someone who loves it. Similarly, people will be drawn to Christ if they are with someone who truly models Christlikeness. But we can't change people. That's up to God.

Meanwhile, you can show genuine love to those who need to see love. You can spend time with them. You can be an example, not hiding your faith, but not forcing it or trying to find ways to manipulate conversations. When the Holy Spirit has prepared the person, either they will ask or He will make it clear. As you and I wait for an opportunity, let's be patient and trust God to work in people we care about.

Kingdom Thinking: Have you ever been surprised when someone you thought had no interest in being a Christian was suddenly open to it? How did that come about?

Going It Alone at Disneyland, and in Life

I used to go to Disneyland primarily with friends or family, but often I went alone—and it was fun. Sometimes my best friend, Andy, and I went together, and that was always a special kind of fun. And once my wife, Faye, and I got annual passes and started going together it was no longer nearly as much fun to go by myself. There's something to be said for sharing the experiences, developing the "inside jokes," and building memories together that going alone simply can't duplicate.

Even when he envisioned it, Walt wanted Disneyland to be a place where parents and their children could have fun together. It was designed to be enjoyed with others.

The Christian life is the same way. In theory, you can "do it on your own," but the only way to truly "get everything out of it" that there is to get out of it—to learn all you can, to grow all you can, to serve all you can, to love all you can—you must experience that life with others. There must be fellowship. There must be companionship on the journey. There must be others to experience life together in community.

The New Testament uses the phrase "one another" or the similar phrase "each other" over 50 times. Here's a short list:

- Love one another (John 13:34)
- Be devoted to one another (Romans 12:10)
- Build up one another (Romans 14:19, 1 Thessalonians 5:11)
- Accept one another (Romans 15:7)
- Admonish one another (Romans 15:14, Colossians 3:16)
- Serve one another (Galatians 5:13)
- Bear one another's burdens (Galatians 6:2)
- Forgive one another (Ephesians 4:2, 32; Colossians 3:13)

- Be patient with one another (Ephesians 4:2, Colossians 3:13)
- Be kind and compassionate to one another (Ephesians 4:32)
- Submit to one another (Ephesians 5:21, 1 Peter 5:5)
- Bear with one another (Colossians 3:13)
- Teach one another (Colossians 3:16)
- Comfort one another (1 Thessalonians 4:18)
- Encourage one another (1 Thessalonians 5:11)
- Encourage (or exhort) one another (Hebrews 3:13)

These instructions are all part of what it means to follow Jesus and to obey Him. How many can you do by yourself?

Now, this list does not necessarily need to occur in the context of the "traditional church," but there must be a group of believers with whom you share mutual commitment. This comes easier for some of us than others (I'm definitely in the latter category), but it is vital to growth.

As believers we need to share each other's struggles, rejoice in victories, meet needs, give our love, and provide opportunities for others to give theirs. Not being part of a faith community not only robs you of the chance to be obedient to God but it robs others of it as well. After all, if you have a need God wants someone to meet, and you isolate and insulate yourself, how can they do what God has called them to do?

People get busy. We don't want to be hurt. We don't want to be selfless. There are countless reasons to try to go it alone. But there's one excellent reason not to. We were designed for community. That's enough for me. Is it for you?

> **Kingdom Thinking:** Have you avoided (intentionally or unintentionally) being part of a faith community? Have you noticed a difference in the way you live your life as a Christian either way?

Going 101: Not Operating as Designed

Go to Disneyland often enough and you're sure to experience an attraction "going 101." This is the radio code for a ride being nonoperational. If you happen to hear it said while you're in the park, it usually refers to the attraction being down unexpectedly. It had been operating normally and then something (either major or minor) went wrong.

As often as I go, I have experienced this delay several times myself—sometimes in line, and sometimes on the attraction. The ones I can recall are:

- Splash Mountain (on ride)
- Matterhorn (on ride)
- Snow White's Scary Adventures (in line)
- Indiana Jones Adventure (in line, more than once)
- Big Thunder Mountain Railroad (in line)

Honestly, I am surprised it has not happened more often … and there are a few attractions I have not been on when they've gone 101 that I'd like to experience!

Attractions have all kinds of ups and downs within their storylines. They may have thrilling components, mysterious sections, peaceful times, and even scary moments. But these are all part of the attraction operating as designed. When an attraction goes 101, something stops working the way it's supposed to.

In Romans 7, the apostle Paul talks about the experience of his walk with Christ "going 101."

> I do not understand what I do. For what I want to do I do not do, but what I hate I do. And if I do what I do not want to do, I agree that the law is good. As it is, it is no longer I myself who do it, but it is sin living in me. I know that nothing good lives in me, that is, in my sinful nature. For I have the desire to do what is good, but I cannot carry it out. For what I do is not the good I want to do; no, the evil I do not want to do—this I keep on doing. Now if I do what I do not want to do, it is no longer I who do it, but it is sin living in me that does it.
>
> So I find this law at work: When I want to do good, evil is right there with me. For in my inner being I delight in God's law; but I see another law at work in the members of my body, waging war against the law of my mind and making me a prisoner of the law of sin at work within my members.[14]

Paul says that in his life, he knows how it should operate, what he should and shouldn't do. But more often than he'd like, he goes 101. Things don't work like they're supposed to. He does what he knows he should not do, and does not do what he knows he should.

Does that sound familiar? It does to me. I can relate much more often than I would care to admit.

Now, what happens when a Disneyland attraction goes 101? They turn the lights on, and the maintenance staff comes in, diagnoses, and fixes the problem—whenever possible trying to make sure the problem doesn't recur.

As Christians we must deal with a 101 in our lives the same way. Our inclination is to leave the lights off and ignore it, or try to fix the problem in the dark. We don't want light shed on these

---

[14] Romans 7:15–23

matters—certainly not the full light of God's truth. But that's exactly what we need to do.

The psalmist admitted this struggle:

Search me, O God, and know my heart: try me, and know my thoughts: And see if there be any wicked way in me, and lead me in the way everlasting.[15]

And the apostle John exhorts believers:

This is the message we have heard from Him and declare to you: God is light; in Him there is no darkness at all. If we claim to have fellowship with Him yet walk in the darkness, we lie and do not live by the truth. But if we walk in the light, as He is in the light, we have fellowship with one another, and the blood of Jesus, His Son, purifies us from all sin. If we claim to be without sin, we deceive ourselves and the truth is not in us. If we confess our sins, He is faithful and just and will forgive us our sins and purify us from all unrighteousness. If we claim we have not sinned, we make Him out to be a liar and His word has no place in our lives.[16]

Fortunately, we have help. One of the main reasons that we do not want to confess our sins or truly examine our lives is fear. What if I'm worse than I think I am? Will God forgive me? How could God possibly love me?

But we need not fear the answers to these questions, for they have been answered for us already.

What a wretched man I am! Who will rescue me from this body of death? Thanks be to God—through Jesus Christ our Lord! So then, I myself in my mind am a slave to God's law, but in

---

[15] Psalm 139:23–24
[16] 1 John 1:5–10

the sinful nature a slave to the law of sin. Therefore, there is now no condemnation for those who are in Christ Jesus, because through Christ Jesus the law of the Spirit of life set me free from the law of sin and death.[17]

Because of what Jesus did for us through His life, death, and resurrection, we have no need to fear condemnation or separation. We can ask God to truly examine our hearts. We can endure the difficulty—even pain sometimes—of being made clean. It is not easy. But an attraction that doesn't work properly is of no use to the guests, no matter how difficult the repairs. And a life that isn't inspected, cleaned, and brought back into good repair when we go off course cannot serve God the way He wants us to—the way He made us to.

Kingdom Thinking: How can you tell when your life is starting to "go 101"? What is one thing you can do to "turn the lights on" and help get it back on track?

Cast Members: A Chosen People

When we think of what makes Disneyland—and all the Disney parks—special, a number of factors may come to mind. Maybe it's the rides, the shows, the theming, the food, the atmosphere, the fireworks, or the parades. Maybe it's a particular one of those that holds a special memory.

All of those features are valuable, and they do all work together to make these places unique. But there's something else, something without which the rest would be nothing: the Cast Members.

---

[17] Romans 7:24–8:2

Walt Disney said, "You can design and create, and build the most wonderful place in the world. But it takes people to make the dream a reality." That's really true. I've been to many places, and while each of them has good people, the level of quality, service, dedication, and show provided by Disney Cast Members is second to none anywhere that I've ever experienced.

Disney Cast Members are a special group of people. And, as Christians, so are we.

> Therefore, as God's chosen people, holy and dearly loved, clothe yourselves with compassion, kindness, humility, gentleness and patience.[18]

We are God's *chosen* people, *holy* and *dearly loved*. Let's look at each of those descriptors a little more closely.

Chosen

Disney employs a careful selection process when hiring Cast Members. It used to be even more stringent than it is now, but it still holds true that not just anyone can walk in off the street and work for Disney. And the really good ones remain there for years. A few have even been there 50+ years. Disney Cast Members are not merely *hired* but *chosen*.

Believers in Christ have also been chosen:

> For He chose us in Him before the creation of the world to be holy and blameless in his sight. In love He predestined us to be adopted as His sons through Jesus Christ, in accordance with His pleasure and will—to the praise of His glorious grace, which He has freely given us in the One He loves.[19]

---

[18] Colossians 3:12
[19] Ephesians 1:4–6

We have been adopted into God's family of "heavenly Cast Members."

Holy

The Greek word for *holy* means, when applied to people, "to be set apart for a specific purpose." Cast Members certainly fit that description. They are set apart for a specific purpose: to be employed by one of the most well-respected companies in the world to operate the park in their various capacities. Each has their own role to play. Walt Disney said, "Disneyland is the star, everything else is in the supporting role." Being hired as a Disneyland Cast Member means being set apart for a purpose, as one with a role to play.

The apostle Peter described how holy people, in light of their chosen position, ought to live:

> Therefore, prepare your minds for action; be self-controlled; set your hope fully on the grace to be given you when Jesus Christ is revealed. As obedient children, do not conform to the evil desires you had when you lived in ignorance. But just as He who called you is holy, so be holy in all you do; for it is written: "Be holy, because I am holy."[20]

To call a person holy is to say that he/she belongs to God; she is to be used in His service or dedicated to Him, and in some special way is His property. Nothing or nobody, except for God, is holy of itself or by nature. A person becomes holy by being dedicated to God and His service.

---

[20] 1 Peter 1:13–16

Dearly Loved

The analogy breaks down a little here, but not because of an inherent flaw. It happens because of how rarely Cast Members receive appreciation from guests.

I don't know fully how recognition works inside the company itself, but I often see Cast Members get criticized, yelled at, or even insulted by guests for doing their jobs. I do see *some* guests thank them, and that's always encouraging. Most of the time, what I see is guests ignoring them, as though they were just part of the scenery.

My wife and I always thank Cast Members for doing their job, whether it's directing us to a line, giving us our food, or helping us onto or off a ride. It's why I created the *Stories of the Magic* podcast[21] in 2012. One step we have taken to really show our appreciation, though, is by cementing our experience through autograph books.

Of course, we have one book for the characters, but we also have a separate one for Cast Members. We carry it with us to the Disney parks as often as we can, and if a Cast Member does something that creates a magical moment for us or exemplifies what Walt wanted his people to be, we ask them to sign our autograph book.

Cast Members' responses have been uplifting. They are always touched, and a few were near tears. For many, no one has ever asked them to do that before. I don't understand why. They are such an important part of our trip that I can't imagine Disneyland or Walt Disney World without them.

Again, Scripture is instructive.

Be imitators of God, therefore, as dearly loved children and live a life of love, just as Christ loved us and gave Himself up for us as a fragrant offering and sacrifice to God.[22]

---

[21]Randy Crane, "Stories of the Magic," http://storiesofthemagic.com
[22] Ephesians 5:1–2

I have been crucified with Christ and I no longer live, but Christ lives in me. The life I live in the body, I live by faith in the Son of God, who loved me and gave Himself for me.[23]

Here's the bottom line: Cast Members are chosen, set apart, appreciated, and valued. What they do comes from that identity, and the more they grasp it, the better they tend to be as Cast Members. It's not hard to tell which ones really "get it."

Believers are God's chosen people, holy and dearly loved. Who we are comes from our identity. The more fully we understand and internalize this truth, the more we live out the characteristics in this verse—and His love. It's not performance—trying to earn His approval. It's a natural expression of knowing who we truly are and acting out of love and gratitude.

Kingdom Thinking: Do you truly see yourself as chosen, holy, and dearly loved? If so, what has been the result? If not, how will your life look different when you do?

Meeting Characters: Stepping into the Story

One of the biggest draws to Disneyland is to meet the characters. It may not mean much to some adults, but there are a lot of kids who can't wait to go to Disneyland not for the rides, but to "meet Mickey Mouse!" One of the reasons the Give Kids the World Village was established in Central Florida was in response to the high percentage of Wish Kids whose wish is exactly that.

You can meet characters all over the parks, but some of the best encounters come when you meet them in their unique

---

[23] Galatians 2:20

environments—like many of the princesses in Fantasy Faire, Snow White by her wishing well, the Fab Five in Toontown, or Woody and Jessie in Frontierland. Visitors step into *their* world and meet them in their own story. Pixie Hollow, a meet and greet attraction, is a great recent example of the popularity of this park feature (see Chapter 8).

There's something special about becoming part of someone's story. At Christmas (also called the Advent season), we remember when God did that for us and then took the story even further.

John 1:14 says, "The Word became flesh and made His dwelling among us. We have seen His glory, the glory of the One and Only, who came from the Father, full of grace and truth." The word translated "made his dwelling" literally means "to pitch a tent." John used it to remind his readers of God dwelling among them in the Tabernacle while they wandered in the wilderness.

In the Incarnation, when God Himself, in the person of Jesus, physically stepped into history and became a man, He entered our story. The miracle of Christmas is that the Word became flesh. "For what the law was powerless to do in that it was weakened by the sinful nature, God did by sending his own Son in the likeness of sinful man to be a sin offering."[24]

What makes Christmas even more significant, though, is that Jesus became like us so that we could become like Him. He did not merely *enter* our story, He *elevated* our stories by inviting us into His own. He stepped down into history to build a bridge that brings us back into a right relationship with God!

Consider these "unusual" Advent passages:

> Your attitude should be the same as that of Christ Jesus:
> Who, being in very nature God,
> did not consider equality with God something to be grasped,
> but made Himself nothing,
> taking the very nature of a servant,

---

[24] Romans 8:2

being made in human likeness. And being found in appearance as a man,

He humbled Himself

and became obedient to death—

even death on a cross! Therefore God exalted Him to the highest place

and gave Him the name that is above every name, that at the name of Jesus every knee should bow,

in heaven and on earth and under the earth,

and every tongue confess that Jesus Christ is Lord,

to the glory of God the Father.[25]

In bringing many sons to glory, it was fitting that God, for Whom and through Whom everything exists, should make the author of their salvation perfect through suffering. Both the One who makes men holy and those who are made holy are of the same family. So Jesus is not ashamed to call them brothers. He says,

"I will declare Your name to my brothers;
in the presence of the congregation I will sing your praises."

And again,

"I will put my trust in Him."

And again He says,

"Here am I, and the children God has given Me."

Since the children have flesh and blood, He too shared in their humanity so that by His death He might destroy him who holds the power of death—that is, the devil—and free those

---

[25] Philippians 2:5–11 (This passage [or part of this passage] was cited earlier, but God's Word applies to various purposes, times, and aspects of life; thus we highlight these words again and this principle will apply later in the book as well.)

who all their lives were held in slavery by their fear of death. For surely it is not angels He helps, but Abraham's descendants. For this reason He had to be made like His brothers in every way, in order that He might become a merciful and faithful high priest in service to God, and that He might make atonement for the sins of the people. Because He Himself suffered when He was tempted, He is able to help those who are being tempted.[26]

By the way, the same word used for "dwelling" in John 1:14 is used again in Revelation 21:3, "And I heard a loud voice from the throne saying, 'Now the dwelling of God is with men, and He will live with them. They will be His people, and God Himself will be with them and be their God.'"

Jesus came to earth to provide fallen humanity with the way back to God. It is not through our own "goodness," nor through our own efforts. But simply by accepting His free gift of salvation and stepping into His story, "heaven's hollow," forever.

Kingdom Thinking: How have you seen God "step into your story" and elevate it to show you how it fits into His story?

---

[26] Hebrews 2:10–18

Chapter 2: Entrance Plaza

Is Narrow and Exclusive Wrong?

*B*efore we can explore the Happiest Place on Earth, we have to get in, right? And how do you get in? You buy a ticket. Ah, if only it was that simple.

One-day? Two-day? Park hopper or not? Annual pass? Which one?

There are so many choices. But there is a restriction. Only a ticket to Disneyland will gain you admission to Disneyland. Seems obvious, doesn't it?

You can't use a ticket for Knott's Berry Farm or Magic Mountain—or even for the LA Philharmonic at the Walt Disney Concert Hall. That one's closer, but it still won't work. That makes perfect sense. So why do people have trouble when it comes to something much more important than Disneyland: heaven?

If you got upset that a Disneyland entrance Cast Member wouldn't let you in with a Knott's ticket, you'd get laughed at. But when Jesus says, "I am the way and the truth and the life. No one comes to the Father except through Me,"[27] people accuse Him— and us—of being arrogant and intolerant.

Just because something is narrow and exclusive does not automatically make it wrong. Life is full of things that are narrow and yet still true. For example, airplane passengers want the pilot to land on the runway, not the highway; to land right-side up, not upside down. Truth is always exclusive of error. "Two plus two equals four" is very narrow, but it's still right.

Christianity is not the only religion that makes exclusive claims. Judaism and Islam, among other religions, also make exclusive claims. Not all religions can be true, because they disagree with each other on major issues, such as whether the universe was created or not, and how to be saved (whether from sin, lack of enlightenment, or other). "Two plus two" cannot equal both four *and* five.

For example, Christianity says that salvation from sin is a free gift from God. Every other religion that I'm familiar with says that we must earn it. How can salvation be free and earned at the same time?

One school of thinking goes something like this: "It doesn't matter what you believe, as long as you are sincere." But sincerity cannot determine whether something is true. It is possible to be sincerely wrong, because faith is only as good as its object. Simply believing something doesn't make it true. We believe something *because* it is true, not to make it true.

Let's say that I put all of my trust into a potted plant to teach me calculus. Will I learn calculus from the plant? No, because it's the wrong object.

In the same way, a person cannot get to heaven by trusting in religion or good works, because that is trusting in the wrong

---

[27] John 14:6

object—these things cannot pay the penalty for our sin. Only Jesus could.

It takes more than sincerity to make something true. Faith in a lie has serious consequences. It *does* matter what a person believes. If you want to drive from New York to Seattle, no amount of sincerity will get you there if the road you take leads to Orlando. Truth is vitally important.

Is refusing to call a belief false always the right thing to do? For instance, is it right to say that racism and Nazism are simply alternate belief systems that we should not pass judgment on? Or, should we condemn these beliefs as being morally wrong? If someone believes they have the right to rob or murder whomever they please, should we accept their beliefs as an alternate lifestyle, or denounce them?

Tolerance is admirable in many circumstances, but tolerating wrong (or evil) by refusing to say it's wrong is in itself wrong. (Read that sentence again if you have to, it's a bit convoluted—but so is the belief it describes.) If Christianity is true, then there is only one God and salvation comes only through Jesus. Therefore religions that deny this truth aren't just alternate forms of spiritual expression; they prevent their adherents from obtaining salvation.

Writer Philip K. Dick said, "Reality is that which, when you stop believing in it, doesn't go away." Denying reality isn't tolerant.

If Jesus Christ is the only way to God, then to claim that He's not is both false and dangerous. If someone has a fatal disease, telling him that he doesn't need to seek medical treatment is wrong. If someone can obtain salvation only by trusting Christ as Savior, then to tell him he does *not* need to accept Christ is even more wrong, no matter how tolerant or well-meaning it may seem.

The Walt Disney Company owns Disneyland. Walt himself created it. They can set whatever conditions on admission they want to, because it's theirs.

God created everything, including heaven. He has provided the way to be redeemed and obtain eternal life. And He can set whatever conditions on eternity that He wants to. Part of the conditions He's set—and there really isn't much—is that Jesus is the only way. The Bible says it. Jesus declared it to be so. And there are very good reasons to believe Jesus is telling the truth—one of those being that He is the Truth.

Of course, if it's not true, if there really is more than one way to God, then the whole thing is a sham. If Jesus said He is the Son of God and the only way to be saved and He is not, then Christianity is futile. It can't be just one of many ways.

There is *one* way, whether it agrees with our sensibilities and what we want to be true or not.

Kingdom Thinking: Where do you stand on this "narrow and exclusive" statement? Is Jesus the only way to God? Do you live like it's true?

The Free Gift of Admission

Imagine yourself at Disneyland but just outside the gates. You desperately want in, but there's a problem. You know which admission ticket you want and you know it needs to be for Disneyland, not somewhere else, but you can't afford it. After all, at the time of this writing it's more than $90 for a one-day, one-park ticket, and almost $140 for a park hopper. (Which is actually still a pretty good value given what you get, but that's another topic.) Even knowing what you need to get into Disneyland, it may be difficult—maybe even impossible—for some families.

No one has that problem when becoming a Christian. We'll get to that in a minute.

Now, imagine you're at the ticket booth, and you don't have enough money for a ticket. Maybe you left your wallet at home— in Maine. At that moment, John Lasseter—or better, Bob Iger, the Walt Disney Company CEO—comes up and says, "Don't worry, I've got it covered," and he offers you a premium annual pass. All you have to do is follow him over to Guest Services and take it. {DISCLAIMER: This does not actually happen, just go with the story.}

Would you hold onto your pride and tell Bob, "No, thanks, I'm fine," even though you know you're not? You have no way to get in without that gift. Or would you say, "Why should I have to go to Guest Services with you? I want you to give it to me right here!" You're being offered a gift, but you won't accept it because of the conditions. Stubborn pride prevents you from receiving a generous gift.

Now imagine a slightly different Disneyland scenario. Again, you are just outside the entrance and can see the joy that awaits you. You've dreamed of going here since you were a child and for a long time you didn't know if you'd ever get to, but now you're there! Unfortunately, for whatever reason, you don't have the money for a ticket. You thought you had enough, or almost enough, but not quite. You figured you would do some bargaining. Maybe you thought you were just $10 short, but really you're nowhere close. You're heartbroken. And then Bob Iger comes up and offers you a premium annual pass, if you'll just walk with him over to Guest Services and pick it up.

Would you do it? Or would you complain that you can't get in *your* way?

There's a bit more to salvation than that, but really, that's what God has done for us.

Romans 6:23 says, "… the gift of God is eternal life in Christ Jesus our Lord."

Ephesians 2:8 says, "For it is by grace you have been saved, through faith—and this not from yourselves, it is the gift of God...."

There's no way to buy your way into heaven, and no way to earn your way into heaven. Eternal life is the gift of God. But "free" and "without condition" are not the same thing. The condition doesn't make it any less free or any less valuable.

In our hypothetical story Bob Iger offers the free annual pass, but with the condition that you walk over to Guest Relations with him to pick it up. If you don't do what he says to do in order to get it, you don't get into Disneyland. You choose to refuse to accept the gift.

God offers us eternal life, but with the condition that we believe in His Son, Jesus Christ. If we don't do that, we choose to refuse to accept His gift. If we *do* believe, we receive a gift beyond our childhood imaginations.

> **Kingdom Thinking:** Have you accepted God's condition, and received His gift of eternal life to you?

Incomplete Commitment

The Esplanade is that area between Disneyland Park and Disney California Adventure Park. When you're there, it means you've parked and made it through the bag/security check. When you make it this far you get to enjoy *some* of the fun of being at Disneyland. But let's be clear: you are *not yet* in the park.

There's area music playing. The monorail passes overhead. You can see the Disneyland Railroad trains as they stop at the Main Street station. You may get to hear the Disneyland Band playing or see characters greeting guests. If you go right up to the gates, you may even be able to take some unobstructed pictures.

Now, imagine that this is all you did. Would anyone call a day spent like this "going to Disneyland"? Sure you got to see and hear some of it, but all from outside the gates, and missing out on a lot! Even though you paid a price (parking, at the very least) just being in the Esplanade isn't "going to Disneyland."

And yet, somehow many of us are content with this much of Jesus Christ. We get close enough to hear the words, the music, and catch a glimpse, but never actually make the commitment. We may *say* we do, but do our actions match our words? We say we believe. We go to church. We might pray before meals. But how much of a difference has Christ made in our lives, our character, our families, our community?

Here is how our life in Christ should be characterized:

"Put on the full armor of God so that you can take your stand against the devil's schemes."[28] Put on not just part of the armor, not just what you think you need at the moment, but the *full* armor.

"You are all sons of God through faith in Christ Jesus, for all of you who were baptized into Christ have clothed yourselves with Christ."[29] The transliterated Greek word for "baptism" is "*baptizo*" and it literally means to immerse or plunge. This verse describes a complete submersion into Christ and being completely covered with Him.

Here is another description of the Christian life from Paul.

I have been crucified with Christ and I no longer live, but Christ lives in me. The life I live in the body, I live by faith in the Son of God, who loved me and gave Himself for me.[30]

---

[28] Ephesians 6:11
[29] Galatians 3:26–27
[30] Galatians 2:20

Paul's entire identity was found in Christ, to the point where he could say that the life he lived was Christ living in him.

"Now if we died with Christ, we believe that we will also live with Him."[31] Commitment does not get much stronger than death!

Gospel author Mark describes a Christ-follower's commitment.

Then He called the crowd to Him along with His disciples and said: "If anyone would come after Me, he must deny himself and take up his cross and follow Me. For whoever wants to save his life will lose it, but whoever loses his life for Me and for the gospel will save it."[32]

Strong words from Jesus. Again, commitment doesn't get much more complete than this calling.

Is this what your commitment to Christ, your daily Christian life, looks like? Mine doesn't always—certainly not as much as I want it to. But where I am is more fully committed to Him than where I used to be, and where I will be is more than where I am now. That's part of grace, and of growing in the grace and knowledge of Jesus.[33]

I would never claim that hanging out in the Esplanade was the same as going to Disneyland, but some days I'm content with a casual commitment to following Jesus. If you're the same, there is hope. We can grow. We're commanded to grow. And He who began a good work in you will carry it on to completion until the day of Christ Jesus.[34] It's not about earning favor; it's seeking His best for us—which is only found in complete commitment to Him.

---

[31] Romans 6:8
[32] Mark 8:34–35
[33] 2 Peter 3:18
[34] Philippians 1:6

> **Kingdom Thinking:** On a scale of 1–10, how would you rate your level of commitment to Jesus Christ? How can you increase that number?

The Berm: Define Your Worldview

(This one is a bit more complex and may be harder to follow. Please stick with it!)

When you "officially" enter Disneyland, it means you've paid your admission, had your ticket scanned, and crossed through the gates––unlike the Esplanade, you are now technically in the park. And yet, that is no place to stay if you really want to be "in" Disneyland. Sure, from there you can see the train and the train station and hear some of the music. You may be lucky and meet a character or even see the Disneyland band. You wouldn't spend a day in that location and think you'd "been to the park" though, would you?

Of course not. From here, you have to go through one of the tunnels to get to Main Street U.S.A. and actually be in Disneyland. Those tunnels pass under the train tracks, which sit on something called "the berm."

Think of a berm as an artificial hill that encircles Disneyland to control the view, and to really be "in" Disneyland means to be inside the confines of the berm. If you're not looking for it, you'll probably never notice the berm, but it's there serving that very important purpose. In *The Vatican to Vegas*, Norman Klein says,

Technically a berm was a shoulder of earth that obscured Anaheim from visitors. As a narrative, the berm was the proscenium arch, marking the reassuring boundaries of the scripted space.[35]

The berm creates your horizon and helps you define what belongs in your experience and what doesn't.

Your worldview does something very similar for your life. In *A World of Difference*, Kenneth Samples says,

> In the simplest terms, a worldview may be defined as how one sees life and the world at large. In this manner it can be compared to a pair of glasses. How a person makes sense of the world depends upon that person's "vision," so to speak. The interpretive "lens" helps people make sense of life and comprehend the world around them. Sometimes the lens brings clarity, and other times it can distort reality.[36]

Your worldview provides a framework for your beliefs, values, and how you live your life day-to-day. It gives you a context for answering the "big questions." It's not meant to give you an excuse to stop thinking critically. Quite the opposite, in fact. A worldview provides a methodology to view and interpret new information and a rationale to accept or reject claims that are counter to your worldview. The more aware of it and intentional you are about it, the better your worldview serves that purpose. Of course, most people never take time to examine their worldview, just as they don't notice Disneyland's berm.

Disneyland without the berm would spill over into the surrounding neighborhood and the neighborhood would "intrude" on Disneyland. Walt couldn't count on a berm to just appear on its own. He was intentional about creating it based on

---

[35] Norman M. Klein, *The Vatican to Vegas: A History of Special Effects* (New York: The New Press, 2004), 308.
[36] Kenneth Richard Samples, *A World of Difference: Putting Christian Truth-Claims to the Worldview Test* (Grand Rapids, MI: Baker Books, 2007), 20.

what needed to be contained within it and what needed to be kept out to maintain a cohesive story.

There have been times when it was necessary for the Imagineers to "think outside the berm," if you will. There just wasn't room inside for changes of a certain scope and scale. Some of the show buildings for headliner attractions (Pirates of the Caribbean, the Haunted Mansion, and the Indiana Jones Adventure, for example) actually exist *outside* the berm. Mickey's Toontown is entirely outside the original one (though "berm" has now been redefined to be "the threshold...isolating the visitor from the street, and inviting a theatrical suspension of disbelief").[37] By that new definition, the "hills" behind Toontown replace the earthen berm as the new threshold.

Sometimes, when presented with significant new information or a dramatic change in life circumstances—something completely outside what one's current worldview can handle or interpret—a worldview must be totally reexamined. It may hold in its original form, or it may change based on the "new reality." The more intentionally and purposefully you conduct that reexamination, though, the more effective it will be. If it's done subconsciously and haphazardly, the result will be mental, emotional, and spiritual chaos—or worse, the attempt to discard a worldview entirely (which is itself a worldview—see, you can't escape it).

This seems consistent with what Paul is talking about when he says, "We demolish arguments and every pretension that sets itself up against the knowledge of God, and we take captive every thought to make it obedient to Christ."[38] Being able to have a clear, coherent, internally consistent belief and value system, one that is rooted and grounded in what God says in the Bible, enables us to take every thought and either fit it into that worldview or discard it as being incompatible or inconsistent.

---

[37] Klein, *Vatican to Vegas*, 308.
[38] 2 Corinthians 10:5

Paul also says,

> Therefore, I urge you, brothers and sisters, in view of God's mercy, to offer your bodies as a living sacrifice, holy and pleasing to God—this is your true and proper worship. Do not conform to the pattern of this world, but be transformed by the renewing of your mind. Then you will be able to test and approve what God's will is—His good, pleasing and perfect will.[39]

To put that in the current context, Paul says that in light of your "new reality" as believers in Christ, saved by God and adopted into His family, examine your worldview. What had once been completely informed by and conformed to the world needs to be reworked. Change your thinking. Start looking for His perspective, and choose to base your worldview on that.

So, how do you do that? What questions do you need to answer to clearly identify what your worldview is, and then determine if it is what it should be? There are several ways to approach this examination, but for now, let me suggest five questions you can answer.

1. Is there a God?
2. If so, what is this God like?
3. Why am I here?
4. What is wrong with the world?
5. How can it be fixed (and what role, if any, do I have in doing so)?

---

[39] Romans 12:1–2

If you'd like a more extensive list of questions, see Kenneth Samples' blog post "What in the World is a Worldview?"[40] or his book *A World of Difference*.[41]

Answering these questions identifies where your berm is, what's inside of it, and what's outside of it. They dictate what you do, why you do it, and how you do it. These answers form your script for how you live your life. If your answer to any of them reflects a contradiction between your belief and your behavior (for instance, you answer #4 with "Humans have no respect for nature," but you litter regularly), that warrants some extra examination. Do you believe something different than you claim to, or do you need to modify your behavior to align with your belief?

You can't function for long if what happens inside your berm is inconsistent with the story it was built to tell. The longer you try, the worse life gets, until eventually you'll come apart at the seams mentally, emotionally, spiritually, and maybe even physically.

It's that important.

> **Kingdom Thinking:** How would you answer the preceding five questions (honestly)? Are your behavior and attitudes consistent with those answers?

---

[40] Kenneth Samples, "What in the World is a Worldview," http://reflectionsbyken.wordpress.com/2011/08/23/what-in-the-world-is-a-worldview/, accessed July 6, 2013.
[41] Samples, *A World of Difference*, 21–22.

Chapter 3: Main Street U.S.A.

Lay of the Land

Hyperreality and Faith

*M*ore than twenty-five years ago, Umberto Eco described a concept called "Hyperreality." Basically, hyperreality is the idea that a simulation is—or at least can be—more "real" than the reality itself.[42]

In an episode of *Gilmore Girls*, Rory and Paris get an apartment. At one point, Rory hears a loud bang and thinks it's gunfire. Paris tells her, "No. That was just a car backfiring. The real gunfire actually sounds fake." Rory had gotten so used to hearing fake

---

[42] Thanks to Kevin Yee for initially introducing this concept to me via his articles on the subject at MiceAge.com back in 2005.

gunfire on TV that the sound of it was more real to her than the sound of actual gunfire. The fake sound had become a hyperreal sound.

Main Street U.S.A. is a classic example. The Main Street at Disneyland never really existed. True, it's based on Walt's hometown of Marceline, Missouri, but it's not a strict re-creation of that town's main street. A lot of the look and feel of Disneyland's Main Street is also based on Fort Collins, Colorado. It's really the Main Street that never was. Yet, when many people think of "small town America main street," they think of Disneyland's Main Street U.S.A., often to the point where they are disappointed if they ever do see a small town's main road.

And why not? Disneyland's "main drive" has almost everything we would expect Main Street to have: a bakery, a town hall, a bank, a fire station, a penny arcade, a barbershop, clothing shops, a photo supply company, even a cinema. It employs happy, gracious people, giving it something of that "small town charm." It has various modes of transportation—an omnibus, a horse-drawn streetcar, a horseless carriage, even a fire engine—all moving smoothly and efficiently down the center of the street, reinforcing the vision that all is as it should be in this quaint, rustic place.

Most people have never seen a turn-of-the-twentieth-century American small town. But we *have* seen Main Street U.S.A. It becomes our hyperreal version of the actual reality. And so what we expect to be true carries more weight than what the so-called real world shows us.

In some ways, this concept is a good description of what biblical faith means. The difference is that instead of a false reality being more real than actual reality, faith tells us that what we believe by faith to be true actually is more real, and has more substance, than what we can see, hear, and feel.

Genesis 22 tells of the time God tested Abraham. He was told to take his son, Isaac, and sacrifice him as a burnt offering to God.

Abraham did as he was told. Of course, God stopped him at the last minute, saying, "Do not lay your hand on the lad or do anything to him; for now I know that you fear and revere God, since you have not held back from Me or begrudged giving Me your son, your only son."[43]

When Abraham stepped out on faith, he did so because he believed a reality that he knew was more real than what he could see around him. He knew that God was faithful, no matter what it seemed like at the moment. That's why he said things like, "*We* will worship and then *we* will come back to you,"[44] to one of the servants. Notice he did not say, "*I* will come back." He says "*we* will." When Isaac asks, "but where is the lamb for the burnt offering?"[45] Abraham answered, "God Himself will provide the lamb for the burnt offering, my son"[46] All Abraham knew was that God had promised him many descendants, these descendants would come through his son Isaac, and that God was faithful to keep His word. So Abraham acted in faith.

Hebrews 11, called the "Faith Chapter," is full of such stories. And that chapter starts by saying, "Now faith is being sure of what we hope for and certain of what we do not see."[47] Another way to say it is that faith is being sure of the reality that is greater than the reality we see around us.

Right here, on Main Street U.S.A., we get a reminder that what we see around us is not all there is—there is much more that can be grasped only through faith.

---

[43] Genesis 22:12 (AMP)
[44] Genesis 22:5 (emphasis added)
[45] Genesis 22:7
[46] Genesis 22:8
[47] Hebrews 11:1

> **Kingdom Thinking:** When you're going through trials or life doesn't seem to make sense, what is more real to you in that moment, what you see around you or God's character and promises?

I Had to Come Here

I had the privilege of spending the afternoon of September 11, 2011, the tenth anniversary of the 9-11 terrorist attacks on the United States, at Disneyland, watching a very special Flag Retreat ceremony. Being there reminded me of a story that Tim O'Day (former director of publicity at the Disneyland Resort, among other things) shared about the day after the attack.

On September 12, 2001, he was walking across Town Square toward City Hall. There was almost no one in the park that day ("You could throw a bowling ball any direction and not hit anyone," he said), but he saw a woman sitting by herself on a bench sobbing. He walked up to her and asked if she was all right, if there was anything he could do to help her. She continued to cry for a few more minutes as he sat next to her. When she could finally talk, she said, "I had to come here. I just couldn't watch it anymore."

Doesn't that resonate? For this woman, Disneyland was an escape, a safe place, and a place of reassurance. She was so distraught that she sought refuge at Disneyland. I have to be honest. Disneyland has been a haven for me on more than one occasion, though not on that particular day.

There are times when we all seek refuge. The world batters or overwhelms us. We've seen all we can stand, and we have to get away. We reach a point where we must escape and find a safe place.

Fortunately, as believers, we have such a refuge, as these many comforting passages attest.

> But let all who take refuge in You be glad; let them ever sing for joy. Spread Your protection over them, that those who love Your Name may rejoice in You.[48]

> The LORD is a refuge for the oppressed, a stronghold in times of trouble.[49]

> The LORD is my rock, my fortress and my deliverer; my God is my rock, in whom I take refuge. He is my shield and the horn of my salvation, my stronghold.[50]

> God is our refuge and strength, an ever-present help in trouble.[51]

> But I will sing of Your strength, in the morning I will sing of Your love; for You are my fortress, my refuge in times of trouble.[52]

> It is better to take refuge in the LORD than to trust in man. It is better to take refuge in the LORD than to trust in princes. All the nations surrounded me, but in the name of the LORD I cut them off. They surrounded me on every side, but in the name of the LORD I cut them off. They swarmed around me like bees, but they died out as quickly as burning thorns; in the name of the LORD I cut them off. I was pushed back and

---

[48] Psalm 5:11
[49] Psalm 9:9
[50] Psalm 18:2
[51] Psalm 46:1—In fact, read all of Psalm 46.
[52] Psalm 59:16

about to fall, but the LORD helped me. The LORD is my strength and my song; He has become my salvation.[53]

The LORD is good, a refuge in times of trouble. He cares for those who trust in Him.[54]

So do not fear, for I am with you; do not be dismayed, for I am your God. I will strengthen you and help you; I will uphold you with My righteous right hand.[55]

God is our refuge from a harsh and cruel world. He is our strength when we have none left of our own. That doesn't mean He takes us out of the world (though sometimes we do get that much-needed respite), but He gives us all we need to stand, as long as we are standing in Him. And that means spending time with Him, knowing who He is, and being able to trust Him (and you can only fully trust one you know well). Sometimes that's easier said than done, but that does not make it any less true.

Praise be to the God and Father of our Lord Jesus Christ, the Father of compassion and the God of all comfort, who comforts us in all our troubles, so that we can comfort those in any trouble with the comfort we ourselves have received from God. For just as the sufferings of Christ flow over into our lives, so also through Christ our comfort overflows.[56]

Come to Me, all you who are weary and burdened, and I will give you rest. Take My yoke upon you and learn from Me, for I am gentle and humble in heart, and you will find rest for your souls. For My yoke is easy and My burden is light.[57]

---

[53] Psalm 118:8–14
[54] Nahum 1:7
[55] Isaiah 41:10
[56] 2 Corinthians 1:3–5
[57] Matthew 11:28–30

When you can't watch anymore, when you've been battered and beaten and have to get away, stop looking around and look up! Take comfort, listen, and be restored. Then act.

A popular hymn powerfully captures the sentiment.

> O soul, are you weary and troubled?
> No light in the darkness you see?
> There's light for a look at the Savior,
> And life more abundant and free!
>
> Turn your eyes upon Jesus,
> Look full in His wonderful face,
> And the things of earth will grow strangely dim,
> In the light of His glory and grace.
>
> Through death into life everlasting
> He passed, and we follow Him there;
> O'er us sin no more hath dominion—
> For more than conqu'rors we are!
>
> Turn your eyes upon Jesus,
> Look full in His wonderful face,
> And the things of earth will grow strangely dim,
> In the light of His glory and grace.
>
> His Word shall not fail you—He promised;
> Believe Him, and all will be well:
> Then go to a world that is dying,
> His perfect salvation to tell!
>
> Turn your eyes upon Jesus,
> Look full in His wonderful face,
> And the things of earth will grow strangely dim,
> In the light of His glory and grace.[58]

---

[58] "Turn Your Eyes Upon Jesus," Helen H. Lemmel, 1922, Public Domain.

> **Kingdom Thinking:** How is God your refuge? What is one way you can choose to rely on Him even more in that capacity?

Park Plaque

Leaving Here to Enter There

"Here you leave today and enter the world of yesterday, tomorrow, and fantasy."

So reads the plaque over the tunnels that take guests beneath the railroad tracks and onto Main Street U.S.A. Before passing under that sign you're technically "in Disneyland," but there's little to see, do, and discover. In order to really experience Disneyland, you must pass through this portal, leave today, and enter the place that is wholly "other."

The same is true about life as a believer comes to faith in Christ. It's possible to know about Him, go to church, and generally "dip your toe in." But that better place takes a conscious, deliberate step of choosing to follow Jesus. When you do, you become new. You are different. You have left one life behind and entered a life that is wholly "other."

Scripture describes this "passing through" in various passages, including these:

Therefore, if anyone is in Christ, he is a new creation; the old has gone, the new has come!...God made Him who had no sin to be sin for us, so that in Him we might become the righteousness of God.[59]

---

[59] 2 Corinthians 5:17, 21

We know that we have passed from death to life, because we love our brothers. Anyone who does not love remains in death.[60]

Do you not know that the wicked will not inherit the kingdom of God? Do not be deceived: Neither the sexually immoral nor idolaters nor adulterers nor male prostitutes nor homosexual offenders nor thieves nor the greedy nor drunkards nor slanderers nor swindlers will inherit the kingdom of God. And that is what some of you were. But you were washed, you were sanctified, you were justified in the name of the Lord Jesus Christ and by the Spirit of our God.[61]

Kingdom Thinking: What was your moment of "passing through the portal?" What is your life like now?

Disneyland Railroad

Why We Need a Blowdown

My brother-in-law, Stuart, and I had the opportunity/privilege of getting a Tender Ride on Engine 1 of the Disneyland Railroad, the C.K. Holliday. We got to talk to the engineer and the fireman, see the train controls, and learn a great deal (as much as one can in twenty minutes) about the operations of a steam train, particularly one at Disneyland.

One of the things Barbara, the engineer, and Jacob, the fireman, explained to us was the importance of the steam pressure

---

[60] 1 John 3:14
[61] 1 Corinthians 6:9–11

and maintaining it at the proper levels. One primary way of doing that is performing a "blowdown" as needed at the Frontierland Station.

Blowing down the boiler several times a day is a critical procedure to ensure the safe operation of a steam locomotive. According to Steve DeGaetano, author of *Welcome Aboard the Disneyland Railroad*, up to twelve pounds of dissolved sediments accumulates to every 500 gallons of water, not to mention the residue from the several pounds of the antifoaming and anticorrosion chemicals that are added to the water several times a day.[62] This sludge can build up inside the boiler. If the sediment is allowed to build up, the result could be a boiler explosion. The blowdown allows this material to be jettisoned from the boiler, in dramatic fashion.

We didn't get to see it on that day (they don't allow tender rides if they're going to do a blowdown), but if you've ever been near the Frontierland/New Orleans Square station, you've probably seen it happen—and heard it. If you've been near that station and heard a sudden loud hiss, and then saw a jet of white steam come from the left side of the engine, that was a blowdown. They blow out the sediment, and then refill with fresh water to continue the run.

Barbara and Jacob told us that they do these blowdowns about once an hour, or every two to three trips around. However, on some days the water is exceptionally "hard," and they have to do it every time. The more minerals and impurities that are in the water, the more often they have to blow down the boiler and refill it with fresh water.

Think about the pressure in our own lives. We are always under pressure. From work. From home. From friends. From other organizations we may be part of. Even from ourselves. When that

---

[62] Steve DeGaetano, "Will It Go Round in Circles," http://miceage.micechat.com/stevedegaetano/sd050107b.htm, accessed July 22, 2013.

happens, we may want to just push through and keep going. We don't have time to stop and do anything else.

But when we keep going along that way, the sediment builds up in our hearts. The impurities get in when we don't take time to flush them out. And we risk an explosion. We blow up at our spouses. We become passive-aggressive with our coworkers. We become resentful of the demands of others. And we avoid church and other believers because we feel like we have to keep struggling to keep our lives together. And yet, the harder the circumstances, the more often we need the blowdown.

God knows this. That's why He created the Sabbath. Not to force rules or legalism on us, but to make sure we're taken care of. "The Sabbath was made for man, not man for the Sabbath."[63] One of my favorite verses in the Gospels comes just before the feeding of the 5,000.

> Then, because so many people were coming and going that they did not even have a chance to eat, he said to them, "Come with me by yourselves to a quiet place and get some rest." So they went away by themselves in a boat to a solitary place.[64]

In the midst of busyness, Jesus says, "Come with Me by yourselves to a quiet place and get some rest." He says the same thing now. At the very times when we're at our most harried, He says, come away with Me. At those times, the most "spiritual" thing you can do may be to take a nap…or go to Disneyland.

Scripture repeatedly reminds us of the dangers of not taking time to "blow down" the boiler of our hearts and clean out the sediment. That cleansing comes when we spend time with God and with other believers.

---

[63] Mark 2:27
[64] Mark 6:31–32

Let us not give up meeting together, as some are in the habit of doing, but let us encourage one another—and all the more as you see the Day approaching.[65]

Sometimes we just need some time "away from it all." A massage. A vacation (short or long). Maybe even a game or a funny movie. As Milton Berle said, "Laughter is an instant vacation."

When we get too much sediment in our system and haven't taken time to blow down the boilers we risk trouble. But once we've done that blowdown, we have to refill with something.

Jesus answered, "Everyone who drinks this water will be thirsty again, but whoever drinks the water I give him will never thirst. Indeed, the water I give him will become in him a spring of water welling up to eternal life."[66]

Do not get drunk on wine, which leads to debauchery. Instead, be filled with the Spirit.[67]

When it's hardest to find time to refill, when we most don't want to do it, that's exactly when we most need God's infilling. If we keep running without clearing out the bad stuff and going back to the fresh water of life, the boiler will explode.

Next time you hear that blowdown or see the steam, ask yourself, "Am I running too hard, too long, without a blowdown?" If you are, then make some time to spend resting with God, and meeting with other believers. It is far better in the long run, because it's how you were designed to operate.

---

[65] Hebrews 10:25
[66] John 4:13–14
[67] Ephesians 5:18

> **Kingdom Thinking:** Do you find it difficult to make time for rest? What's one thing you can do today to create intentional time for rest and renewal?

Keep Your Level Full!

A set of sensors monitors the boiler water level above the brakeman. On our ride the fireman asked us, "On a steam train, which do you think is worse: the boiler having too much water or having too little water?" My brother-in-law and I thought about it, and both said, "Too little water." That's correct. If the boiler has too much water, it may not be able to heat sufficiently to generate steam. If it has too little, once it reaches a certain temperature the water will all flash evaporate at once and the boiler will explode.

That's consistent with how the Ohio Valley Systems railroad explains what happens in their steam locomotive operations manual:

Too much water in the boiler and it won't heat up quickly enough to generate enough steam. It can also cause Priming (water collecting in the cylinders). Too little water in the boiler and the crown sheet (the top of the firebox/bottom of the boiler) will overheat and cause a boiler explosion. A boiler explosion levels everything within several hundred feet, starting with the engine crew.[68]

It doesn't get much worse than this in steam train operations. That's why the Disneyland Railroad crew constantly monitors the

---

[68] Steam Locomotive Operation, OVS Training Institute 2006, http://www.ovsrails.com/OVSTI/SteamLocoManual.htm, accessed July 27, 2013.

water level and makes sure the engine is always operating with plenty of water in the boiler.

Previously, I likened the boiler to our spirit. The same parallel applies again. Are you trying to work/minister/serve/live out of a *full* spirit or a dangerously *empty* one? Ephesians 3:16–19 says,

> I pray that out of His glorious riches He may strengthen you with power through His Spirit in your inner being, so that Christ may dwell in your hearts through faith. And I pray that you, being rooted and established in love, may have power, together with all the Lord's holy people, to grasp how wide and long and high and deep is the love of Christ, and to know this love that surpasses knowledge—that you may be filled to the measure of all the fullness of God.

As believers, we want God's strength and power, and to really understand the scope of His love for us, but we usually want to do it ourselves. We try. We struggle. We fail and wonder what went wrong.

> This is what the LORD says:
> "Cursed is the one who trusts in man,
> who draws strength from mere flesh
> and whose heart turns away from the LORD.
> That person will be like a bush in the wastelands;
> they will not see prosperity when it comes.
> They will dwell in the parched places of the desert,
> in a salt land where no one lives.
> But blessed is the one who trusts in the LORD,
> whose confidence is in him.
> They will be like a tree planted by the water
> that sends out its roots by the stream.
> It does not fear when heat comes;
> its leaves are always green.

It has no worries in a year of drought
and never fails to bear fruit."[69]

Trouble results when we rely on our own strength. We try to serve and love others out of our own efforts. That works for a while, but eventually our levels get too low and we burn out, or we snap at people, or we may even blow up. What little steam we have left gets used up and our "internal boiler" explodes. Then we feel guilty, ashamed, and fearful that we've let God down. We tried and we failed.

But the truth is usually that we didn't allow ourselves the time to refill. It's easy to stay busy and not take time to spend with God. We think we know what needs to be done and when and we don't "wait upon the Lord to renew our strength." We think we can do our part and then let God do His part. But in John 15:5–6, Jesus said,

> "I am the vine; you are the branches. If you remain in Me and I in you, you will bear much fruit; apart from Me you can do nothing. If you do not remain in Me, you are like a branch that is thrown away and withers; such branches are picked up, thrown into the fire and burned."

Notice that Jesus does not say, "Apart from Me you can do some things," or even "Apart from Me you can do a little." The imagery is clear. A branch separated from the vine will live for a little while but it dies quickly. It must remain attachedto the vine. That's why Jesus made a regular practice of spending time alone with His Father.

Now this attachment does not require a thirty-minute "quiet time" first thing in the morning every day, unless that is what works for you and your relationship with God. It does not entail going through the motions or making the means the goal. But it does

---

[69] Jeremiah 17:5–8

mean that prayer, time in the Bible, time with other believers, and rest must be a part of your "spiritual rhythm."

Each of us needs to keep a close watch on our levels and make sure we are not running low, and ask God for wisdom and discernment if this is a blind spot. The Disneyland Railroad crew refills their train's boiler when it gets down to about half full, so that it never risks getting too low. Our internal boiler needs the same kind of attention and refilling.

Every puff of steam from the engine serves as a reminder of the water level in the boiler that created that steam, and as a reminder to not let our boiler level get too low, or the boiler could explode—with considerable damage to ourselves and those around us.

> **Kingdom Thinking:** How do you "refill" spiritually? Have you ever let your internal boiler get too low? How could you tell?

City Hall

"What Do You Want Me to Do for You?"

The Gospel of Mark chapter 10 has a pair of interesting stories back-to-back.

In verses 46–52, Jesus and the crowd of people with Him come near a blind man named Bartimaeus, who is begging by the side of the road. Bartimaeus shouts, "Jesus, Son of David, have mercy on me!" Jesus has this man brought to Him and asks, "What do you want Me to do for you?" The blind man asks for his sight, and Jesus responds, "Go, your faith has healed you." Immediately Bartimaeus received his sight.

There are very few reasons a park visitor might go to Main Street's City Hall. Offhand, the only ones I can think of are to get a celebration button, put in a compliment (for a Cast Member, show, etc.), or lodge a complaint. There aren't many other reasons to go inside. If you do enter, as you approach the counter you will be asked one question, "How can I help you?"

How do you respond? One hundred percent of the time, it's with a specific request, like these:

- I'd like to compliment _____.
- I need to complain about _____.
- It's my birthday (or anniversary, or whatever).
- I have this problem. Is there anything you can do for me?

All are specific, direct requests. A guest never says anything like, "Oh, I'm not sure." We don't respond, "If you don't mind, and if it wouldn't take up too much of your time or inconvenience you, I was wondering if I could get a birthday button, unless maybe something else would be better." We tell them exactly what we want.

Bartimaeus did the same thing. Jesus asked, "What do you want Me to do for you?" and the blind man told Him his request directly, specifically, and without hesitation. Do you do the same?

I didn't—not often, anyway—though that is changing. As a learning Christian I made vague requests and couched them in caveats so much that it was clear I did not really expect Him to give me whatever it is I asked.

When we pray we say, "If it's Your will...," which is wise, but often we really mean, "You're probably not going to do this, so now I have an out, a way to justify what seems to me to be an unanswered prayer without actually having to wrestle with anything." What happened to asking specifically, directly, and in faith? I'm not talking about material things, though asking for "our daily bread" is certainly legitimate. (More on this in the next section.)

I don't know about you, but I have asked for too little, and done it in a way that if nothing happened I could just say, "Well, it must not have been His will," thereby staying safe, settling, and missing out. After all, Bartimaeus didn't have to ask for his sight. That was risky. It meant he would have to completely change the way he lived and "saw" the world (so to speak). He could have asked for a more comfortable mat, or for more people to give money to him, or even for a warmer cloak. But he didn't. He asked for much more than that. He asked that his greatest need—and his greatest desire—be met.

"Ask Me for anything in My Name," says Jesus.[70]

Jesus again: "Ask and you will receive."[71]

"You do not have, because you do not ask God," says James.[72]

Here we see clear and direct statements, where God essentially says to us, "What do you want Me to do for you?" Do you ever directly answer His question, and actually believe He'll do what you ask?

Not asking, or skirting the issue, is really taking the matter out of God's hands. It's saying to Him, "I don't think You're going to do this for me, so I just won't ask, certainly not in a way that I have to actually put my faith in You for the answer and risk Your saying no."

---

[70] John 14:14
[71] John 16:24
[72] James 4:2a

Kingdom Thinking: Answer God's question. Clearly and specifically, what do you want Jesus to do for you? Are you willing to actually say it?

What's the Catch?

Let's back up a few verses from the previous story, because if we leave it where we did, though the story provides a valuable lesson, we run the risk of missing an important part of the picture.

In Mark 10:35–45, James and John come to Jesus with a request. "What do you want Me to do for you?" Jesus asks them (v. 36). They replied, "Let one of us sit at Your right and the other at Your left in your glory" (v. 37). Not only does Jesus not grant their request but also He tells them that they don't even really understand what it is they're asking and explains to them that their priorities are wrong.

The same question from Jesus is posed to James and John and Bartimaeus. They offer two very different responses.

The second lesson from City Hall is this: You won't always get what you ask for. If you go into City Hall and say, "It's my birthday. Can I have a birthday button and free dinner at the Blue Bayou?" you'll get the button, but not the dinner. If you say, "I didn't get the scene combination I wanted on Star Tours. I want my admission for the day comped." you're not going to get it.

There are criteria for granting requests. At Disneyland, one must ask for something reasonable for the situation, comparable to the problem, and/or within Disney's power to do. Don't try asking them to make it stop raining. It won't work.

James continues in chapter 4:

> When you ask, you do not receive, because you ask with wrong motives, that you may spend what you get on your pleasures.[73]

Here again is Jesus:

> If you remain in Me and My words remain in you, ask whatever you wish, and it will be done for you.[74]

And from John:

> Dear friends, if our hearts do not condemn us, we have confidence before God and receive from Him anything we ask, because we keep His commands and do what pleases Him.[75]

Again, John:

> This is the confidence we have in approaching God: that if we ask anything according to His will, He hears us. And if we know that He hears us—whatever we ask—we know that we have what we asked of Him.[76]

I'm not advocating "name-it-and-claim-it." There are certain conditions (not rules or formulas to compel God to act), but they're not surprising, are they?

Think of a child growing up in her parents' house. She is disrespectful to her parents, never wants to spend any time with them, and disobeys. If she asks for something, are they going to give it to her? Maybe, but probably not. She doesn't respect them. She's just using them.

---

[73] James 4:2b
[74] John 15:7
[75] 1 John 3:21–22
[76] 1 John 5:14–15

If the opposite is true and she shows love to her parents, spending time with them, being respectful and obedient, are they not more likely to grant her request? Of course they are. It's not a guarantee, though. She may have asked for something that they know to be harmful. There may be something she needs to learn by *not* having it…at least not right away. The parents may have something better in mind for her. Still, she can ask, and be confident in her request.

Let me encourage you to do the same thing. It is likely that there's something on your heart that you want to ask God, but haven't. He has said to you, "What do you want Me to do for you?" but you haven't answered. Ask Him, and if necessary keep asking. Either you'll receive it, or He'll change your heart and desires. He will give you what you need, which may also be what you want, as long as your desire is to please Him. But this won't happen if you don't ask.

Also keep in mind that "confident" and "arrogant" are not the same thing. Consider Jacob's prayer when he was on the way to face Esau.

O God of my father Abraham, God of my father Isaac, O Lord, who said to me, "Go back to your country and your relatives, and I will make you prosper," I am unworthy of all the kindness and faithfulness you have shown your servant. I had only my staff when I crossed this Jordan, but now I have become two groups. Save me, I pray, from the hand of my brother Esau, for I am afraid he will come and attack me, and also the mothers with their children. But you have said, "I will surely make you prosper and will make your descendants like the sand of the sea, which cannot be counted."[77]

Do your prayers sound anything like Jacob's?

---

[77] Genesis 32:9–12

- Rooted in Who God is
- Humble
- Specific and direct
- Recalling God's promises

First, do a self-check, asking the Holy Spirit to help. Are you actually spending time with Him and in His word, or do you only come to Him when you want something? Are you doing what you already know He's told you to do, or is He only Santa Claus and not your Lord? Are you approaching Him with a sense of entitlement and arrogance? Are you asking for something for selfish and sinful reasons?

That last question bears a bit more attention. Clearly it isn't sinful or wrong to ask for something for yourself. Bartimaeus did, and his request was granted. The question is, what are you going to do with what He gives you? Use it selfishly? Over-indulge in it? Waste it? Or are you going to use God's gift also for the benefit of others? Be wise with it? Use it to glorify God?

If your heart is right, ask confidently and clearly. Ask in faith, trusting Him to do it. He may say no (though not in an audible voice), but that's up to Him, not you. If He does deny a request, live with it at the time. For now, answer His question.

Kingdom Thinking: Revisit your request from before. Now, do the heart check. Do you need to reconsider or revise your request? If so, now is a great time to do that. If not, be confident and bold (though not arrogant or entitled).

Walt's Apartment

Never Will I Leave You

It's one of those little details that is so easy to overlook, yet it's in plain sight. Just above the Fire Station (next to Town Hall) is a window with a light in it. So what?

While Disneyland was being built, Walt Disney wanted a place he and his family could stay so he could keep an eye on things. He had an apartment constructed on the second floor of the Main Street U.S.A. Firehouse—private, and hidden from the rest of the park. When he worked in the apartment, he often sat at a small wooden desk near the window facing Main Street.

Sharon Baird, one of the original Mouseketeers, was there Opening Day:

> On the opening day of Disneyland, we (Mouseketeers) were in Walt Disney's private apartment above the Main Street Fire Station when the gates of the park opened for the first time. I was standing next to him at the window, watching the guests come pouring through the gates. When I looked up at him, he had his hands behind his back, a grin from ear to ear, I could see a lump in his throat and a tear streaming down his cheek. He had realized his dream. I was only twelve years old at the time, so it didn't mean as much to me then. But as the years go by, that image of him becomes more and more endearing.[78]

That's the window you see when you look above the fire station. That's where Walt Disney sat, worked, and looked out to watch people come to his Magic Kingdom for the very first time.

---

[78] "Walt's Private Apartment,"
http://www.justdisney.com/Features/Apartment.html, accessed July 27, 2013.

Over the next decade, whenever Walt was in Disneyland the light in his apartment window was on. This became well-known to the Cast Members who worked during this time, and they would look for this light to know if Walt was there or not. Since his death, the window light has been left on, and it symbolizes Walt Disney's spirit and presence at Disneyland. The only exceptions are at Christmas time (when a small, illuminated Christmas tree stands in the window), and when his daughter Diane Disney Miller is in the park, out of respect for her.

The light in the window is a reminder of where this enchanting place came from, whose dream it was, and who we have to thank for it. Every time I leave—and most of the time when I enter—I take a moment to glance at the window and say a silent "thank you" to Walt Disney.

That reminder of the presence of the creator has a parallel in Christian Communion, but it also serves as a connection to a promise that was made in Scripture. It's made more than once, but we'll look at just one instance.

Keep your lives free from the love of money and be content with what you have, because God has said,
   "Never will I leave you;
never will I forsake you."
So we say with confidence,
   "The Lord is my helper; I will not be afraid.
What can man do to me?"[79]

I do not cite the original Greek (the language the New Testament was written in) often, but in this instance it is very important. In English grammar, a double negative cancels itself out, but in Greek grammar multiple negatives reinforce the strength of the statement. In the phrases, "Never will I leave you; never will I forsake you," the first is a double negative, and the

---

[79] Hebrews 13:5–6

second is a triple negative. This is not a casual statement. It says, in effect, "Never, ever will I leave you; never, ever, ever will I forsake you."

God makes a promise that you or I cannot undo. If you are His child, He will not leave you…ever! You may have been abandoned—because a loved one left, or even died. You may have been betrayed. You may be afraid of what the future holds or convinced that your past (or present) makes you unlovable. But if you've accepted Jesus Christ, you have been adopted into His family. You don't have to achieve a certain status or worry about whether you have (or are) enough of anything. He chose you. He loves you. And He will never leave you or forsake you.

Next time you enter Disneyland, and again when you leave, don't hurry through Town Square. Take a moment to look above the Fire Station. Think for a moment about Walt Disney, and the light that reminds us that his spirit is always there, because he remains an integral part of Disneyland. Then let it remind you of Someone Else who is always present, not just in memory, but in present reality.

Kingdom Thinking: What reminds you of God's presence in your life? What do you do when life gets hard and you don't feel that presence?

Main Street Windows

Who Are You Thankful For?

When you enter Disneyland, once you pass through the archway and enter Main Street, what's the first thing you do? Make a mad dash for Space Mountain or Indiana Jones? Head up to the train station to start your day with a "grand circle tour"? Get dragged to Fantasyland by your kids as fast as their little legs will take them? Stroll down Main Street U.S.A. and observe the second-floor windows?

Wait…stroll down Main Street and observe the second-floor windows? Who does that, and why in the world would they waste their time like that? Well, the *who* would be "not very many people," and the *why* would be the point to this section.

These windows are a tradition started by Walt Disney himself. In the Introduction of the excellent book *Windows on Main Street* author Chuck Snyder says,

> This book is about the men and women whose creative vision, tireless efforts, "can-do" attitudes, teamwork, and ability to dream have brought a smile to the face of anyone who has visited a Disney Park. The ultimate honor for these Cast Members, as employees are known, is to have their names emblazoned on a window in the Main Street U.S.A. area. To the typical park Guest, these names appear to be the calling cards of make-believe shopkeepers. In reality, the names belong to the "all-stars" of the parks' histories. As one walks around the Main Street U.S.A. area, these names are the opening credits to a show like no other.[80]

In the Foreword to the same book, Executive V.P. and Imagineering Ambassador Marty Sklar says, "This tradition was established by Walt Disney for Disneyland Park. He personally selected the names that would be revealed on the Main Street windows on Opening Day, July 17, 1955."

---

[80] Chuck Snyder, *Windows on Main Street: Discover the Real Stories of the Talented People Featured on the Windows of Main Street, U.S.A.* (New York: Disney Editions, 2009), 5.

Walt knew that, though this was his dream, his vision, he could not have done it by himself. He wasn't one to give compliments or express gratitude very often—especially not directly. And so, the windows on Main Street are Walt's tribute, his special "thank you" to those men and women who helped make the dream a reality, starting with his father, Elias. It's a tradition that continues to this day.

In the United States, Thanksgiving Day is a time for reflecting on the gifts we've been given, the people in our lives who mean so much to us, and everything else that we have to be thankful for. And yet, how often do we spend more than a few minutes—if any time at all—actually reflecting and expressing our thanks? For many, it has become a day of watching football, overeating, and getting ready for Black Friday shopping.

The apostle Paul remembered and gave thanks. In Philippians 1, he tells the recipients of his letter, "I thank my God every time I remember you. In all my prayers for all of you, I always pray with joy because of your partnership in the gospel from the first day until now..."[81] He expresses his gratitude for people again in Acts 28:15, Romans 1:8, 1 Corinthians 1:4, Ephesians 1:15–16, and elsewhere. He repeatedly emphasized the importance of giving thanks, and not just when things were going well. In fact, as I read through the Bible, the importance and value of thankfulness is clear.

I have a lot to be thankful for—and a lot of people to be thankful for. So, in the spirit of Disneyland's Main Street U.S.A. windows, here are just a few of the many people (or, in some cases, groups of people) that I'm thankful for.

- Of course, my wife, Faye. We will celebrate our thirteenth wedding anniversary this year (2013), and I am so grateful for her love, support, encouragement, and dedication to me and our family as a whole for the last thirteen-plus years.

---

[81] Philippians 1:3–5

- My cater-cousin, Andy. He lives a couple of states away, so we don't get to see each other very often, but he's still a valuable friend to me and an important part of my life. He's also the one who was there at the very beginning of my fascination with Disneyland, when over the course of a couple of years or so we would go nearly every Friday night—along with many other times—to the park.

- My parents, and my parents-in-love (aka, Faye's parents). Their support and encouragement will always be greatly prized.

- Coworkers who are friends as well as associates, and a supervisor/boss who respects me and works with me as an equal, even though I report to him.

- Other friends who have become extended family over the years (Zia, Robyn, Tim, Leslie, Tricia [both of them], Rachel, Debbie, Billy, Danielle, and more).

- The people who take the time and effort to create many of the podcasts I listen to, and their related websites. It may sound silly, but they are how I learn, stay informed, and expand my mind and horizons at times when I don't have a lot of spare time to read as much as I'd like.

- The Cast Members at Walt Disney World, and the other Team Members and employees we met during our Central Florida vacation in 2010 who went out of the way to make our day special, who took extra time to talk to us and visit with us, and who generally "made the magic happen." Thank you Sara (our "sister" and server at 50's Prime Time Café), Judy (our photographer at Epcot's ImageWorks – The Kodak "What If" Labs), Skipper Jennifer (our Jungle Cruise skipper), Steven (a Hall of Presidents Cast Member), Elicia (our server at Whispering Canyon Café), Jessica (a Cast Member at Pecos Bill's in the Magic Kingdom), Kelli (a lifeguard at Discovery Cove), and more!

That's just a part of my particular list.

On Thanksgiving Day, and every day, try to spend more than just a minute or two before you eat to remember who and what you're thankful for. No matter how good or bad things are, there's always someone and something to be thankful for—most especially God Himself and our Lord Jesus Christ, but don't stop there!

(Oh, and in case you're wondering, Walt Disney has a window of his own, but it's not on Main Street. Do you know where it is?)

Kingdom Thinking: Who is on your Thanksgiving list…and do they know it?

Main Street Opera House

The Griffith Park Bench: Salvation, an Event…and a Process

In the Main Street Opera House, just inside the doors, sits a bench. It is the very bench that Walt Disney referred to when he said,

> [Disneyland] came about when my daughters were very young and Saturday was always daddy's day with the two daughters. So we'd start out and try to go someplace, you know, different things, and I'd take them to the merry-go-round and I took them different places and as I'd sit while they rode the merry-go-round and did all these things—sit on a bench, you know, eating peanuts—I felt that there should be something built, some kind of amusement enterprise built, where the parents and the children could have fun together. So that's how

Disneyland started. Well, it took many years…it was a period of maybe 15 years developing. I started with many ideas, threw them away, started all over again. And eventually, it evolved into what you see today at Disneyland. But it all started from a daddy with two daughters wondering where he could take them where he could have a little fun with them too.[82]

Now, some people will doubt that this is the whole story, and probably with good reason. Walt was a master storyteller, and sometimes he didn't let the mundane facts get in the way of a good story. Still, it's pretty safe to assume that—while there were many events and experiences both before and after this day that led to the creation of Disneyland—this was a significant milestone in the development of the concept.

There was a process to the conception, construction, and completion of Disneyland, with significant milestones along the way. But at some point the idea for Disneyland did not exist in any form…and then it did.

Our salvation is the same way. One moment we were not saved, and then the next moment we were. Exactly when that moment is may be the subject of at least as much debate as when Walt really first dreamed up the idea for Disneyland. Nevertheless, the Bible says,

But because of His great love for us, God, Who is rich in mercy, made us alive with Christ even when we were dead in transgressions—it is by grace you have been saved.[83]

At the same time, though, salvation is more than a singular event, it is a process.

---

[82] As described by Walt Disney on the "Walt Disney's Dream" plaque in the lobby of the Main Street Opera House.
[83] Ephesians 2:4–5

For the message of the cross is foolishness to those who are perishing, but to us who are being saved it is the power of God.[84]

We *have been* saved, and we *are being* saved. The theological term for the former is "justification," and for the latter, "sanctification."

Justification means that your eternal destiny has changed. Sanctification means God is working in you to move you along the path toward that destiny. Neither result from your effort alone. Justification is a gift, and sanctification is God working in you and through you to conform you to the likeness of His Son. And yet, you accept the gift of salvation, and you "work out your salvation," through His power and for His purpose and pleasure.

Therefore, my dear friends, as you have always obeyed—not only in my presence, but now much more in my absence—continue to work out your salvation with fear and trembling, for it is God Who works in you to will and to act according to His good purpose.[85]

The way he told the story, Walt sat on a park bench and imagined a place where parents and children could have fun together. But it took years of development to actually create it, and even then, he said that "Disneyland will never be completed." True to his word, even today there are changes, improvements, and even expansions at Disneyland—now the "Disneyland Resort."

You are not what you *will be*, but you're also not what you *once were*! You have been saved, and you are being saved. Through your life, you will continue to grow, to learn, and to experience His grace in new and fresh ways as you follow Him.

---

[84] Ephesians 1:18
[85] Philippians 2:12–13

Being confident of this, that He who began a good work in you will carry it on to completion until the day of Christ Jesus.[86]

Kingdom Thinking: How does it encourage you to know that you are still being saved, as well as having been saved?

Great Moments with Mr. Lincoln

Your Place in His Plan

As with the Carousel of Progress and it's a small world, Great Moments with Mr. Lincoln was introduced at the 1964–65 New York World's Fair. It was sponsored by the State of Illinois and marked the first use of a human-like Audio Animatronic. All that the Imagineers had learned over the preceding several years of designing mechanical figures and developing Audio Animatronics culminated in this figure—and then carried well beyond in Pirates of the Caribbean and more!

Originally, Mr. Lincoln was planned to be part of the Hall of Presidents in the never-developed Liberty Street (which has since found a home in Liberty Square at Walt Disney World). A 1963 issue of *National Geographic* described it like this:

The illusion was alarming. The tall, lonely man sits in a chair much as in the Lincoln Memorial in Washington, D. C. But this is no cold stone figure; this Lincoln is "man-size" and so realistic it seems made of flesh and blood.[87]

---

[86] Philippians 1:6
[87] *National Geographic*, August 1963, 206–07.

Wathel Rogers made adjustments at an electronic console, and Lincoln's eyes ranged the room. His tongue moved as if to moisten his lips and he cleared his throat. Then with a slight frown, he clasped the arms of his chair, stood up, and began to talk in measured tones.

"What constitutes the bulwark of our own liberty and independence?" he asked.

And then he answered: "Our reliance is in the love of liberty which God has planted in us...."

To get an idea of the tremendous animation job this is, try it yourself. Sit in an armchair and pull yourself to your feet, observing how many muscles are called into play and the subtle balance required.

The Lincoln skin is the same Duraflex that has worked so well on the other Audio-Animatronic figures.

"Duraflex has a consistency much like human skin," Rogers said. "It flexes as well as compresses. Rubber, for example, will flex, but won't compress correctly for our needs."

Rogers described the mechanics: 16 air lines to the Lincoln head, 10 air lines to the hands and wrists, 14 hydraulic lines to control the body, and two pairs of wires for every line. Rogers ran the Lincoln face through some of its 15 expressions. "Lincoln smiled at me (first on one side of his face, then the other). He raised each eyebrow quizzically, one at a time, then, fixing me with a glance, frowned and chilled my marrow. And just to show he wasn't really angry, he ended by giving me a genial wink."[88]

---

[88] Robert De Roos, "The Magic Worlds of Walt Disney," in Modern

Great Moments with Mr. Lincoln has changed a few times over the years, always updating the Audio Animatronic technology, and at times changing the script, in one way or another. The current version is my favorite, though. The script is the same one that was used from 1984 to 2001. However, Royal Dano's voice (the actor who gives voice to Mr. Lincoln) is from a newly discovered recording that is cleaner than the original performance.

In this show Abraham Lincoln says some powerful words, but there is one portion in particular I would like to focus on. He says,

> I know there is a God, and that He hates injustice and slavery. I see the storm coming. I know His hand is in it. If He has a place and work for me—and I think He has—I believe I'm ready, and with God's help, I shall not fail.

Can you say that? Do you see a storm coming—or already here? Does He have a place and a work for you, and do you know what it is? Are you ready?

> For it is by grace you have been saved, through faith—and this not from yourselves, it is the gift of God—not by works, so that no one can boast. For we are God's workmanship, created in Christ Jesus to do good works, which God prepared in advance for us to do.[89]

What has God prepared for you to do? And how do you know? Well, one way is to really examine your heart and see what He has put on it as a burden or deep concern.

Mechanics: Yesterday's Tomorrow Today, http://blog.modernmechanix.com/the-magic-worlds-of-walt-disney-part-1/, accessed July 27, 2013.

[89] Ephesians 2:8–10

We might express our devotion and say, "Let my heart be broken by that which breaks the heart of God." Scott Krippayne even wrote a song to that effect called *What Breaks Your Heart*:[90]

God, what breaks your heart, what makes you cry,
What will I see if I look through your eyes?

But have you ever thought about what that means? What breaks *His* heart? Injustice. Suffering. Sickness. Abuse. Poverty. Sin. And more. His heart breaks for anything that hurts His children or keeps people from Him.

If our hearts were broken by everything that breaks God's heart, we would be catatonic all the time. We couldn't function. But, if you are a Christian, surely there is something that breaks His heart which also breaks yours. Something that resonates with you and moves you beyond sympathy. For President Lincoln, it was injustice and slavery. This wasn't a pet project of his. He knew God well enough to know that these things were wrong, and that God had placed him in the world at that time and place to do something about it.

Kingdom Thinking: What stirs your heart? And what are you doing with/about it?

---

[90] Scott Krippayne, "What Breaks Your Heart," *All of Me* (Brentwood, TN: Spring Hill Music Group, 2001).

Main Street Vehicles

Horse-Drawn Streetcar: How Committed Are You?

The Horse-Drawn Streetcar on Main Street U.S.A. is another attraction with a personal Disney history. All of the Cast Members who operate this attraction are very knowledgeable—about the horses, and about the attraction's past. According to one I had a chance to talk with recently, there's an exceptionally good reason for that knowledge.

Back in late June or early July of 1955, as Disneyland was nearing completion, Walt Disney was told that funding was not available for the Horse-Drawn Streetcar. All the money (and more) had gone to other parts of the park. Walt insisted that he had to have that attraction, and he was again told there was not enough money.

Walt asked, "How much would it cost?" He was given the figure, and immediately pulled out his checkbook and wrote a check for that amount on the spot. He really wanted that attraction! The streetcar also has the distinction of being one of only four attractions that Walt Disney (through his personal company, Retlaw Enterprises) owned personally. The others were the Disneyland Railroad, the Monorail, and the Viewliner.

This same helpful Cast Member told me that the attraction's own history is part of the reason—maybe a large part—that the Horse-Drawn Streetcar is the only "horse-powered" vehicle still operating today. Originally there were two others, the Surrey and the Horse-Drawn Fire Wagon, but they have both since been retired. Only this one remains.

Walt Disney wanted this attraction in his park—and he wanted it badly enough that he was willing to pay the price himself to have it.

Are you willing to show similar sacrifice (though not necessarily monetary) for anything, or anyone? Is there anything that means enough to you that you will sacrifice whatever it takes to have it without a moment's hesitation? What about following Jesus? Do you express that kind of commitment to Him? It's what He calls us to.

Consider these biblical passages:

As they were walking along the road, a man said to Him, "I will follow You wherever You go."

Jesus replied, "Foxes have holes and birds of the air have nests, but the Son of Man has no place to lay his head."

He said to another man, "Follow me."

But the man replied, "Lord, first let me go and bury my father."

Jesus said to him, "Let the dead bury their own dead, but you go and proclaim the kingdom of God."

Still another said, "I will follow you, Lord; but first let me go back and say good-bye to my family."

Jesus replied, "No one who puts his hand to the plow and looks back is fit for service in the kingdom of God."[91]

The kingdom of heaven is like treasure hidden in a field. When a man found it, he hid it again, and then in his joy went and sold all he had and bought that field.

Again, the kingdom of heaven is like a merchant looking for fine pearls. When he found one of great value, he went away and sold everything he had and bought it.[92]

You won't necessarily be called to sell everything or move to a foreign country (though you might). But we are *all* called to "put our money where our mouth is" every day. There is always something that can interfere with following Jesus. Maybe it's your

---

[91] Luke 9:57–62
[92] Matthew 13:44–46

job. Maybe it's your family. Maybe it's fear. Maybe it's comfort. Maybe it's a lack of understanding who God is and how much He loves you.

But whatever it is, every day Jesus says, "Follow Me," and every day—maybe many times a day—we make a decision. Do you want to follow Him badly enough, do you love Him enough that you'll do whatever it takes to follow Him, in whatever form that takes in your life?

Kingdom Thinking: What is your Horse-Drawn Streetcar? What do you want as badly as Walt Disney wanted that? If it's not Jesus, what's in His place, and why?

Omnibus: The Tourist Christian

On Disneyland's Opening Day, all the vehicles on Main Street U.S.A. had "natural" horsepower: the Horse-Drawn Fire Wagon, Surrey, and Streetcar.

Only the last one continues to operate today. In place of the others are three "newfangled" vehicles. The red Horseless Carriage entered service on May 12, 1956, and a yellow one joined it in December. Summer of 1956 saw the addition of the Omnibus (the green double-decker bus) and August of 1958 added the last of the motorized vehicles, the Fire Engine. As of today, the vehicles in operation are the same ones from the 1950s (with some replacement parts, I'm sure), so if you want to touch a bit of history, give these a ride next time you need to get from one end of Main Street U.S.A. to the other.

Consider the three different motorized vehicles and the purposes they traditionally serve:

- The Omnibus is for sightseeing; it's leisurely and recreational.
- The Fire Engine is for emergencies, being reactive and making sure blazes are put out. (Mrs. Thelma Bird, from the Market House Party Line, could have used one! You'll see why a little later in this chapter.)
- The Horseless Carriage is practical, used by nearly everyone, and as a replacement for horse-drawn carriages served as a transition between eras—moving toward the future and progress.

You've probably heard that there are three kinds of people in the world (or four, or two, or whatever). In fact, here are some of my favorite ways to distinguish between people.

- There are 3 kinds of people in the world: those who can count and those who can't.
- There are 10 kinds of people in the world: those who understand binary and those who don't.
- There are 2 kinds of people in the world: those who can extrapolate from incomplete data.

Here's another way: The Omnibus, Fire Engine, and Horseless Carriage provide a great vehicle (so to speak) to describe three approaches to being a Christian. We'll look at each one individually.

Modeled after the large busses used for tours of New York's Manhattan borough in the 1930s, the Omnibus is a purely recreational vehicle. Guests ride to see the sights—and in some cases, to be seen. It provides a different perspective on Main Street, especially the upper deck of the bus, but with no practical application at the time. No matter what you see, you can't go into a store, stop to admire a window, or get some ice cream.

"Tourist Christians" are the same way. Their question is, "What's in it for me?" If they do anything at all, it is done to be seen by others and get recognition from people. Mostly, though, they just want to go along for the ride. They come to church only to feel good, serve when they'll get applause, and leave if things get too hard. They claim to be followers of Christ, but it makes no practical difference in their lives, especially if that difference might involve suffering, sacrifice, or challenge. They prefer to just ride along "above it all." The problem? Eventually they have to come down and get off the bus. Then what?

Now, that's not to say that there aren't benefits to being a Christian. Christians are blessed in many ways. But Tourist Christians are in it only (or primarily) for the blessings.

These are the kinds of followers we see in John 6:60–66. The scene is shortly after Jesus has fed the 5,000. He had just finished teaching that He is the Bread of Life and talking about his followers eating His flesh and drinking His blood.

> On hearing [this teaching], many of His disciples said, "This is a hard teaching. Who can accept it?" Aware that His disciples were grumbling about this, Jesus said to them, "Does this offend you? Then what if you see the Son of Man ascend to where He was before! The Spirit gives life; the flesh counts for nothing. The words I have spoken to you—they are full of the Spirit and life. Yet there are some of you who do not believe." For Jesus had known from the beginning which of them did not believe and who would betray Him. He went on to say, "This is why I told you that no one can come to Me unless the Father has enabled them."

> From this time many of his disciples turned back and no longer followed Him.

They stuck with Him for the healing, the feeding, the show, and being part of the "in crowd." But when the teaching got hard or the way difficult, they left. These were tourist disciples.

Not everyone left, though. As we continue to read John 6, Jesus asks the Twelve Apostles, "You do not want to leave too, do you?" Peter responds, "Lord, to whom shall we go? You have the words of eternal life. We have come to believe and to know that you are the Holy One of God."[93] This recognition of His deity and divine mission is "what was in it for them," and it impacted their lives every day.

> **Kingdom Thinking:** How can you recognize a Tourist Christian? Have you had the tendency to be one?

Fire Engine: The "Fire Escape" Christian

Main Street U.S.A.'s Fire Engine was based on a turn-of-the-century hose-carrying fire engine. It's not quite that antique, though. The bell and siren are authentic, but the rest was created in the Studio Coach shop, designed by the talented Bob Gurr. He has often said that if it moves on wheels at Disneyland, he probably designed it. That certainly proves true on Main Street U.S.A., as all of the motorized Main Street vehicles were designed by him. In fact, it's also unique because in order to get it to the park from the location where it was built, Gurr drove it a good distance down the Santa Ana Freeway!

The fire engine has a very different purpose from the Omnibus. It represents turn-of-the-century America and, by analogy, a different way some people live the Christian life.

---

[93] John 6:67–69

Rarely will you find a fire engine cruising around town. There's no sightseeing or recreation to be done. It answers the call to put fires out, and then leaves. As a rule, it is reactive—not seeking out ways or locations to prevent fires, but just coming to stop the ones that have started. That's what they were made for, and there's nothing wrong with that—for fire engines.

Fire Escape Christians have the same strategy. It's not that these people don't genuinely believe—often, they do. But the motivation is messed up. Their question is, "What do I have to do to avoid punishment?"

Accept Christ to avoid hell. Do what you must out of fear that not doing "enough" means you'll end up there anyway. There's no room for grace here, no room for love, or faith, or joy. It's a reactive way to be a Christian—doing things (and not doing other things) strictly to escape hell and not to draw near to God. It means serving out of obligation and, again, fear of consequences. Avoiding hell is a good thing, but it's not enough to have the "abundant life" Jesus promised.

Of course, this is assuming these people do anything at all. The other variation of this kind of Christian is the one who "accepts Christ" and that's it. It goes no further. They figure they've got their "Get Out of Hell Free" card, so that's sufficient. No need to grow, or change, or repent, or serve, or anything else. Just claim the name of Jesus and then go about one's merry way.

These disciples run the risk of being exactly the kind of people Jesus talked about in Matthew 7:

Not everyone who says to Me, "Lord, Lord," will enter the kingdom of heaven, but only the one who does the will of My Father who is in heaven. Many will say to Me on that day, "Lord, Lord, did we not prophesy in Your name and in Your name drive out demons and in Your name perform many miracles?" Then I will tell them plainly, "I never knew you. Away from Me, you evildoers!"[94]

Or of being the ones Paul described in 1 Corinthians 3:

> If anyone builds on this foundation using gold, silver, costly stones, wood, hay or straw, their work will be shown for what it is, because the Day will bring it to light. It will be revealed with fire, and the fire will test the quality of each person's work. If what has been built survives, the builder will receive a reward. If it is burned up, the builder will suffer loss but yet will be saved—even though only as one escaping through the flames.[95]

Rather than take a chance at getting burned for being a Fire Escape Christian, we ought to commit ourselves to getting as far from the fire as possible, and helping others stay out of it.

Kingdom Thinking: How can you recognize a Fire Escape Christian…or your own tendency to be one?

Horseless Carriage: The Intentionally Growing Christian

The Horseless Carriage was the first of the motorized Main Street vehicles introduced to the park. Some claim it is a replica of an Oldsmobile; others say a Franklin touring car; but it was actually designed as a composite of many gas-driven cars of the early years

---

[94] Matthew 7:21–23
[95] 1 Corinthians 3:12–15

in automobile history. Though its parts were nearly all fabricated by Disney staff, some of the external parts, like the lights, are authentic pieces from the turn of the century—1903 or so.

This vehicle marks the transition between two eras. As America moved out of the age of horses and into the age of machines for transportation, the horseless carriage led the way. Gas lights gave way to electric lights (as they do on the Magic Kingdom's Main Street U.S.A. in Walt Disney World), and horse-drawn carriages gave way to horseless carriages.

Of the three vehicles on Main Street, the Horseless Carriage represents the most accessible mode of transportation to the average family. Only certain people could drive a tour bus like the Omnibus, and everyone else had to pay to ride in it. Only certain people would even be allowed on a fire engine. But a horseless carriage was for everyone. Families could ride it and so could friends. Even strangers could be given a lift.

The Intentionally Growing Christian recognizes both of these realities—forward progress, and availability to everyone—of the life of faith. Vibrant faith assumes forward progress, and it is available to everyone. Their question is, "How can I grow in Christ and show Him to others?"

The New Testament records many calls to maturity, and Timothy is a great example of an Intentionally Growing Christian. Paul recognized his willingness and desire to grow and to teach others. (Not everyone who fits into this category will formally teach, but everyone will share their faith and disciple others in some way.) Timothy was acquainted with grace, and also with suffering.

You then, my son, be strong in the grace that is in Christ Jesus. And the things you have heard me say in the presence of many witnesses entrust to reliable people who will also be qualified to teach others. Join with me in suffering, like a good soldier of Christ Jesus.[96]

This commitment does not come from fear or obligation. There's a reason Paul starts with a reminder of God's grace. The attitude flows from gratitude and love for the grace and love God has given us.

Intentionally Growing Christians also recognize that a relationship with Jesus is not something to be hoarded or hidden. Jesus said, "Come to Me, all you who are weary and burdened, and I will give you rest,"[97] and "For God so loved the world that He gave His one and only Son, that whoever believes in Him shall not perish but have eternal life."[98] Peter reminded his readers, "The Lord is not slow in keeping His promise, as some understand slowness. Instead He is patient with you, not wanting anyone to perish, but everyone to come to repentance."[99]

Growing in Christ means more than *internal* growth; it also bears fruit—and one way to bear fruit as a Christian is by introducing others to Jesus, through your words and actions.

Three different vehicles, with three different histories and purposes. As each rolls down Main Street U.S.A., it asks the question, which of us are you?

Kingdom Thinking: How can you recognize an Intentionally Growing Christian, or your own tendency to be one? What is one step you can take toward being one more consistently?

---

[96] 2 Timothy 2:1–3
[97] Matthew 11:28
[98] John 3:16
[99] 2 Peter 3:9

Main Street Cinema

Getting Past the Noise

One of the "hidden in plain sight" gems of Main Street U.S.A. is the Main Street Cinema. An Opening Day attraction, the Main Street Cinema shows (in black and white) six animated shorts from the early years of Mickey and the Gang while a recorded musical accompaniment plays.

As of this writing, the six shorts playing are:

- *Mickey's Polo Team*
- *Traffic Troubles*
- *The Dognapper*
- *The Moose Hunt*
- *Steamboat Willie*
- *Plane Crazy*

This theatre is a great place to get out of the sun (or rain) and enjoy some classic cartoons. It also contains something that most people aren't aware of, and it's here we find our lesson.

Of the six cartoon shorts playing, only one plays its own soundtrack. All the rest have musical accompaniment playing throughout the room as their only soundtrack. The one that plays its own? *Steamboat Willie*.

What makes this factoid interesting and significant is that you must pay close attention to even notice it. The music playing in the room is good, and it fits the Cinema, but it's relatively loud. The soundtrack for *Steamboat Willie*, by comparison, is quiet. You have to be standing right in front of it and paying attention to hear it clearly. If you don't listen for it, you probably will miss it. Only *Steamboat Willie* has a unique soundtrack, but you must listen carefully and filter out the other (good) music and sound to hear it.

There's a lot of "noise" in the world today, and not all of it is bad. Worthwhile movies and TV shows vie for our attention, as do countless good books. Thanks to Live365, Pandora, Spotify, and other services there is almost no limit to the music you can listen to. Thousands of podcasts on almost every conceivable subject are available on iTunes, Stitcher Radio, and other services.

Technology has brought us a wealth of content that is encouraging, fun, entertaining, educational, and even valuable. But it's easy to get caught up in the "noise," and when we do, we miss the sound that's constantly playing in the background.

> Whether you turn to the right or to the left, your ears will hear a voice behind you, saying, "This is the way; walk in it."[100]

People make time for a favorite TV show (or shows, the average person over age fifteen spends 2.7 hours per day watching TV—that's nineteen hours per week, or 983 hours per year, almost forty-one days!). We also listen to podcasts, go to movies and parties, read reports or the newspaper, etc. But how much time do we spend listening to God? Reading His Word? Praying? Spending time in natural surroundings and listening to Him speak through His creation?

This lesson is not about "guilting" us into action (or inaction, as the case may be), it's about helping us to become intentionally aware of our priorities and encouraging us to listen better. God's voice is always there, but we can miss it through the noise of life, or because what we're listening for (i.e. the way out of a troubled relationship) is not what He's saying ("Let Me work in your heart and change you").

Listen carefully. Filter out the noise—even if it's "good" noise. His voice is there.

---

[100] Isaiah 30:21

Kingdom Thinking: What is one way you can filter out some of the noise in your life and listen for Him?

Market House

Market House Party Line: Preoccupied with Position

One of those often-overlooked gems at Disneyland are phones hanging on the walls in the Market House on Main Street U.S.A. Most guests think of them as just decorative props—if they notice them at all—but there's more to them than that.

Pick one up and you get to listen in on a "party line" conversation. Two recordings have been featured over the years, and the current one actually has two parts that loop into each other. My favorite part is the second half of the conversation, where Mrs. Thelma Bird calls Quentin Spoon, Fire Chief, to report her barn being on fire.

The transcript of the entire three-minute or so conversation is long, but here are the key parts:

Quentin Spoon: Hello? I've got it, Eugenia!

Mrs. Thelma Bird: Hello? Oh, thank goodness! I want to report a fire! My barn is burning, and there's lots of smoke, and I can see the flames coming through the door! Please, come quick!

QS: A fire, did you say? Well, then you'll need to speak to the Fire Chief.

MTB: Who are you?

QS: Quentin Spoon, City Postmaster, at your service.

MTB: But I thought, I rang the fire station...

QS: This is a fire station, and the post office, and the general store..

MTB: I need the Fire Chief, my barn is burning down!

QS All righty, just a minute!

(more sounds of the fire, and a donkey braying)

QS: Hello! Quentin Spoon, City Fire Chief here!

MTB: You're the Fire Chief, too?!

QS: Yep, a fella's gotta wear many hats in this town.

MTB: Why didn't you say so?

QS: I had to get my Fire Chief's hat! Ain't official without it!

MTB: Now can we please get back to my barn?

…

Gertrude Anderson: Thelma Bird! You can show a little more respect to our dear Quentin Spoon!

MTB: Who is this? Gertrude? Gertrude Anderson? You get off this line right now!

QS: Now what can I do for you, Gertrude?

GA: Well, Quentin, I just wanted to know if my package of peacock feathers has arrived yet.

QS: Oooh, sounds like this call is for my postmaster's hat. Be right back!

MTB: Wait! Gertude, get off the line! This is an emergency!

GA: Hmmph! And I suppose my missing package of peacock feathers is NOT an emergency?!

MTB: Gertrude! HANG UP!!

GA: Well!! I never!! You'd think her house was burning down!

MTB: Now! Can we get back to the fire?

…

(more terrible sounds coming from the barn)

MTB: Oooh!

QS: Oh, don't worry, Mrs. Ird. We'll have a fire truck out there in no time.

MTB: Never mind, Chief Spoon. Don't bother to send a truck.

QS: What? Are you telling me there's no fire?

MTB: No, no fire.

QS: Hmmm....

MTB: There is nothing left to put out. Good day, Mr. Spoon.

QS: Well, don't that just beat all!!

(hangs up the phone)

Quentin Spoon had to wear a lot of hats, and he insisted on doing so, literally. His job was to serve the town as the Postmaster, Fire Chief, and whatever else he may have been. But he was very concerned with his *position*, too. He was so concerned about his titles that a woman's barn burned down while he was busy making sure he was exercising his proper authority.

Spoon wasn't being intentionally malicious or destructive about what he was doing, but he was so preoccupied with who he was, what he was "supposed" to be doing, and making sure he was in the right position that he forgot to serve.

That's pretty normal for Christians, too, but it can also be just as destructive. Paul says in Ephesians and in 1 Corinthians that we are all part of the body of Christ, and we all have a role to play in it. We shouldn't think less of others who aren't like us or think less of ourselves because we wish we were more like someone else. Yet at the same time, our purpose in having such roles is not for our benefit.

And in the church God has appointed first of all apostles, second prophets, third teachers, then workers of miracles, also those having gifts of healing, those able to help others, those with gifts of administration, and those speaking in different kinds of tongues.[101]

---

[101] 1 Corinthians 12:28

It was He who gave some to be apostles, some to be prophets, some to be evangelists, and some to be pastors and teachers, to prepare God's people for works of service, so that the body of Christ may be built up.[102]

The purpose of our roles, of our gifts, is to serve others. It would be easy to say, "Oh, I'm a teacher, I don't do communion preparation," or "I'm an evangelist, I don't do homeless ministry."

Yes, we should serve using the gifts God has given us, but sometimes needs arise among the body, and it's up to whoever is available to meet them. Don't worry about your specific role. Nor about whether you'll be any good at it. Don't worry about whether you're wearing the right hat at the right time. If you sense God's nudge to do something to serve others, do it!

Don't let a spiritual house burn down while you're switching hats...or claiming someone else is wearing that hat instead.

Kingdom Thinking: When have you been nudged to do something that you didn't think was "your thing" and were blessed by serving in that way?

Jolly Holiday Bakery

The Wisdom of Mary Poppins

When it comes to iconic Disney characters, particularly from the live-action films, it's hard to top *Mary Poppins*. Sadly, she's not

---

[102] Ephesians 4:11–12

represented much in the parks. In fact, I can only think of three places:

- In meet-and-greets and parades (like "Mickey's Soundsational Parade");
- The Jolly Holiday Bakery is themed to Mary Poppins; and
- The lead horse on King Arthur Carrousel, named Jingles, is dedicated to Julie Andrews—the actress who played Mary Poppins in the movie—and has a couple of symbols related to Mary Poppins.

Still, this is enough to give us the opportunity to think about the wisdom of Mary Poppins. Now, even though she's "practically perfect in every way," she's not a "Proverbs 31 woman" by any means. But her movie affords us great reminders of practical wisdom.

I Love to Laugh

A cheerful heart is good medicine,
but a crushed spirit dries up the bones.[103]

In the scene with Uncle Albert, laughter is literally "uplifting." The characters sing about the different ways people laugh, and then they laugh themselves. Uncle Albert and Bert, in particular get—literally—carried away by the laughter. Recall that they float to the ceiling—table, chairs, teacups, and all—while laughing uproariously. And when they force themselves to get sad, the sadness brings them back down to the floor.

When my parents joined my wife and me for their fortieth anniversary at Disneyland, Mary Poppins and Bert had an extended

---

[103] Proverbs 17:22

conversation with them about different laughs. It was one of my favorite memories of that trip!

We've all felt that way, haven't we? Laughter lightens our mood and our spirit. Cheerfulness expresses itself in smiles and laughter.

Medical science has proven again and again the health benefits of laughter. And this scene in *Mary Poppins* gives a visual illustration to what the Bible says.

A Spoonful of Sugar

> Speak to one another with psalms, hymns and spiritual songs. Sing and make music in your heart to the Lord, always giving thanks to God the Father for everything, in the name of our Lord Jesus Christ.[104]

When the Banks children didn't want to clean their room, Mary Poppins sang a song to them about making drudgery fun and making work a game. Soon the children "took the medicine" and cleaned up rapidly. It comes down to a choice of attitude.

This Bible verse is one of several that reminds us of that very truth. Not everything in life will be fun and pleasant. In fact, sometimes life will be very difficult. But we still choose to "sing and make music in [our] heart to the Lord...." Notice Paul doesn't say to do that if you *feel* like it, or if things are going well. It's a choice.

A Jolly Holiday

> He who walks with the wise grows wise,
> but a companion of fools suffers harm.[105]

---

[104] Ephesians 5:19–20
[105] Proverbs 13:20

Have you ever noticed that some people are just pleasant to be around? They're not necessarily "the life of the party," but they don't have to be. When you're around them, you're a better person. Of course, some are the opposite—some people seem like they can bring you down by being in the same room. They are always pessimistic, or mean, or irritable, and when you're around them, you find these characteristics coming out in yourself, too.

Mary Poppins is the former. Bert and others liked to be around her. "Oh, it's a jolly 'oliday with Mary / Mary makes your 'eart so light / When the day is gray and ordinary / Mary makes the sun shine bright!"

Everybody has a responsibility to choose who they will associate with. Will it be people like Mary Poppins—people that lift you up and inspire you—people like the ones this Proverb refers to? The apostle Paul warned, "Do not be misled: 'Bad company corrupts good character.'"[106] It matters.

Kingdom Thinking: What wisdom from *Mary Poppins* is most needed in your life today?

Partners Statue

An Extravagant Gift

As guests walk down Main Street U.S.A., two sights greet them at the end of the street. One is Sleeping Beauty Castle, the icon, the symbol of Walt Disney's Magic Kingdom. But standing in front of it, in the center of the Central Hub, from which extend the paths

---

[106] 1 Corinthians 15:33

that will take visitors to the lands of adventure, fantasy, frontiers, the future, and more, stands a bronze statue known as the "Partners" statue.

I want to draw your attention to the plaque at its base.

I think most of all what I want Disneyland to be is a happy place…where parents and children can have fun, together. —*Walt Disney*

Disneyland was created with that primary purpose in mind. Walt Disney World, Disneyland Paris, Hong Kong Disneyland, and all the other Disney parks owe their existence to this one reality: a father wanted to give a gift to his family, and to other families.

Walt was a man who loved spending time with his family. The creation of Disneyland took a lot of time and a lot of different ideas. By the time Disneyland was completed, Walt's two daughters had grown up. The day Disneyland opened, Sharon was nineteen and Diane was twenty-one.

Nevertheless, it was on those "daddy-and-daughter" outings that the idea for Disneyland was born, and it came out of a desire for parents and children to have fun together. It started as a desire for his own family, a gift *to* them and *for* them to have a place to have fun as a family. Then that dream, that gift, expanded to not only his daughters' families but also "to all who come to this happy place." "Uncle Walt" died December 15, 1966, but his dream, his legacy, his gift, lives on today.

Sure, the parks all cost money to get into, but their existence is a gift because of the magic, the wonder, the dreams they foster, whether one has set foot in a Disney park or not. And for those who have dreamed of going, and who choose to allow themselves to set aside their cynicism and become absorbed by the magic, just setting foot inside a Magic Kingdom for the first time realizes all those dreams and begins to create memories that are worth far more than the price of an admission ticket.

That's quite an extravagant gift from a father to his children, isn't it? And yet our God has given us a far more extravagant gift than that.

> For to us a child is born,
>> to us a son is given,
>> and the government will be on His shoulders.
> And He will be called
> Wonderful Counselor, Mighty God,
> Everlasting Father, Prince of Peace.[107]

Christmas is more about gift-giving than anything else. Even retailers, whose primary goal seems to be to separate us from as much of our money as possible, spend most of their advertising promoting what they sell as gifts for others. We give gifts at Christmas because the Magi gave gifts (even if it was quite some time after Jesus was born—why let the facts of the story spoil a perfectly good nativity scene?). We give gifts at Christmas because it's a way we can express our love to others. But most of all, we give gifts at Christmas because God gave His most precious gift to us on that first Christmas.

Next time you see the Partners statue, take a moment to stop and read the plaque. Remember why Walt Disney wanted to build Disneyland, and what an extravagant gift and expression of love that was. And then remember how much more extravagant was the gift that God gave you, planned from the foundations of the world, delivered on Christmas Day, and fully opened on a Friday, Saturday, and (ultimately) Sunday morning some thirty-three years later, when this little baby, the Son of God, willingly gave Himself

---

[107] Isaiah 9:6

in our place, so that we could have "the gift of God [which] is eternal life in Christ Jesus our Lord."[108]

Thanks be to God for His indescribable gift![109]

> **Kingdom Thinking:** Which of God's gifts is most valuable to you? Why?

Keep Your Vision Clear

As mentioned previously, right in the middle of Disneyland, in the Central Plaza, or "Hub," stands the Partners Statue. But guests who have been going to Disneyland for only the last twenty years or so may not realize that this statue wasn't always there.

The Partners Statue only became part of Disneyland in 1993. At first, planters occupied that spot. In the mid-1980s, various promotions made use of that space in a bid to increase attendance. Among them were a gigantic jukebox (with a DJ at the bottom) for "Blast to the Past" and a "Cage of Death" (a huge metal globe with a motorcycle rider inside performing various stunts) during "Circus Fantasy."

The disruption to the carefully laid out theme and storytelling——to say nothing of almost totally obscuring the view of Sleeping Beauty Castle—greatly upset the Imagineers. To help keep this from happening again, and to honor Walt Disney, who had passed away almost three decades earlier, the idea for the Partners Statue was born.

All kinds of "great ideas" had been placed in the Central Hub to promote various events, but they had a tendency to obscure the

---

[108] Romans 6:23b
[109] 2 Corinthians 9:15

view of the park icon—or what Disney called the "wienie" that draws you forward. So the Imagineers came up with a tribute to Walt Disney, which also served to ensure that our view could never again be blocked by something that didn't really belong there.

Our natural tendency as believers in Christ is to do the same thing. We get distracted. We find "good" things (some very good, some not so much) and we set them up at the center of our lives, focusing our attention—and maybe even our adoration—on them. When we do, they block our view and we lose our focus on the One who should be the main focus, the One who calls to us and draws us forward.

Since, then, you have been raised with Christ, set your hearts on things above, where Christ is seated at the right hand of God.[110]

But seek first His kingdom and His righteousness, and all these things will be given to you as well.[111]

Those who live according to the sinful nature have their minds set on what that nature desires; but those who live in accordance with the Spirit have their minds set on what the Spirit desires.[112]

You will keep in perfect peace
him whose mind is steadfast,
because he trusts in You.[113]

So how do we keep our focus on God? It sounds easy, but in reality it can be difficult to do. After all, does it mean to just think

---

[110] Colossians 3:1
[111] Matthew 6:33
[112] Romans 8:5
[113] Isaiah 26:3

about God *all the time*? If so, how do we do our jobs? How do we drive? Can we only watch TV programs or movies or listen to music that explicitly talks about Him (in a positive way) in every line? I don't think so. Paul gave some great encouragement to the Philippian church that should serve us well in this regard:

Finally, brothers, whatever is true, whatever is noble, whatever is right, whatever is pure, whatever is lovely, whatever is admirable—if anything is excellent or praiseworthy—think about such things. Whatever you have learned or received or heard from me, or seen in me—put it into practice. And the God of peace will be with you.[114]

As usual, it's not rules. It's not a set of steps. It's character and relationship. Scripture's words are our guideline. The more we focus on these true, noble, right, pure, lovely, admirable things, the closer we relate to God and are shaped into the image and likeness of His Son. Our lives and our hearts will keep Him at the center, and our view of Him who matters most is unobscured.

It's a process, a journey. Don't beat yourself up if you're not there yet. Just keep loving Him and following Him as He gives you strength. You are not what you will be, but—thanks be to God— you also aren't what you once were!

Kingdom Thinking: What do you most often put in the "Central Hub" of your life that blocks your view of God?

---

[114] Philippians 4:8–9

Parades

You Have Been Chosen

Not everyone who visits Disneyland or Walt Disney World is a "parade person," but I am. I love to watch the Disney parades, even just for a few minutes as I'm on my way somewhere.

Aside from, "What time is the three o'clock parade?" the next most commonly asked question by guests about the parades may be, "How can I be *in* the parade?"

Well, the short answer is usually, "You can't." Unless you're a Cast Member, you don't get to be in the parade. You have to be part of that exclusive group—unless you're chosen.

You see, in some parades, the performers come to the crowd and choose some to participate. Even beyond that, at the time of this writing Walt Disney World has a Grand Marshall Coordinator. I had the privilege of interviewing Dean Gaschler, who held that role for fourteen years, on the *Stories of the Magic* podcast.[115] He told me several stories of how he chose Grand Marshalls from among the park guests for the day's parade.

Some people were in the park celebrating a special occasion. Some were suffering in some way—often children with a debilitating illness. Others desperately wanted to be part of the parade. And still others had no idea it was possible. But do you know what none of them did?

None of them *earned* it. Whether chosen by Dean or by the parade performers more informally, Guests became part of the parade not because of anything they had done to earn it or deserve it. They were chosen and they accepted the invitation. That's it.

You've been chosen, too.

---

[115] *Stories of the Magic* podcast, episodes 14 and 15, http://storiesofthemagic.com.

Praise be to the God and Father of our Lord Jesus Christ, who has blessed us in the heavenly realms with every spiritual blessing in Christ. For He chose us in him before the creation of the world to be holy and blameless in His sight. In love He predestined us for adoption to sonship through Jesus Christ, in accordance with His pleasure and will—to the praise of His glorious grace, which He has freely given us in the One He loves. ... In Him we were also chosen, having been predestined according to the plan of Him who works out everything in conformity with the purpose of His will, in order that we, who were the first to put our hope in Christ, might be for the praise of his glory. And you also were included in Christ when you heard the message of truth, the gospel of your salvation. When you believed, you were marked in Him with a seal, the promised Holy Spirit, who is a deposit guaranteeing our inheritance until the redemption of those who are God's possession—to the praise of His glory.[116]

Do you see what that says about you? As a believer in Christ, you have been chosen. You have been adopted. You have been included in Christ. You are God's possession.

What did you do to deserve it? Nothing. What merit do you bring to this transaction? None. How did you earn this? You didn't. If you are in Christ—and even being "in Christ" is not of yourself, it is the gift of God—these amazing features simply describe who you are. It is a part of your Supernatural Kingdom Identity.

No one can take it away from you. No one can devalue you. No one can legitimately say you are inferior, unloved, or worthless. To be blunt, you can't even say such negative things about yourself. God has made a statement of fact. Who are we to disagree with Him—especially since He's the one who chose you in the first place?

---

[116] Ephesians 1:3–14

This is important enough that I'm going to say it again. You have been *chosen, adopted, included*. A key aspect of your Supernatural Kingdom Identity is that you belong to Christ and are valued. It simply is true of you. Period. You can't earn it, and you don't have to. Just live in that truth.

Kingdom Thinking: With this truth foremost in mind, what is one thing you can do differently to really embrace this part of your Supernatural Kingdom Identity?

Chapter 4: Adventureland

Lay of the Land

A Step into the Unknown

*E*ach of the lands of Disneyland is unique and tells its own story. But of all the lands off the Hub (Main Street U.S.A., Adventureland, Frontierland, Fantasyland, and Tomorrowland), one is missing something that each of the others have. Adventureland does not have this one thing that all the others do.

What's absent from Adventureland is a "wienie," which in Disney parlance refers to a visual icon in the park that draws guests in.

Former Imagineer and current Disney Legend John Hench defined it this way: "A beckoning hand [that] promises something worthwhile; its friendly beckoning fingers say, 'Come this way. You'll have a good time.' ...Imagineers have found that people respond to a wienie at the end of a corridor because it beckons them to continue further in their journey....The wienie promises that you will be rewarded for the time and effort to walk down that corridor."[117]

All of the other original lands have such visual icons.

- Main Street U.S.A. – Sleeping Beauty Castle (when you're coming in from outside); The train station (looking from the Hub back down it)
- Tomorrowland – The Astro Orbitor (when it was up above the PeopleMover track, not so much up front where it is now)
- Fantasyland – Depending on what direction you approach from, this could be the Matterhorn, the Carrousel (seen through the castle), or even Dumbo
- Frontierland – The smoke stack on the Mark Twain (especially before the trees grew as much as they have)

Part of the purpose of the wienie is to give guests an idea of what they're going to experience in that land. It gives them a visual cue as to what they can expect. Adventureland does not have anything like this. The Tiki Room has *some* visual interest, but it sits at an entrance, and can't be seen from the other side. Tarzan's Treehouse is similar. There is nothing that beckons you forward, except the promise of adventure. And some of what you see *can* even seem menacing at first.

But there's a good reason for that. Urban planner (and blogger, published author,[118] and speaker at the Walt Disney Family

---

[117] John Hench, *Designing Disney* (New York: Disney Editions, 2008), 50.
[118] Sam has written an excellent book about the development of the Disney theme parks from a design and architectural standpoint, called *Walt and the Promise of Progress City*, and another about the growth and evolution of Disneyland itself called, *The Disneyland Story*. I highly recommend both.

Museum) Sam Gennawey explains it this way: "If you knew what was coming, it wouldn't be an adventure."[119]

When we think about what we most want out of life, one of the first things that comes to people's minds is security, or safety. But that's not what being a Christian is all about. Sure, we know that heaven is our ultimate future, but between now and then, life is pretty unpredictable. We're never promised the long view. We are told only to take the next step.

Paul (Saul at the time) experienced this uncertainty firsthand: "Now get up and go into the city, and you will be told what you must do."[120]

Old Testament patriarch Abram didn't get much more:

The LORD had said to Abram, "Leave your country, your people and your father's household and go to the land I will show you.
I will make you into a great nation
and I will bless you;
I will make your name great,
and you will be a blessing.
I will bless those who bless you,
and whoever curses you I will curse;
and all peoples on earth
will be blessed through you."
So Abram left, as the LORD had told him; and Lot went with him. Abram was seventy-five years old when he set out from Haran.[121]

God guides us (when we're open to receiving it), but one step at a time. "Your Word is a lamp to my feet and a light for my

[119] "WEDWay Radio Episode 104,
http://wedwayradio.squarespace.com/sn/2012/1/8/adventure-awaits-show-notes-for-episode-104.html.
[120] Acts 9:6
[121] Genesis 12:1–4

path."[122] A lamp illuminates only a small distance in front of us. Sometimes God provides a flashlight, not a floodlight.

When you first step into Adventureland you know only what's right in front of you, or right next to you. As you explore further, you get to see more and more, and wonderful adventures await you. But you would have never known them had you not gone into unknown territory to find out what was there—with only the promise of a sign to entice you.

As you follow God and His will and desires, you get to see more and more of what He has in store for you—and the farther in you get, the more you can look back at the adventure you've had.

It's not easy sometimes, but God never promised it would be. He did promise peace and security, but only in Himself. Sometimes following Him feels risky, but it's never as risky as *not* following, and just "playing it safe." And to really follow Him into this adventure of the Christian life means to do it completely—with all your heart, mind, soul, and strength (to paraphrase the context a bit).

It means loving, and risking hurt and separation (as when someone dies or moves far away). It means serving, and risking being taken advantage of. It means giving, sometimes out of great abundance and sometimes when it seems like you've got nothing to give. It means following, even when the way seems unclear, and when feeling woefully unqualified to do what He's calling you to do. And it means being true to who He made you to be, living your own adventure, not someone else's.

Your journey may be one of sacrifice, but also of joy. The adventure is always worth it. Often we won't have the "wienie" drawing us in and telling us what's to come. We have only a sign, a bridge, and the willingness to explore in faith. When we do, we discover that adventure, a great adventure, really is out there, and we wonder why we spent so much time avoiding it.

---

[122] Psalm 119:105

> **Kingdom Thinking:** How have you experienced God leading you into adventure recently—and what are you doing to follow Him?

Challenges and Companions on the Journey

As I write this section, it has been a very unordinary, trying week or so. My Mom was taken to the hospital Monday of last week with acute kidney failure, along with other health issues. She lives 1,800 miles away, so it was very difficult for my wife, Faye, and me to be so far away and unable to really do anything other than call and talk to her a couple of times—and pray. We were very grateful, of course, that my Dad and Aunt (her husband and her sister) were there with her.

At the same time, I had a coworker ask how I was doing one morning, listen to me, and give me a hug and some words of encouragement. For that, I am very grateful, more than she may realize, as it was exactly what I needed at that moment. Thankfully, I can report that my Mom came home from the hospital a day earlier than the doctors had originally anticipated, and she is healing very well as of this writing.

Then, Faye and I spent this past weekend in San Diego with some good friends. We were up late every night talking, laughing, and playing games. We spent our days exploring familiar San Diego sights, as well as visiting a new church. This is not to say that it was all fun and games, of course. We had some problems with the room where we were staying, and even fixing the problem had its share of struggles. Our emotions varied, and, while many of our conversations were light and fun, several were serious and deep.

As I reflected on the weekend, I realized again the importance and value of companions—of friends and family to share in our adventures. And that experience, of course, took me (mentally first, then physically later) to Adventureland. Two things stand out in this context about Adventureland, specifically the attractions based on stories (i.e. Aladdin's Oasis, The Indiana Jones Adventure, and the tree house—first Swiss Family Robinson and currently Tarzan). First, all of the stories begin with some kind of tragedy, disaster, or difficult situation. Second, the progress from peril or challenge to resolution hinges on the companions' resourcefulness and determination along the journey. More than any other land, with the possible exception of Fantasyland, this land highlights both of those realities: difficulties and the role of companions on our journey.

The story of Aladdin starts with him as a lone orphan scavenging and stealing what he needed in order to survive. His journey toward redemption begins when he meets the Genie and the Magic Carpet, and kicks into high gear when Jasmine becomes an important part of his group of companions. He started his journey alone, and ended with people he cared about—and who cared about him.

The Indiana Jones Adventure is its own self-contained story, not directly tied into any movie. However, we know it is set in 1935, right around the same time as *The Temple of Doom* movie, before *Raiders of the Lost Ark* or *The Last Crusade*. As far as Indiana Jones knows at this time, his father is dead, but he does have friends in Sallah, Dr. Marcus Brody, and others. In this attraction, Indy is lost in the Temple of the Forbidden Eye. Part of the purpose the "tours" serve is to try to locate and rescue Dr. Jones. He is alone, but his friends are seeking to save him.

The Swiss Family Treehouse is obviously based on the *Swiss Family Robinson* movie. One of the themes of this film is the importance of family sticking together and working together to overcome seemingly insurmountable obstacles.

Tarzan's Treehouse, which replaced the Swiss Family Treehouse, tells the story of Tarzan. His parents were killed when he was a baby, and he was raised by Kala, a gorilla whose own son was killed and eaten by the same vicious leopardess that killed Tarzan's parents. The bulk of the story takes place when Tarzan is an adult, isolated from humans. The companionship he first experiences is partially pure, but some characters reveal ulterior motives (which is always a risk when we form relationships). Still, Tarzan's nonhuman companions serve important roles as friends, guides, and even protectors, and ultimately Jane joins his group of companions as well.

Adventures must have challenges, otherwise they're not adventures. Nowhere are we guaranteed that we will enjoy every step of all our adventures, but we're neither expected to nor required to. David says in Psalm 23, "Even though I walk through the valley of the shadow of death, I will fear no evil, for You are with me."[123] That doesn't sound like fun—in fact, it sounds miserable, depressing, and frightening—but it's part of the journey, part of the adventure. Without the valley of the shadow of death, would David have learned to trust God, and to follow wherever the path may lead? Life consists of contrasts. For every high, there seems to be a low. And yet we wouldn't trade certain days, or even just moments, for anything. The adventure of life consists of both, and everything in between. Adventureland reminds us of that journey.

This land also illustrates the importance of companions—friends and family who are there to help us on our odyssey. They challenge us, encourage us, inspire us, push us to accept challenges and risks (or to caution us so we don't take stupid risks), even rebuke us when necessary. The song "For Good" from the musical *Wicked* sums it up well. Here are a few lines from that song:

GLINDA
I've heard it said
That people come into our lives for a reason

---

[123] Psalm 23:4a

Bringing something we must learn
And we are led
To those who help us most to grow
If we let them
And we help them in return
Well, I don't know if I believe that's true
But I know I'm who I am today
Because I knew you.
. . .

ELPHABA
. . .
So much of me
Is made of what I learned from you
You'll be with me
Like a handprint on my heart
And now whatever way our stories end
I know you have rewritten mine
By being my friend.
. . .
Because I knew you,

BOTH
I have been changed for good.

Companion stories abound. Why? Well, one reason is that we were created for companionship, thus stories like these resonate with us. The Bible emphasizes the importance of companionship, community, and fellowship, and the closer a personal story relates thematically to the Ultimate Story, the more significant and impactful that story is to us. In our darkest times we need people to be with us, to pray for us, to listen to us, to help us, or even to rescue us. God provides these people. It can be hard to seek them out or to be open to them, but the progress in our adventures from darkness to light, from fear to confidence, from despair to hope, from grief to joy, frequently comes through our companions.

The first thing that God called "not good" was a lack of companionship. "It is not good for the man to be alone."[124] Jumping far ahead from that Genesis starting point, during the dark days between Jesus' crucifixion and resurrection, and between His ascension and Pentecost, His disciples sought camaraderie.[125] Jesus Himself said that "By this all men will know you are My disciples, if you love one another."[126] At the end of his life, Paul desired companionship and for people to know he cared.[127]

I have been truly blessed. In addition to the coworker and friends I mentioned earlier, I have Faye, my parents, my Aunt, and other family (in particular my cousins and my "adopted" sisters who I love very much). I also have other valued friends, especially my best friend/cater-cousin, Andy. He lives 1,200 miles away and there are times I would have given my right arm (and more) to be able to see him. I am grateful for our relationship, and that we have Facebook, email, and Skype for those times between visits, though. In His wisdom, God has given these valuable companions to me—and me to them—for us to share our adventures together.

I was reminded over the last week or so of both the fun and the frightening adventures that make up our lives. From now on, as I walk though Adventureland I will be reminded of my companions and will be thankful for them. I will also be reminded that others are counting on me to be one of *their* companions.

I pray that you encounter companions on your journey as well, and that you will be reminded to thank God for them. Be open to receive them, and be that kind of companion for others.

---

[124] Genesis 2:18a
[125] see John 20:19, Acts 2:1
[126] John 13:35
[127] see 2 Timothy 4:9–22

> **Kingdom Thinking**: Who are the most valuable companions on your adventure right now? Who counts you as a companion?

Enchanted Tiki Room

We Need a Song

In 2010 I had the opportunity to attend D23's "Destination D: Disneyland '55" event at the Disneyland Hotel. The end of Day 1 was billed as "E-Ticket: Music from Disney Parks," featuring Richard Sherman, of the noted Sherman Brothers, a songwriting duo who wrote more motion-picture musical song scores than any other team in film history. During his portion of the program, Richard reminisced, played songs, and told stories of his days writing music for Walt Disney and Disneyland with his brother, Robert.

In one of those stories, he talked about a day when Walt called the Sherman Brothers and told them he had something to show them. He took them into an area (part of one of the soundstages on the Disney lot, I believe) and showed them some of the Audio Animatronics for what was to become Walt Disney's Enchanted Tiki Room. He showed Richard and Robert some of the figures, what they did, and so on.

Richard said, "That's great, Walt. But what is it?" Walt replied, "That's exactly why you're here! Nobody understands what this is! I need you to write a song to explain this to people!" And from that experience, the Sherman Brothers' first song written exclusively for the theme park, *The Tiki Tiki Tiki Room*, was born. Two days later, I sat in the Tiki Room show thinking, "This song really does exactly what Walt asked for. It tells you everything you need to know about what's supposed to be happening here."

Walt had a similar request for The Carousel of Progress and it's a small world: "I need a song to explain this!"

In my experience, I've noticed that Christians often focus on Bible study, small group or Sunday School curriculum, or the pastor's sermon to be the "teaching part" of our spiritual development. The music is the "worship" part, and if we give any thought to it at all, it's because of how it makes us feel.

But in truth, the songs we sing can be an important part of the "explain this!" Complex theological concepts well-expressed in song make their way deeper into our hearts than any lecture, sermon, or small-group discussion could take them. Some theologically rich songs provide lessons and reminders of God's love, grace, justice, mercy, faithfulness—and our need for all of those—that resonate deeply within us. Sometimes songs convey lessons as clearly as in any spoken word. In fact, when you get right down to it, you can summarize the Christian faith and life fairly accurately—and without missing much crucial truth—with this song:

Jesus loves me! This I know,
For the Bible tells me so;
Little ones to Him belong,
They are weak but He is strong.

Yes, Jesus loves me!
Yes, Jesus loves me!
Yes, Jesus loves me!
The Bible tells me so.

Jesus loves me! He who died,
Heaven's gate to open wide;
He will wash away my sin,
Let His little child come in.

Yes, Jesus loves me!
Yes, Jesus loves me!
Yes, Jesus loves me!
The Bible tells me so.

Jesus loves me! loves me still,
When I'm very weak and ill;
From His shining throne on high,
Comes to watch me where I lie.

Yes, Jesus loves me!
Yes, Jesus loves me!
Yes, Jesus loves me!
The Bible tells me so.

Jesus loves me! He will stay,
Close beside me all the way;
He's prepared a home for me,
And some day His face I'll see.

Yes, Jesus loves me!
Yes, Jesus loves me!
Yes, Jesus loves me!
The Bible tells me so.[128]

Remember, The Psalms are the hymnbook, the songbook, of the Children of Israel. Songs are important enough that there is an entire book of the Bible devoted just to them, and many other books have songs in them as well.

Is teaching important? Sure. Is study necessary? Absolutely. But let us not forget the value of songs, and of singing together.

---

[128] Anna B. Warner, "Jesus Loves Me," 1860.

Let the word of Christ dwell in you richly as you teach and admonish one another with all wisdom, and as you sing psalms, hymns and spiritual songs with gratitude in your hearts to God.[129]

Sometimes we just "need a song to explain this!"

Kingdom Thinking: What songs "explain this" for you?

Aladdin's Oasis

A Whole New World Through New Eyes

Aladdin's Oasis was a semi-improvised show for children based on the 31st animated feature produced by Walt Disney Feature Animation, *Aladdin*. One of the common features of our two main characters, Aladdin and Jasmine, is that they are both trapped in a world they don't want. Aladdin's plight results from poverty and Jasmine's is due to her station in life (as Princess and daughter of the Sultan). Neither can see a way out. All they know and expect to ever know is their day-to-day, just-getting-by existence. It's a life that in some ways could be pleasant, but was often difficult. Neither expected to experience any adventure other than just their daily lives, never knowing what was just beyond the horizon.

When Jafar tricked Aladdin into entering the Cave of Wonders to retrieve the Magic Lamp, Aladdin's life was changed forever, and he—for selfish reasons at first—shared that change of perspective with Jasmine. Consider some of the lyrics of their

---

[129] Colossians 3:16

featured song, *A Whole New World*. Sure, the song is a love song, and as such major portions don't apply here, yet some of the lines prove instructive.

> (Aladdin) I can show you the world / Shining, shimmering, splendid...I can open your eyes / Take you wonder by wonder / Over, sideways and under / On a magic carpet ride / A whole new world / A new fantastic point of view ...

> (Jasmine) A whole new world / A dazzling place I never knew / But when I'm way up here / It's crystal clear / That now I'm in a whole new world with you...

> (Jasmine) I'm like a shooting star / I've come so far / I can't go back to where I used to be

> (Aladdin) A whole new world

> (Jasmine) Every turn a surprise

> (Aladdin) With new horizons to pursue

> (Jasmine) Every moment red-letter

> (Both) I'll chase them anywhere...[130]

It took a change in perspective for Aladdin and Jasmine to see "a whole new world" that had been out there the whole time, but that they never knew existed.

The same is true for us. We live our lives, and for most of us we can't even conceive of anything other than what seems normal. All we can see is what surrounds us, and our view of reality is

---

[130] Alan Menken and Tim Rice, "A Whole New World," Walt Disney, 1992.

determined mostly—even wholly—by what we see and hear. But consider this verse:

> Since, then, you have been raised with Christ, set your hearts on things above, where Christ is seated at the right hand of God. Set your minds on things above, not on earthly things.[131]

Paul says that because we have been raised with Christ, we gain a new perspective. The reality of what we see and hear is not the only reality there is. We can choose to change our perspective and set our hearts and minds on things above—on heaven, on Christ, on God. And when we do that, not only does the scale of our problems change but also the scale of our accomplishments and achievements.

Problems still exist, but they become smaller compared to the greatness of our God. Remember, in Isaiah's prophecy of the coming Messiah, which is often quoted around Christmas, he says, "And he will be called Wonderful Counselor, Mighty God, Everlasting Father, Prince of Peace."[132] Which of your problems is too big for a God that is described by those names? And yet, if our eyes are fixed on earthly things, we lose sight of the greatness of our God who can and does care for us. He is bigger than all our problems and fears, and we need not depend only on ourselves, which leads to more problems.

At the same time, our achievements and accomplishments take on their proper perspective. In Philippians 3 Paul says,

> But whatever was to my profit I now consider loss for the sake of Christ. What is more, I consider everything a loss compared to the surpassing greatness of knowing Christ Jesus my Lord, for whose sake I have lost all things. I consider them rubbish, that I may gain Christ and be found in him, not having a

---

[131] Colossians 3:1–2
[132] Isaiah 9:6b

righteousness of my own that comes from the law, but that which is through faith in Christ—the righteousness that comes from God and is by faith. I want to know Christ and the power of his resurrection and the fellowship of sharing in his sufferings, becoming like him in his death, and so, somehow, to attain to the resurrection from the dead.[133]

The apostle had a lot to brag about, but when his perspective was changed he saw that it really wasn't worth that much compared to knowing Christ. Does that mean accomplishments have no purpose? No. But it does mean that the most important thing about us is not what we do, it is Who we know, and Whose we are. You don't have to look at others and compete with them for value and significance. A change of perspective gives us a view of "a whole new world."

Aladdin was trapped at the bottom of society. Jasmine was trapped at the top. Both found their new life of adventure when their view was transformed to outside what they could see and into "a whole new world." No matter where you find yourself in life, "set your minds on things above, not on earthly things" and see what "a whole new world" may look like.

Let us fix our eyes on Jesus, the author and perfecter of our faith, who for the joy set before him endured the cross, scorning its shame, and sat down at the right hand of the throne of God. Consider him who endured such opposition from sinful men, so that you will not grow weary and lose heart.[134]

---

[133] Philippians 3:7–11
[134] Hebrews 12:2–3

> **Kingdom Thinking:** How can you change your perspective—or have it changed—to get a more God's-eye view of the world?

Jungle Cruise

A True-Life Adventure

Here is adventure. Here is romance. Here is mystery. Tropical Rivers, silently flowing into the unknown. The unbelievable splendor of exotic flowers...the eerie sounds of the jungle...with eyes that are always watching. This is Adventureland, the wonderland of nature's own design.[135]

When Disneyland was in its formative stages, Walt Disney planned an area where the studio's *True-Life Adventures* series of nature films could be shown right in front of the park visitors. It was to be called, appropriately enough, "True Life Adventureland." The land was originally supposed to include real animals from Africa to inhabit a jungle river, but after zoologists told Walt the animals would lay around, sleep, or hide, the Imagineers built Animatronic animals instead and the term "True-Life" was eventually dropped from "True-Life Adventureland."

Consider the true-life adventures represented by the quintessential Adventureland attraction, the Jungle Cruise. Passengers get:

- Ruins of an ancient shrine
- An elephant bathing pool

---

[135] From Walt Disney's Opening Day dedication speech for Adventureland, 1955.

- A safari base camp and gorillas
- The Nile River
- An encounter with African bull elephants
- A group of baboons and a family of lions "protecting a sleeping zebra"
- Safari party on the pole
- Hippo pool
- An example of native arts & crafts ("That's Art there on top.")
- The world famous "back side of water"
- Piranhas
- Trader Sam
- The dreaded return to civilization

Alright, so they're not all "true-life," but they're all based on real events and sights, only with a twist. And—while all later instances including the current version have made use of a comedic spiel—the original intent of the ride was to provide a realistic, believable voyage through the world's jungles. The original spiel had no jokes and sounded much like the narration of a nature documentary.

Think about the ride; especially imagine (or remember) riding it as a child for the first time. Some moments are scary, like when the piranhas appear. Some are difficult, like what the safari party encountered (an angry rhino). Some are thrilling, like cruising by the back side of water! OK, I'm kidding, like the close-up look at the elephants and hippos.

Some parts can be boring. One of the times I rode the Jungle Cruise, we had to wait for a few minutes before we could return to the dock. While waiting, the skipper pointed out some of the local flora to us. "There's some. And there's some more over there. And more over there." That's still one of my favorite Jungle Cruise jokes for some reason, but the truth is that nothing was happening and we were staring at shrubs.

When you get off the ride, you look back and realize it was fun. Depending on how good your perspective is, you may be enjoying it while you're on it, but maybe not all of it, until later. And sometimes, it gets more fun in the retelling and remembering.

Like the tales portrayed in Adventureland, the Christian life is a true-life adventure. Sometimes it's scary. Sometimes it's hard. Sometimes it's exciting. Sometimes it's boring. And it's not fun all the time. That's OK, because fun isn't the purpose of life. Rather, the purpose is Christlikeness: growth, maturity, love, grace, joy. Fun is a periodic byproduct.

Mark Lowry put it this way (paraphrased a bit):

Christ said, "I've come to give you life, but not just life, but life more abundant!" First you've got to know what life is. You know what life is?

Life is a series of emotions and experiences, a mountain after a valley, a wife to feed, a husband to clothe, children to raise, a boss to put up with, car loans, taxes, April 15th. Life is life!

Christ said, "I've come to give you life...more abundant!"

If I could put the Christian life into one word, you know what it would be? It wouldn't be joyous, it wouldn't be victorious, it wouldn't be sad, it wouldn't be depressing even though it has been all these things at some point in time. If I could put it into one word, if I could put my entire Christian experience into one word, it would be this; the Christian life is...interesting![136]

---

[136] Adapted from Mark Lowry, "First Class, Wrong Flight," *Mouth in Motion* (Nashville, TN: Word Music, 1994).

For whatever else it may or may not be at any given moment, overall life is an adventure! Take it!

Kingdom Thinking: What word would you use to summarize your Christian experience? Or, if you are not a Christian, what word do you think you would use to describe the Christians you know?

Are You in De-Nile?

On the "World Famous" Jungle Cruise, your skipper takes you on four—or possibly five, depending on who you ask—of the world's major rivers:

- the Irrawaddy and Mekong in Asia;
- the Nile and the Congo in Africa;
- and the Amazon in South America.

On some cruises, depending on who your skipper is you may get a mention of the Irrawaddy, but most of the time only one river is called by its name: the Nile. "We've now turned down the Nile River, the longest river in Anaheim. No, really, it's the longest river in the world, winding across more than 4,000 miles. And if you don't believe me, you must be in…de-Nile." That pun almost always gets a laugh—or at least a groan.

Whether on the river adventure or the adventure of life, we often come upon a point of "denial." On the Jungle Cruise, passengers pass through it and our reward is a spectacular view of "the back side of water"—where the boat goes under a waterfall.

In life, you have a choice. If you choose denial, your adventure becomes treacherous, dark, and unfulfilling. It seems like the easy way, but it's quite the opposite. If you choose to avoid denial, your adventure can continue in the way it was meant to. Do you want God's presence, provision, and promises? Then don't go down the path of denial.

Denial of what? Sin. Not the sin of everyone around you, but your own. If you want to experience God's presence, provision, and promises, you must embrace God's priorities and perspective, and that starts with an honest self-evaluation of what separates you from Him and what He wants for you.

It's popular and considered polite today to talk about the goodness in people or in ourselves, and how we need to focus on the positive and ignore the negative. Saying something bad about ourselves is considered negative self-talk and should be avoided at all costs. The problem with this view is that it is not what the Bible says.

If we claim to be without sin, we deceive ourselves and the truth is not in us. If we confess our sins, He is faithful and just and will forgive us our sins and purify us from all unrighteousness. If we claim we have not sinned, we make Him out to be a liar and His word is not in us.[137]

A more biblically balanced approach is to engage in some "negative self-talk": getting real with God about our sin. Agree with Him on how we've fallen short of His standard for our lives and His holiness. It is not legalistic, but authentic, transparent, and honest. Claiming we don't need to or avoiding it is living in denial.

As Christians, we still sin. We are not "slaves to sin", as in our unredeemed state, but we still break God's law. And it still separates us from God—not positionally or eternally, but relationally, right now. When God seems distant, and when we feel

---

[137] 1 John 1:8–10

like our prayers aren't being heard (much less answered), or life is overwhelming, it's wise to confess our sins and repent. Sin may not always be the issue, but it would be foolish to discount the need for repentance.

The purpose of this confession is not to remain mired in guilt or to put ourselves down. Nor is it to manufacture or dwell excessively on negativity. It is to accept that we're not perfect, that we are inclined to seek our own self-interest and be petty, greedy, deceitful, arrogant, envious, etc. We take these sins to God and simply agree with what He's already said about them (and us). That's what confession is and it is one of the most important ways to break the power of sin in your life—just talk honestly to God about it.

Confession that's followed by continually choosing to repeat the same behavior rings hollow, though, and that's where repentance comes in. If we confess our sins but keep on committing them, we're right back in denial. Repentance is changing your mind. It is choosing to think differently, and then acting differently. None of us can do this successfully without the Holy Spirit working in us. That's why confession, which reconnects God and sinners because it gets the things that have been separating us out in the open and out of the way, comes first.

What do you want your life to look like? What do you want to be true of you? Do you want to know God's will for your life? Do you want to live powerfully in your Supernatural Kingdom Identity? Do you want to make an impact on your world? Then start here with confession and repentance, and revisit it regularly. None of the rest of the "good stuff" is possible without this regular, honest, and sometimes painful, time of evaluating where sin is getting a foothold in our lives and then choosing to turn away from it.

"De-nile" on the Jungle Cruise is a great pun. Denial of our sin in real life is no laughing matter. Confessing and repenting of it aligns your mind and heart with God, helps make His priorities yours, and clears the way for Him to work powerfully in and through you. And that way is the path of true, exciting, fulfilling adventure—the one you were created for!

Kingdom Thinking: Where has de-nile (or denial) taken you?

Indiana Jones Adventure

Integrity

When it comes to things Disney does best, right at the top of my list are the themed attractions. From the themed queue (line), to the attraction itself, to the exit—the very best attractions tell a unified story from beginning to end. A great example of this complete theming is the Indiana Jones Adventure.

Imagineers call the queue for an attraction "Act I" of the story. This is where the stage is set and the story begins. *The Disneyland Encyclopedia* says of this attraction queue, "At over a quarter-mile long, this would be the longest, and most densely detailed, queue in Disneyland history."

From the moment you cross the entry (under the sign) of the Indiana Jones Adventure and enter the attraction's environment you are immersed in the story of an ancient temple, recently found by Indiana Jones—who has now disappeared. The overgrown foliage, stuttering generator, odd markings throughout the temple, strange noises, and more all tell the story. There are even some hidden surprises—most of which get completely bypassed now thanks to FastPass. When the ride first opened, Cast Members even handed out decoder cards so guests could decode the "maraglyphs" found throughout.

The ride itself takes you on a wild expedition through the deepest interiors of the temple, encountering fire, snakes, insects, skeletons, and much more. And after the ride, the walk back out of the temple keeps you in the story, including more maraglyphs to decipher. Two movie props contribute to the realism of the exit to the Indiana Jones Adventure: the mine car from *Temple of Doom* and the truck from *Raiders of the Lost Ark*.

All facets of this attraction, from the queue through the exit, work together to tell a single story. What you see on the outside is what you find on the inside. The story is consistent. In short, the attraction has integrity.

Dictionary.com defines integrity as:

1. adherence to moral and ethical principles; soundness of moral character; honesty.
2. the state of being whole, entire, or undiminished.[138]

Integrity is highlighted as a critical character trait of godly people. The apostle Paul tells Titus, "In everything set them an example by doing what is good. In your teaching show integrity, seriousness and soundness of speech that cannot be condemned, so that those who oppose you may be ashamed because they have nothing bad to say about us."[139] All the parts work together and give the same message.

Several more biblical passages describe this desirable trait:

Let integrity and uprightness preserve me, for I wait for and expect You.[140]

---

[138] Dictionary.com, s.v. "Integrity," http://dictionary.reference.com/browse/Integrity?s=t, accessed August 16, 2013.
[139] Titus 2:7–8
[140] Psalm 25:11

Vindicate me, O LORD, for I have walked in my integrity, and I have trusted in the LORD without wavering.[141]

Receive instruction in wise dealing and the discipline of wise thoughtfulness, righteousness, justice, and integrity.[142]

Whoever walks in integrity walks securely, but he who makes his ways crooked will be found out.[143]

And endurance (fortitude) develops maturity of character (approved faith and tried integrity). And character [of this sort] produces [the habit of] joyful and confident hope of eternal salvation.[144]

Stand therefore [hold your ground], having tightened the belt of truth around your loins and having put on the breastplate of integrity and of moral rectitude and right standing with God.[145]

This is not a call to perfection—none of us is perfect nor will we be this side of heaven—but that doesn't let us off the hook when it comes to growing in integrity. Part of integrity is acknowledging that we fall short. Contrary to popular belief, hypocrisy is not making mistakes or falling short, it is pretending to be someone or something that you know to be not true.

It's easy to look good on the outside, but how are you on the inside? When people look beneath the surface you present to the world, do they find consistency and honesty? How does your life look from entry to exit? Are your stated values reflected in your daily conduct?

---

[141] Psalm 26:1
[142] Proverbs 1:3
[143] Proverbs 10:9
[144] Romans 5:4 (AMP)
[145] Ephesians 6:14 (AMP)

> **Kingdom Thinking:** What story are you telling with your life, and do you tell it all the way through?

Swiss Family Robinson/Tarzan's Treehouse

Aliens and Strangers

The Swiss Family Treehouse opened November 18, 1962, the first significant attraction added to Adventureland since Opening Day. Based on the popular live action movie, the Disneyland version was not only modeled after the look of the treehouse in the film, but was decorated throughout as though the family was still living there and visitors had just missed them.

Sadly for many, the Robinson family was evicted in the spring of 1999, and in the summer of the same year, Tarzan's Treehouse opened (one day after the animated feature premiered in theaters). A new tree suddenly grew next to the main tree and a suspension bridge connecting the two was built. As with many Disney attractions, homage is still paid to the old one, though. Listen carefully to the music playing on the gramophone and you will recognize a familiar tune from the attraction's past.

The Robinson family and Tarzan have more in common than just living in a treehouse, though. Both were shipwrecked and forced to live in a place that wasn't truly their home. In general, Tarzan adjusted the best, but in both cases, they lived in a place and among a people (or animals) that were not their own. They were "aliens and strangers." The Robinson family in particular was forced to live in one place while knowing they had another home "out there."

Does that sound familiar? Peter and the writer of Hebrews both describe us, followers of Christ, people of God, the same way.

Dear friends, I urge you, as aliens and strangers in the world, to abstain from sinful desires, which war against your soul. Live such good lives among the pagans that, though they accuse you of doing wrong, they may see your good deeds and glorify God on the day He visits us.[146]

All these people were still living by faith when they died. They did not receive the things promised; they only saw them and welcomed them from a distance. And they admitted that they were aliens and strangers on earth. People who say such things show that they are looking for a country of their own. If they had been thinking of the country they had left, they would have had opportunity to return. Instead, they were longing for a better country—a heavenly one. Therefore God is not ashamed to be called their God, for He has prepared a city for them.[147]

This world is not our home. We live here for a while, but our ultimate home is in heaven. The more preoccupied we are with where we live now, the more our troubles seem overwhelming, because there's nothing else to look forward to, no better place. If this earthly home is bad, what hope is there?

But Christians live in one place now and eagerly await another. And God, by His grace, has given us the Holy Spirit so that we have a taste, a promise, and a reminder of that future home now.

Just as a dolphin lives in the water but must breathe the air, so we live on the earth but must be refreshed by God in heaven. If the dolphin only remained in the water, it would die because it never got the air it needed. If we remain only world-focused, we will also appear lifeless. God's refreshing grace, given to us through His spirit, provides a regular reminder of what awaits us in our heavenly home.

---

[146] 1 Peter 2:11–12
[147] Hebrews 11:13–16

Kingdom Thinking: Have you ever felt "homesick for heaven"? What brought it on?

Chapter 5: Frontierland

Lay of the Land

The Bible: Our Historical Foundation

> *"It is here that we experience the story of our country's past.....A tribute to the faith, courage, and ingenuity of our hardy pioneers who blazed the trails and made this progress possible."*[148]

*F*rontierland is about knowing our history, our heritage.

As Christians, the main source for knowing our heritage is the Bible. Sure, there are others—stories about Christians between then and now, hymns and other songs, etc.—but if the Bible is overlooked or underused, we risk getting way off

---

[148] From Walt Disney's Opening Day dedication speech for Frontierland, 1955.

track. We run the same risk if we don't understand and use the Bible properly. Sure, God speaks to us through His written Word, and sometimes He points us right to a verse or story that's just what we need at that moment. But the longer we read the Bible, the easier it can become to misuse Scripture because we haven't taken the time to understand what it really says. We (usually unintentionally) read into it what we want it to say.

The classic example of this mishandling has been 1 Corinthians 10:13.

> No temptation has seized you except what is common to man. And God is faithful; He will not let you be tempted beyond what you can bear. But when you are tempted, He will also provide a way out so that you can stand up under it.

Here's the way I've usually heard people interpret that verse: "God won't give you more than you can handle."

Now, it does say that He will provide a way out, and there's a provision about not being tempted "more than you can bear." But that interpretation is completely off, and that sentiment isn't true. In fact, sometimes we *are* given more than we can handle, so that we learn to stop relying on ourselves and start relying on God. In 2 Corinthians, Paul says,

> We do not want you to be uninformed, brothers, about the hardships we suffered in the province of Asia. We were under great pressure, far beyond our ability to endure, so that we despaired even of life. Indeed, in our hearts we felt the sentence of death. But this happened that we might not rely on ourselves but on God, who raises the dead.[149]

1 Corinthians 10:13 is specifically talking about temptations, not trials, struggles, problems, or suffering. In fact, earlier in the

---

[149] 2 Corinthians 1:8–9

chapter—right before this—Paul warns his readers about what had happened in the past to the nation of Israel. He tells them that the kinds of temptations they are facing—specifically, giving in to idolatry—are not unique to them. It has happened before; thus they have the warnings and examples to learn from and be encouraged by.

It's true that not all passages are that straightforward. And there is room for responsible interpretation with the best and most complete information possible. But too often people read a passage, or hear someone else talk about it, and latch on to what they want to hear, not what was actually said. Or, they fail to check it out to see if the message they're being told is true and accurate. It's easy to do, but it is a dangerous and irresponsible way to read the Bible, and not true to our heritage.

Kingdom Thinking: Do you agree or disagree with the contention that Christians too often mishandle the Scriptures? Why? What verses have you seen or heard used out of context?

Context is Critical

When you first start reading the Bible, you'll probably want to just read it, and that's a good way to start. But as time goes on and you grow in your faith, you need to proceed to more serious study. Some ideas, some principles, are timeless and universal, but it's important not to assume that everything is.

Read the Bible to become familiar with its contents. Study the Bible to understand it better and use it correctly.

To that end, I highly recommend a book called *How to Read the Bible for All Its Worth* by Gordon Fee and Douglas Stuart. It was one of my textbooks when I was in Bible College pursuing my bachelor's degree in Church Ministry. It helps you learn to think contextually as you read. You will learn not just what a text says (the immediate, textual context), but who it's said to and why (the historical context), what form it's said in (the literary context—narrative is different from poetry, which is different from a letter, etc.), and even what type of literature the book itself is. The different types of literature in the Bible serve different purposes.

American history has also been documented in different types of literature. Consider for a moment:

- Lewis & Clark's journal
- Abraham Lincoln's collection of speeches
- Mark Twain's *A Connecticut Yankee in King Arthur's Court*
- Benjamin Franklin's *Poor Richard's Almanack*

All are different types of literature. All serve different purposes. And yet all are valuable in one way or another for a complete understanding of America and our history.

Let's pop back to Frontierland for a minute.

- Some attractions have a historical basis, like the Mark Twain and the Columbia, or even the Shooting Gallery and Big Thunder Mountain Railroad.
- Some are based in fiction, like Tom Sawyer Island.
- And some are a combination, like the Golden Horseshoe.

Each serves a different purpose, but they are all part of the whole.

Now, before you get agitated, I am *not* saying any parts of the Bible are fiction. I *am* saying the Bible contains different types of literature, and they can serve different purposes. For example:

- The Psalms are poetry, often describing people speaking to God, not the other way around.
- The Old Testament books of Joshua, Judges, Ruth, Samuel, Kings, Chronicles, Ezra, Nehemiah, and Esther are historical narratives.
- The gospels are evangelistic narratives (they capture history, and they are narratives, but they have the specific purpose of telling people about Jesus).
- Daniel and Revelation are apocalyptic literature, which is generally more symbolic than other types of literature.
- Books like Job and Proverbs are Wisdom literature.

Of course, within each book, there may be other literary types interspersed. For instance, portions of Genesis are poetry, not narrative.

And each type serves a different purpose. Here is one example to "get you started." Proverbs are just that, proverbs. When properly understood and used, they are helpful resources for living the life of faith. Improperly used, they can provide a basis for selfish, materialistic, shortsighted behavior.

For instance, Proverbs 22:6 says, "Train a child in the way he should go, and when he is old he will not turn from it." In general, that is true, but it's not a promise. Some children who are raised in a Christian family turn away when they grow up. Some come back. Some don't. That does not mean we should give up on them. It does not mean they are a lost cause. But it does mean we should not count on them eventually coming back just because "the Bible says they will."

And, in fact, that common "at a glance" understanding doesn't even address the meaning of the Proverb in the Hebrew. Cynthia Tobias, of Learning Styles Unlimited, pointed out that the *Amplified Bible* does a better job of teasing it out: "Train up a child in the way he should go [and in keeping with his individual gift or bent], and when he is old he will not depart from it."

She talked about this understanding in a seminar at McChord Air Force Base. Afterwards, Chaplain Cecil R. Richardson, who has a Masters Degree in Hebrew Studies came up to her and told her that the original Hebrew of the verb translated "train" is used uniquely here. In those days, it referred to the clearing out of the mouth of a newborn baby and it meant, "create an environment for life."

So, the verse says: "Create an environment for life for that child, in keeping with their individual gifts or bents, and when they're old, they won't depart from it."

In this seminar, Cynthia said,

This is very different from the modern day interpretation where we think we should raise them the way we want to, decide what they need to know, and pound it into their little heads, because we're the ones who know better. We're the adults here.

The biggest homework assignment for parents is to know each individual child, so we can help create an environment for life for them, in order to get across what the Lord wants us to get across and what we need to get across as responsible parents.[150]

This proverb does not promise that they'll stay on "the straight and narrow," but it encourages parents to rely on God to show them who that child is meant to be. It also calls parents to help their children as much as they can to enable them to fulfill their God-given potential.

Now, before you decide to form a lynch mob and come after me (for aborting God's promises), let me show you two verses that make it abundantly clear that Proverbs are just that, *proverbs*, not

---

[150] Cynthia Tobias, "No Two Alike" (Colorado Springs, CO: Focus on the Family, 1994).

promises, and that they cannot be interpreted in isolation from the rest of Scripture.

Proverbs 26:4 says, "Do not answer a fool according to his folly, or you will be like him yourself." Good advice, right?

Proverbs 26:5 says, "Answer a fool according to his folly, or he will be wise in his own eyes."

Two verses in Proverbs, one right after the other, provide two opposite instructions. How do we reconcile the two if the Bible is the word of God and every word is true? By understanding the literary context. These are proverbs—brief, particular expressions of truth. They point to a truth, but must be understood in balance with the rest of Scripture and by using wisdom in the particular situations in which they need to be applied. Context (of all kinds) is critical.

Kingdom Thinking: Think of your favorite verse or passage of Scripture. Do you know the context?

Frontierland Shootin' Exposition

Honesty

Everything has certain characteristics that are critical to "that thing" being considered a good version. For example, a rifle must load efficiently, aim accurately, fire reliably, and shoot straight. If any of these are not true of a certain rifle, then it's not a very good rifle.

In the "Old West" era that Frontierland represents, most rifles were pretty questionable at best. Rifles were often difficult to load, and the quality of the aim varied between reasonably good and random guess (depending on the skill of the marksman). A shooter could expect his gun to fire, but there was a pretty good chance it would jam or misfire, too.

Arguably, the most important characteristic, though, was whether it shot straight. A gun did its rifleman no good—no matter how easily it loaded, accurately it could be aimed, or reliably it fired—if the actual bullet went somewhere other than where it was aimed. The others could be corrected for, either through making adjustments or cleaning the gun well, but a rifle that didn't shoot straight had to be completely overhauled or destroyed. Without that one key trait, it could not be counted on.

The sign in front of the Frontierland Shootin' Exposition (Shooting Gallery) advertises this most important quality, as any shooting gallery might. After all, if the rifles can be suspected of not shooting straight, no one would play the game. If I don't know my shot is going to go where I point it, why bother? Trusting a rifle that you don't know will shoot straight is for suckers. Not to worry, though. Disneyland's rifles are guaranteed to be straight shooters.

A rifle makes an implied claim that it will send a bullet in the direction you aim it. A rifle that shoots straight fulfills that promise. This quality is so important that the phrase "straight shooter" entered the English language in the late 1920s to mean "one who is honest, forthright, and upstanding in their behavior." They can be trusted. Honesty is important to people.

Honesty is important to God, too.

Honest scales and balances are from the Lord;
all the weights in the bag are of His making.[151]

Kings take pleasure in honest lips;
they value a man who speaks the truth.[152]

---

[151] Proverbs 16:11
[152] Proverbs 16:13

An honest answer
is like a kiss on the lips.[153]

Go up and down the streets of Jerusalem,
look around and consider,
search through her squares.
If you can find but one person
who deals honestly and seeks the truth,
I will forgive this city.
Although they say, "As surely as the Lord lives,"
still they are swearing falsely.
O Lord, do not Your eyes look for truth?
You struck them, but they felt no pain;
You crushed them, but they refused correction.
They made their faces harder than stone
and refused to repent.[154]

Honesty matters. Of course, it doesn't function in isolation. Left to itself, it is possible for honesty to be as much of a weapon as a rifle. Honesty must be matched with grace and love.

The Word became flesh and made His dwelling among us. We have seen His glory, the glory of the One and Only, who came from the Father, full of grace and truth.[155]

For the law was given through Moses; grace and truth came through Jesus Christ.[156]

Instead, speaking the truth in love, we will in all things grow up into Him who is the Head, that is, Christ.[157]

---

153 Proverbs 24:26
154 Jeremiah 5:1–3
155 John 1:14
156 John 1:17
157 Ephesians 4:15

Honesty is one of the most crucial characteristics of the Christian. If people can't trust our word about mundane matters, how can they trust us about placing faith in Jesus? If we are not honest with people in our conversations, what does that say to them about our God?

That does not mean saying exactly what's on our mind all the time. A filter is wise and healthy. Words can hurt. They can be destructive. If you're about to say something that's true, ask yourself first if it's beneficial, helpful, and loving. If not, don't say it. That's grace and love. At the same time, grace and love without truth are hollow and meaningless. As with most aspects of the Christian life, it is all about balance.

It's easy to fudge, fib, tell a little white lie, skirt the truth, or whatever pretty face we may want to put on an ugly reality. Don't let that be you. Be known as a straight shooter.

Kingdom Thinking: How do you feel when someone isn't honest with you? What does that say to you about their character and what's important to them?

Billy Hill and the Hillbillies

Unique, Just Like Everyone Else

Billy Hill and the Hillbillies was not the first show performed at the Golden Horseshoe Saloon. That honor goes to Slue Foot Sue's Golden Horseshoe Revue, which ran from July 16, 1955, until October 12, 1986. This variety show had over 50,000 performances and is listed in the *Guinness Book of Records* as the longest-running musical of all time. Since 1986 there have been a few different productions on that stage, with the current one being Billy Hill and the Hillbillies.

It's a fairly complicated history, but the short version is that the Billys first performed in Critter Country, beginning at the same time as the opening of Splash Mountain (July 17, 1989), and moved into the Golden Horseshoe Saloon in late December of 1994. Billy Hill and the Hillbillies is made up of four members (or at least four members perform at a time), and part of the "gimmick" is that all of them are named Billy Hill. Even when they introduce each other for solos or spotlight features, the intro always consists of something like, "Please welcome my brother, Billy Hill!"

The show is a mix of comedy and impressive musicianship. They perform a bluegrass/country music centered show, but they also throw in classic rock and rap (performed in a bluegrass style—go ahead, wrap your head around that). But what's the purpose of talking about it here (besides to persuade you to go see them next time you're at Disneyland—which I hope you do!)? To answer that question, let's first take a look at a conversation between Helen Parr and her son Dash in the Disney/Pixar movie *The Incredibles*.

> Dash: You always say "Do your best," but you don't really mean it. Why can't I do the best that I can do?
> Helen: Right now, honey, the world just wants us to fit in, and to fit in, we gotta be like everyone else.
> Dash: But Dad always said our powers were nothing to be ashamed of, our powers made us special. (Dash ran *very* fast, as you'll recall.)
> Helen: Everyone's special, Dash.
> Dash: [muttering] Which is another way of saying no one is.

We all want to be special. Our identity is often wrapped up in making sure we stand out from everyone else and have made a name for ourselves. We want to be unique.

And we are. But that quality must be balanced with and find its full expression in being part of something else—or Someone else.

Just as each of us has one body with many members, and these members do not all have the same function, so in Christ we who are many form one body, and each member belongs to all the others.[158]

The members of Billy Hill and the Hillbillies are unique. They each have different talents and skills, different personalities, and probably even different preferred performance styles. They even all have different real names. But for the sake of the show, they are all called "Billy Hill." They combine their skills, talents, and abilities for the sake of the group and the show. They play various instruments during the show and particular Billys are highlighted in different portions of the show. Yet they are all still "Billy Hill."

Believers are each unique and special. That comes from Christ, and finds its truest expression in Christ and in His body. Is "everyone's special" really another way of saying "no one is"? Do we have to stand out from, or even above, everyone else to have value in who we are? Not at all! Just as each Billy is unique, but identified with the others by their name, all who are in Christ are unique but are identified with the others by His name (we are "Christ"-ians, after all), and as part of His body. For the sake of each other, and Christ, we submit our uniqueness to Him.

You don't have to be "better" to be unique, and uniquely valuable. You just need to be found *in* Him, embracing your identity in Him.

Kingdom Thinking: How have you seen God's unique design in you, and how are you using it to benefit His body?

---

[158] Romans 12:4–5

Big Thunder Mountain Railroad

Facing Your Fears

Big Thunder Mountain Railroad opened in September of 1979, and became the third member of the Disneyland "Mountain Range" (The Matterhorn and Space Mountain preceded it in 1959 and 1977 respectively, and Splash Mountain followed it in 1989).

Taking the place of the Nature's Wonderland area, but paying tribute to it in multiple ways, this roller coaster became one of the fastest rides in Disneyland at the time and was proclaimed "the wildest ride in the wilderness!" by both the attraction poster and the narrator at the beginning of the attraction. It also marked my first real roller coaster ride and the beginning of facing my fear of them—a fear that dates back to when I was eight years old (maybe younger) and was traumatized by a roller coaster at a county fair.

Big Thunder Mountain Railroad is a perfect vehicle (so to speak) for facing your fears. From a pragmatic standpoint it is a great "starter coaster." Taking a broader look, it seems built to remind guests that it's perfectly natural to be afraid of some things. Consider some of the visuals in the attraction:

- A runaway train hurtling through an abandoned mine
- Mysterious glowing pools of water
- A goat chewing a stick of dynamite
- An earthquake (it's often unnoticed, but that's what you're supposed to be experiencing on the third lift hill)
- A population that has plummeted from 2,015 to 38. Where did everybody go, and why?
- Dark tunnels
- Entering a "blasting area" (the sign even says "Danger!")

The storytelling elements depict a place to fear. Yet something tells us we'll be OK—the names of the trains themselves:

- I.B. Hearty
- I.M. Brave
- I.M. Fearless
- U.B. Bold
- U.R. Courageous
- U.R. Daring

With a reassuring name, the vehicle that carries you through the ride proclaims victory over the fearful elements that surround you.

Do you know what the most-often repeated command in the Bible is? "Don't be afraid." This command, or a variation of it, appears more than 100 times in the Bible. And it is not all front-loaded in the Old Testament. It is Jesus' most-repeated command, too—yes, even more than "love one another." A quick search of BibleGateway shows the phrases "do not be afraid," "don't be afraid," and "do not fear" a combined total of 103 times! Not all of them are commands, but most are.

Here are our reassuring words from Scripture:

Have I not commanded you? Be strong and courageous. Do not be afraid; do not be discouraged, for the Lord your God will be with you wherever you go.[159]

So do not fear, for I am with you;
do not be dismayed, for I am your God.
I will strengthen you and help you;
I will uphold you with My righteous right hand.[160]

---

[159] Joshua 1:9
[160] Isaiah 41:10

So don't be afraid; you are worth more than many sparrows.[161]

Do not be afraid, little flock, for your Father has been pleased to give you the kingdom.[162]

Peace I leave with you; My peace I give you. I do not give to you as the world gives. Do not let your hearts be troubled and do not be afraid.[163]

Wherever this life carries you and whatever you do (or don't do), you will encounter fear-inducing situations. In fact, you're probably thinking of one right now. What does God say in those moments? "Don't be afraid." He is with you. He loves you. He will show Himself strong on your behalf—as long as you trust Him.

No matter how careful you try to be, how safe you try to play it, there will always be things to fear. Trying to avoid fear entirely is like trying to ride Big Thunder Mountain Railroad without actually getting on the ride. It doesn't work—never has, never will. Even if you claim to not be fearful, let me challenge you with this thought: when you are stressed about something, it is because you are afraid of the outcome. Stress is just another form of fear.

Do you fear rejection by people? Trust His love.

Do you fear an overwhelming task? Trust His strength.

Do you fear failure? Trust His grace.

Do you fear a difficult or hopeless circumstance? Trust His peace and comfort.

Do you fear suffering? Trust the promise of His presence.

Fear not, for He is with you and you are in His firm, faithful grip.

---

[161] Matthew 10:31
[162] Luke 12:32
[163] John 14:27

> **Kingdom Thinking:** What have you avoided out of fear, but which you also know is the direction in life God has for you?

Big Thunder Ranch

Petting Zoo: On Being Sheep

The Big Thunder Ranch Petting Zoo is tucked away along Big Thunder Trail in Frontierland, the path between Big Thunder Mountain Railroad and Fantasyland. Formerly part of the Mine Train Through Nature's Wonderland (as far back as 1960), when that attraction was closed in 1977 this patch of land sat unused for nearly a decade. Big Thunder Ranch, including the petting zoo, opened in 1986.

Inspired by the western ranches of the 1880s, Big Thunder Ranch features a small wooden ranch house and petting barnyard where young cowpokes can meet and pet barnyard animals, such as cows, goats, sheep, donkeys, and pigs. From time to time, the ranch has even served as home to the Thanksgiving turkeys that used to be pardoned by the president of the United States.

When I think of petting zoos, and this one in particular, I think of sheep. Sure, there are other animals, but mainly sheep. The obvious connection here? Christians are called the sheep of God's pasture, and Jesus the Good Shepherd. For now, I want to focus on us, the sheep.

> Yet for Your sake we face death all day long;
> we are considered as sheep to be slaughtered.[164]

---

[164] Psalm 44:22

But He brought His people out like a flock;
He led them like sheep through the desert.[165]

We all, like sheep, have gone astray,
each of us has turned to his own way;
and the LORD has laid on Him
the iniquity of us all.[166]

When He saw the crowds, He had compassion on them, because they were harassed and helpless, like sheep without a shepherd.[167]

My sheep listen to My voice; I know them, and they follow Me.[168]

When we imagine sheep, we might imagine cute, fluffy, and gentle creatures. We may think of Jesus holding a little lamb in His arms. People who have spent a great deal of time around sheep will tell you a different story, though. Sheep are:

- Stupid (or foolish, if we want to be a little nicer)
- Slow learners
- Stubborn
- Unattractive
- Totally dependent
- Straying
- Single-minded
- Skittish or fearful
- Restless

---

[165] Psalm 78:52
[166] Isaiah 53:6
[167] Matthew 9:36
[168] John 10:27

And believers in Christ are called sheep. Not a very flattering picture, is it? If we're honest with ourselves, though, these characteristics are true, especially when we compare ourselves not to other sheep, but to the Shepherd.

We wander off at the least provocation. We're fearful. We're slow to learn the lessons God tries to teach us. We are totally dependent on God (though some may not want to admit it). We're stubborn beyond reason. And we are restless. When hungry, afraid, not at peace with each other, or bothered by insects, sheep will not lie down. Are we any different?

But sheep have one other characteristic: they are valuable to people. People use sheep for wool, milk, and meat. Their horns were (and in some cases, still are) used to make musical instruments or to hold oil. And under Jewish law, they were used for sacrifices.

Their value is not recognized by other sheep (as far as I know). Their intrinsic worth doesn't come from how good they are at being sheep, or whether they obey the shepherd. Rather, their value emanates from the shepherd who cares for them.

That's you and me. You may not be all that pleasing or appealing when you look at yourself, or compare yourself to others—but you are valuable to God. He made you. He loves you.

So when you visit the petting zoo, look more closely at the sheep. Then remember that you are one of God's sheep, and that He knows you, has compassion on you, and considers you valuable.

Kingdom Thinking: Which of the above "sheep characteristics" do you most identify with? What changes when you remember your intrinsic value?

Mark Twain Riverboat

Six Keys to Checking Your Spiritual Depth Level

The Mark Twain Riverboat is another Opening Day attraction. A look at early concept drawing of Disneyland shows that Walt always wanted something like this in his park. There is quite a bit of history associated with this ship, and for that, I encourage you to check out its entry in *The Disneyland Encyclopedia.*[169]

A trip on the Mark Twain is a leisurely twelve- to fifteen-minute cruise around the Rivers of America. Along the way, the narrator points out interesting sights along both coasts. Much of the narration that relates to the operation of the ship itself is a pretty good historical representation.

Part of the audio includes the leadsman sounding off the depth markers. On Mississippi riverboats in the mid-1800s the leadsman's job was to monitor the depth of the water to keep the ship from running aground. He had to regularly check it and call out the depth ("Mark Three," "Half Twain," "Mark Twain," etc.). "Mark Twain" is the depth they wanted to hear, because that meant the water was two (or "twain") fathoms deep—safe for riverboats.

If the leadsman did not do his job—or if the captain did not listen to him—the ship would run aground. He had to keep an eye out to make sure they stayed in the proper depth. Otherwise, the whole ship was in trouble.

Believers need to do the same thing in our spiritual journeys. Regular checkups of our spiritual health will prevent drifting into unsafe waters. Recall David's words in the Psalms:

---

[169] Chris Strodder, *The Disneyland Encyclopedia: The Unofficial, Unauthorized, and Unprecedented History of Every Land, Attraction, Restaurant, Shop, and Major Event in the Original Magic Kingdom* (Solana Beach, CA: Santa Monica Press, 2008), 267–68.

Search me, God, and know my heart;
test me and know my anxious thoughts.
See if there is any offensive way in me,
and lead me in the way everlasting.[170]

He's asking God to check the depth markings in his life.

The great nineteenth century preacher Charles Spurgeon offered six "depth markers" (though he didn't call them that) we can apply to check our spiritual health.

1. Conviction of sin;
2. Simple faith in Christ;
3. Unfeigned repentance from sin;
4. Real change of life;
5. True prayer;
6. A willingness to obey the Lord's commandments.

How would you say you measure in each area? Again, lay aside perfection. That's not the point. The question is, are you growing? Are you making progress? Is your "depth" in each area more than it was last month, last year, or five years ago? The deeper each one is, the safer the spiritual water you're in.

Now, if the Mark Twain's crew discovers they're venturing into shallow waters, what would they do? Take some bearings, figure out where they are and where the deeper water is, and head for it. You can do the same. If one or more of these six depth markers is too shallow, stop. Figure out where you are (get a trusted friend, pastor, or coach to help you if you need it) and what you need to change to get into the deeper water, and then intentionally move in that direction.

---

[170] Psalm 139:23–24

> **Kingdom Thinking:** What is the one area you need to focus on the most, and what is one thing you can do (or stop doing) in that area to get into "deeper, safer water?"

Sailing Ship Columbia

The Upper Story and the Lower Story

Unlike its sister watercraft on the Rivers of America, the Sailing Ship Columbia did not debut on Opening Day. Instead it joined the Mark Twain Riverboat on June 14, 1958.

The Columbia differs from the Mark Twain in two distinct ways. Besides the type of ship it is (a three-masted eighteenth-century merchant ship vs. a paddlewheel riverboat), the Columbia is not built on a forced-perspective scale. While the Mark Twain is built on roughly a 5/8 scale (with some modifications for operational and safety needs at Disneyland), the Columbia is a full-sized replica of the *Columbia Rediviva*, which was the first American ship to circumnavigate the globe in 1790. That ship is also the vessel after which the Columbia River was named.

The Sailing Ship Columbia is also unique from all other park attractions in that it is possible to have two entirely different experiences aboard ship, depending on which deck you're on. No other attraction offers two such different experiences from each other on one vehicle.

On the top deck, you can observe the shore of Tom Sawyer Island glide by on the starboard (right) side, and Frontierland, New Orleans Square, and Critter Country on the port (left) side. The narration points out interesting sights. You feel the wind in your face and hear the detonation of the cannon as it fires.

Below deck, you are totally enclosed. The only way to see what you're passing is if you look through the Captain's quarters. You can explore a nautical museum, which shows what life would have been like for the crew of the original ship. The living quarters are below, as is the galley, pantry, and sick bay. It can feel confining down there, and there is no sense of where the ship might be. In fact, if you miss the narration occasionally heard below deck, only two or three minutes into the trip you'll likely have no idea where you are.

The day-to-day life happens below deck, but the ship is sailed from above.

Our lives—and history—are the same way. In *The Story*, Randy Frazee presents a condensed chronological Bible divided into thirty-one chapters so people can come to understand God's story and how their stories intersect with it. Throughout the work, he draws attention to what he calls The Upper Story and the Lower Story.

The Upper Story is the big picture: God's perspective, plan, and work throughout history to have—and then to restore—a relationship with people: you. The Lower Story is human experience, with all its triumphs and tragedies. Most of the time in the Lower Story, people reject God, run from Him, hide from Him, and even battle Him, yet He relentlessly pursues us. Our day-to-day lives are the Lower Story, and God speaks down into them with lessons, examples, and reminders.

The two stories start out as one, but then the Fall separates them. But the Bible tells us that one day, the two will be rejoined, just as our relationship with God will be fully and completely restored (though Christ's atonement certainly put us back in good standing now).

It's usually through the Lower Story lens that we read, interpret, and understand Scripture, and that is entirely valid. But it doesn't paint the full picture. Without the Upper Story, the Lower Story doesn't make sense, and it becomes all about our efforts, our strategies, and being "good enough" to earn a peek into the Upper Story. All the while, God tells us that not only is the Upper Story the lens by which the Lower Story makes sense but also He has come to us to reunite the two stories through Christ.

On the Sailing Ship Columbia, that day-to-day living happens below deck, the ship's "Lower Story." But the purpose of that life, the reason for being on the ship, can only be seen from the upper deck. The Upper Story gives the crew perspective, direction, and purpose, without which, life below deck can be burdensome, tiring, confining, and even boring.

Inhabitants of the lower deck can get a glimpse of this upper perspective: they have to look through the window in the Captain's Quarters. Only by sharing the same view as the Captain when he is with his crew can they get a partial glimpse of that upper deck view. It's not the whole picture, but sometimes it's enough. The apostle John got that glimpse in Revelation 21.

> Then I saw a new heaven and a new earth, for the first heaven and the first earth had passed away, and there was no longer any sea. I saw the Holy City, the new Jerusalem, coming down out of heaven from God, prepared as a bride beautifully dressed for her husband. And I heard a loud voice from the throne saying, "Look! God's dwelling place is now among the people, and He will dwell with them. They will be His people, and God himself will be with them and be their God. He will wipe every tear from their eyes. There will be no more death or mourning or crying or pain, for the old order of things has passed away."[171]

John "saw" the destination, but he needed the view from the upper deck to see it. And once we have it, it can (and should) inform everything that happens below deck. That's a mark of

---

[171] Revelation 21:1–4

spiritual maturity. Having that Upper Story view, God's perspective, helped Jesus endure the cross,[172] and it can help you endure whatever adversity you're facing.

One other bit of information helps distinguish these two areas of the ship. The sails and the ship's wheel are on the upper deck. The anchor is below. Forward movement—progress toward the ship's destination—comes about through activity on the upper deck. Delay or lack of progress—even working against progress—occurs below.

Again, the same is true in your life and mine. The more time we spend focused on the Lower Story, the more an anchor becomes our only sailing tool. In some people it breeds fear, in others, hubris. Whatever the Captain may want to do, staying below deck with anchor at the ready says, "I'm not willing to follow You completely. I want to stay in the harbor and out of the storm. I'd rather stay where I am, where I think it's 'safe,' than to catch the winds and sail into the unknown."

Focusing on the Upper Story means being willing to obey the Captain's orders, man the sails, fire the cannon, or do whatever He says needs to be done to go wherever His navigation may take you.

The Good News is the Captain came down to the Lower Story, and provided a way into an Upper Story perspective. You must choose the view, intentionally and regularly. It's not always easy, but nothing worthwhile ever is.

Kingdom Thinking: We all find ourselves mired in the Lower Story, for most of us more often than we'd like. What is one way you can get that peek out the Captain's Quarters, or even spend time on the upper deck?

---

[172] Hebrews 12:2

Tom Sawyer Island

Freedom in Christ

Tom Sawyer Island (now called "Pirate's Lair on Tom Sawyer Island") opened eleven months after Disneyland itself, on June 16, 1956. Oh, the man-made island was there at park opening, but it was inaccessible. Once Disneyland was up and running fairly well, Walt Disney turned his attention to this unique piece of real estate.

Many ideas were batted around, including "Mickey Mouse Island" and "Treasure Island" (based on the book and the Disney live-action film of the same name). Eventually the team arrived at "Tom Sawyer Island," and Walt did what he often did at this stage of an attraction's development: he turned it over to an Imagineer to create the actual attraction based on Disney's concept and suggestions.

This time was different, though. Marvin Davis was given the task of developing the island, but his idea was not what Walt had wanted. According to *Walt Disney: An American Original*, Walt told Davis, "Give me that thing," and he took Davis' drawings. That night, Walt worked "for hours in his red-barn workshop. The next morning, he laid tracing paper on Davis' desk and said, 'Now that's the way it should be.' The island was built according to his design."[173] That makes Tom Sawyer Island the only early Disneyland attraction personally designed by Walt Disney himself.

When you put the island (in its original or its present form) up against the rest of Disneyland's attractions, there are some significant differences, but nearly all of them can be summed up in one word: freedom.

The rest of the park's attractions (with the possible exception of Tarzan's Treehouse) are very structured. Guests walk through a

---

[173] Bob Thomas, *Walt Disney: An American Original* (New York: Disney Editions, 1994), 265.

specific queue and then sit in either a theater seat or a ride vehicle. You go where the Imagineers want you to go, when they want you to go, and you see and hear exactly what they want you to see and hear.

But Tom Sawyer Island is different. It has trails, caves, multiple paths, bridges, shortcuts (or scenic routes), a tree house, a fort (now a thing of the past), and more. There are places to sit and relax, or to watch and observe. No shops or restaurants distract you. The island is not a preprogrammed five- or even fifteen-minute experience. Guests can come and go as they please (allowing, of course, for the wait for the rafts—the only way on or off the island), and can stay as long they like—up to dusk, anyway.

Within this grand land of adventure, frontier, and wilderness, people enjoy freedom. Freedom to play. Freedom to imagine—with props and setting to suggest, but nothing to require—a specific outcome. Freedom to discover. Are there limitations to the freedom? Of course, just look at the water surrounding this place. But does that matter when you're caught up in the experience? Not at all.

Author Bob Goff says of Tom Sawyer Island,

> There are no admission requirements at Tom Sawyer Island. It doesn't matter how tall or short you are, old or young, religious or not. There are no lines on Tom Sawyer Island; it can be whatever you want it to be. You can do countless things there. Most of them involve running and jumping and using your creativity and imagination. It's a place where you can just go and do stuff. In that way, it's a place that mirrors life well—at least the opportunity to do much more with our lives. [174]

---

[174] Bob Goff, *Love Does* (Nashville: Thomas Nelson, 2012), xv.

I like this place because a guy named Disney had a hair-brained (sic) scheme to make a magical world where people could go and feel free. And it worked.[175]

Somehow we've missed that this is what life in Christ can be—and most often should be. We get caught up in the do's and don'ts. We rail against what we oppose, but forget to extravagantly embrace what we love. We live either afraid that God will get mad at us, afraid that He already is, or unconcerned whether or not He cares at all.

Even when we claim to be Christians we prefer to live by rules and "how to's" than by freedom, grace, and love. We want Him to tell us exactly where to go, where to sit, what to see, what to experience, and when to move onto the next "thing."

St. Augustine said, "Love God and do whatever you please: for the soul trained in love to God will do nothing to offend the One who is Beloved."[176] But that's too messy. It's unsafe. What if I make a mistake? What if, in trying to do the right thing, I sin? What if someone doesn't like the way I'm living, doesn't think it's "Christian enough?" Join the club.

For he who was a slave when he was called by the Lord is the Lord's freedman; similarly, he who was a free man when he was called is Christ's slave. You were bought at a price; do not become slaves of men.[177]

The people in Jesus' day who thought they were the most "religious" were the rule-followers—the Pharisees. But Jesus

---

[175]"Turning Imagination into Action, http://storylineblog.com/2012/03/27/turning-imagination-into-action-love-does-an-excerpt-from-bob-goff/, accessed August 7, 2013.

[176] This is a modern paraphrase of the full quote from St. Augustine, from Homily #7 of the Homilies on the First Epistle of John (verse 8), "Homilies on the First Epistle of John," *Works of Saint Augustine: A Translation for the 21st Century*, Boniface Ramsey, trans, (Hyde Park, NY: The City Press, 2010), 110.

[177] 1 Corinthians 7:22–23

chastised them for enslaving people with rules, especially when those rules gave them an appearance of "spirituality" and piety, but inside they rotted away because the rules kept them from the One who made the Law to show them their need for Him.

Paul the apostle describes our struggle perfectly:

> It is for freedom that Christ has set us free. Stand firm, then, and do not let yourselves be burdened again by a yoke of slavery.... You who are trying to be justified by law have been alienated from Christ; you have fallen away from grace.... The only thing that counts is faith expressing itself through love. You were running a good race. Who cut in on you and kept you from obeying the truth? That kind of persuasion does not come from the one who calls you.... You, my brothers, were called to be free. But do not use your freedom to indulge the sinful nature; rather, serve one another in love. The entire law is summed up in a single command: "Love your neighbor as yourself." If you keep on biting and devouring each other, watch out or you will be destroyed by each other.[178]

What if you spent time with God every day—in whatever way works best for you—getting to know Him better and opening yourself up to Him more. Then, in every situation in which you find yourself, ask yourself these questions.

- What needs to be done?
- How might God want to use me to serve or love someone else right now?
- What is the most loving thing that I can do?

Have you done it?

---

[178] Galatians 5:1–15, see also Colossians 2

Try it. Take the risk, even if only for one day. You may fail for most of that day. But that's OK. What if you were to succeed just once or twice? What if in those moments you truly lived as a disciple, following Jesus and letting His love flow through you to a lost, hurting, and dying world? How would your life be different?

Christ has set you free to live and love for Him. Following Jesus means to live in that freedom. Not according to a long list of rules and regulations. Not according to fear, but through, in, and by His love. Go and "do" because (to quote Bob Goff again) "love does."

Kingdom Thinking: Spend time with God today (or tomorrow, depending on how late you're reading this), and ask Him to help you live a life of love in His freedom. Then ask and answer the questions above as often as they come to mind throughout the day.

Risk and Reward or Fear and Disappointment

On a recent visit to Disneyland, I revisited Pirate's Lair on Tom Sawyer Island. It was early in the day, so I was able to spend a good hour on the island, exploring on my own with very few other people around most of the time. As I did, I noticed some changes, and I don't just mean the "invasion" of Captain Jack Sparrow and the other pirates.

Tom Sawyer Island was originally conceived by Walt Disney as a place for kids to play and fully engage their imaginations. At the same time, adults could indulge their "inner child" and frolic, too. The caves, bridges, tree house, fort, and more were there to fire the imagination and invite exploration.

Many of those features are still there, but they're "safer" now. It's just not the same. There is one "right way" to go into most caves. There is one direction to cross the bridges, and usually a safety gate at the "wrong" end to keep people out. There is one way into the tree house.

Lookout posts can be found throughout the island, with "telescopes" you can use. But they're all mounted and firmly fixed in place so you can look only in the direction each is already pointing (and in the case of at least one of those, it's pointing into a tree, so there's nothing to see but leaves).

Perhaps worst of all, Fort Wilderness is locked up tight. What was once the culmination of the exploration is now a testament to "you can go no farther."

What was once a place of freedom is now restricted, reigned in, and tamed. Fear and legal concerns have diminished the pleasure of this island, making it a shadow of what it once was.

How often do believers do the same thing to God, and to our faith? In the past we took risks for God. Living out our faith was an adventure as we followed Him wherever He led. Whether after our conversion or after a "mountain top experience" like a church camp, faith was an adventure.

But at some point, that unabashed enthusiasm diminished—maybe after years, maybe after days—and we started to play it safe. Fear and legalism took control. Following God turned into following rules and being "nice." Consequently, we stay on the clearly marked path everyone else follows and miss out on everything around us.

On Tom Sawyer Island, there is good news—if you look long enough and dare to continue the exploration. You can still find places of freedom within the broader confines of the island itself. You can explore caves with no signs to tell you which way to go. You'll happen upon paths without arrows. And best of all, there is a treasure.

Go around the fort and past the cemetery—which serves as a reminder that risk and adventure don't always have a "happily ever after." If you do, you'll discover the hidden surprise on the island. It's a pirate treasure chest spilling over with gold and jewels! If you were dissuaded by the restrictions earlier or disappointed by the fort that held so much promise, you would have missed it. But if you dared to continue to press on, you've been rewarded.

Again, we as followers of Christ have the same dilemma and the same solution. We live within the broader confines of "the island," in this case, the basics of the Christian faith: the death, burial and resurrection of Christ, loving one another, the service of all believers (according to our gifts that He has given us), and the ministry of reconciliation. You may add one or two items to that list or take one or two off, but I think for the most part we can agree on this list.

Within that space, though, there is a lot of freedom. You may have to get past the legalism you're surrounded by—the list of "do's and don'ts." You may have to get past, or through, the expectations others place on you. And you will certainly have to get through your own fear at times.

What lies on the other side of that boundary, though, is freedom like you've never imagined. It's a freedom to live a life of love and truth the way God designed you, and serving Him in the unique way He shaped you. It may not look like something anyone else is doing. It may be big, or it may be very small. It may take you someplace you never imagined or keep you right in your own backyard.

Whatever it looks like, it's what you do and how you live because of who God says you are and what He wants from you— for your good and for His glory (though not necessarily in that order). Your life is characterized this way:

I have been reminded of your sincere faith, which first lived in your grandmother Lois and in your mother Eunice and, I am persuaded, now lives in you also. For this reason I remind you to fan into flame the gift of God, which is in you through the laying on of my hands. For God did not give us a spirit of timidity, but a spirit of power, of love and of self-discipline.[179]

> **Kingdom Thinking:** Have you stepped past the fear and legalism, even briefly, and experienced this true freedom? What was it like?

Fantasmic!

The Power of Imagination

Fantasmic!, the spectacular nighttime show on the Rivers of America remains, after twenty-plus years, one of the most popular attractions at Disneyland. Special effects, water-screen projections, giant Animatronics, a fantastic soundtrack, and a pirate ship set the stage and aid in the telling of an exciting story.

The show takes us inside Mickey Mouse's imagination, and sure enough, it's full of beauty and wonder—and some strange things involving dancing elephants, Pinocchio, the aforementioned pirate ship, and more. But the Disney villains, especially the Wicked Queen from Snow White, can't let this spectacle stand.

The Magic Mirror tells her, "In Mickey's imagination, beauty and love will always survive." She challenges that notion, though, entering Mickey's imagination with Maleficent (human and dragon forms), Ursula, Chernabog, and others to try to show him that good will not always triumph over evil.

---

[179] 2 Timothy 1:5–7

All seems lost until Mickey remembers, "Wait a minute. This is *my* dream!" and he uses the power of his imagination to defeat the dragon and celebrate his "happily ever after."

Is it any wonder that the main stage for Fantasmic! is Tom Sawyer Island, a place that was built to celebrate and cultivate imagination? All of this is set up before the show officially begins, as the narrator tells us:

Nothing is more wonderful than the imagination, for in a moment, you can experience a beautiful fantasy or an exciting adventure. But beware, nothing is more powerful than the imagination, for it can also expand your greatest fears into an overwhelming nightmare.

As it turns out, Christians have a lot in common with Mickey Mouse. At its best, our imagination allows us to look beyond circumstances, beyond what we can see, to realize what is currently only possible. You can dream. You can discover. When combined with prayer, studying God's Word, and living in obedience, faith becomes a kind of imagination—rooted in something (or Someone) solid, and yet, "Faith is being sure of what we hope for and certain of what we do not see."[180]

That's the positive side, but just as it was with Mickey, our imagination can be powerful when we allow it to focus on our fears. I'm sure if I asked you to list your top fears (don't worry, I won't), most of us could list ten or twenty without trying. But how many of those things you fear have actually happened? And of the ones that have, how many of them were as bad as you had imagined?

Fear is normal, and in many cases, healthy. What is *unhealthy* is when our imagination gets involved and "expands your greatest fears into an overwhelming nightmare." Fear is the opposite of

---

[180] Hebrews 11:1

faith. Fear is focusing on what can go wrong and how bad it can be instead of on God and how good He is.

When fear preoccupies us, we call it worry. When worry fills our minds and hearts, we take our eyes off Jesus and fix them squarely on our circumstances. What if Mickey's imagination had been invaded by the Wicked Queen and he did nothing but pay attention to her? What if he had allowed the fear to consume him when the obstacles seemed insurmountable?

What happens when people do that?

The lesson of Fantasmic! (intended or not) is that fear can destroy us—from the inside—but we have a choice. We don't have to fixate on our fear. We can choose to use our imagination—or faith—to focus instead on the future God has for us, where "in all things God works for the good of those who love Him, who have been called according to His purpose."[181]

It's your choice: beauty and adventure or an overwhelming nightmare. Both can come from that place of imagination. Which will you experience today?

Kingdom Thinking: When have you had a Mickey Mouse, "Wait a minute. This is my dream!" moment, when you intentionally chose faith over fear and worry?

---

[181] Romans 8:28

Chapter 6: New Orleans Square

Lay of the Land

Be on Your Guard

*W*ith the possible exception of Main Street U.S.A., only New Orleans Square exhibits a unique feature: It has nothing clearly indicating its entrance. (If you call the arches you pass under to get into Main Street's Town Square a clear entry sign, then New Orleans Square definitely counts as the only one.)

Think about it. Off the Central Hub there are signs at the entrances of Frontierland, Adventureland, and Tomorrowland. Fantasyland has Sleeping Beauty Castle—a pretty clear entry. Mickey's Toontown has a large sign over its entrance. Even Critter Country has its own sign. Only New Orleans Square lacks a clear demarcation.

Why? As far as I know, there is no "official" reason (though if you know of one, please let me know![182]). However, when we think about what New Orleans Square represents, a reason and a lesson emerge.

The setting of New Orleans Square is Mardi Gras, Fat Tuesday—the day before Ash Wednesday. Subtle (and not-so-subtle) decorative and place-making clues set the stage for that particular day. In some religious traditions, Ash Wednesday begins the forty-day period of fasting known as Lent, leading up to Easter Sunday. In anticipation of this period of fasting, a "celebration" is held the day before. Basically it affords a chance to do all the stuff you want to do before you have to behave and deprive yourself for six weeks.

Mardi Gras is known for its festive atmosphere—and often for its rowdiness, excessive consumption of alcohol, and debauchery. The family-friendly version of this festival is what's intended to be captured in New Orleans Square.

As nice a face as Disney puts on it, and as much fun as this sanitized version is, what's celebrated in New Orleans Square is sin.

It's easy for us as humans—Christian or not—to wander into that same kind of spiritual territory unaware or unintentionally. That's not the biggest problem—the biggest problem is becoming aware of it and choosing to stay there—but if we stay out of it to begin with, we're that much better off. Of course, Satan would like nothing better than to lure us straight into a bad quarter.

Is there any wonder that there is no warning or announcement of entry into this land?

At times the church as a whole has been focused on sin, atonement, escaping hell, etc., even to the point of legalism. Now there is a strong push back in the direction of grace. That's a good thing.

---

[182] randy@faithandthemagickingdom.net

You are saved by grace. Nothing you do can make God love you more, or less. You can't earn His favor, and you don't have to. He came to us right where we are, as sinners, and saved us because of His love for us. That's the Good News.

However, some of that push toward grace has led people to forget a key truth. When we sin, we are forgiven, but that does not mean that we just go on as we are with no attempt to change. It does not mean that we don't try to avoid sin and resist temptation. Scripture exhorts us to be on guard:

Be on your guard; stand firm in the faith; be men of courage; be strong.[183]

Then He said to them, "Watch out! Be on your guard against all kinds of greed; a man's life does not consist in the abundance of his possessions."[184]

Therefore, dear friends, since you already know this, be on your guard so that you may not be carried away by the error of lawless men and fall from your secure position. But grow in the grace and knowledge of our Lord and Savior Jesus Christ. To Him be glory both now and forever! Amen.[185]

Believers are told very clearly to be on guard, to be watchful, to make an effort to avoid sin. Yes, we are free in Christ, but that liberty does not give Christians license to just go through life as we are, never seeking to grow or be perfected through Christ. And that growth doesn't just happen. It requires intentionality on our part. We do not just go on sinning, living our lives knowing that we're loved and forgiven, and leaving it at that.

---

[183] 1 Corinthians 16:13
[184] Luke 12:15
[185] 1 Peter 3:17–18

What shall we say, then? Shall we go on sinning so that grace may increase? By no means! We died to sin; how can we live in it any longer? Or don't you know that all of us who were baptized into Christ Jesus were baptized into His death? We were therefore buried with Him through baptism into death in order that, just as Christ was raised from the dead through the glory of the Father, we too may live a new life.[186]

One of the most destructive lies of the devil is "You'll never be good enough. God could never love you." Another one is, "You're fine just as you are. God already loves you, so just keep doing what you're doing and don't worry about it."

Part of being a Christian is growing in Christ, and that means sinning less. We'll never be perfect this side of heaven, but have you grown from where you were last year? When we do sin, we repent. That doesn't mean trying to not sin, it means agreeing with God that what we've done is sin and choosing to do something different (some people see repentance as only one part or the other, but it's both).

This response comes not from trying to earn favor, but out of gratitude and love. The motivation is grace. The opposite of grace isn't inaction, though; the opposite of grace is merit. Believers cannot earn grace, but that does not mean we do nothing to change and grow.

A swing of the pendulum all the way over to licentiousness and not being concerned about sin, not trying to become better than we have been—takes us straight into New Orleans Square. And with no sign announcing it, before we realize what's happened we've become ensnared.

For the grace of God has appeared that offers salvation to all people. It teaches us to say "No" to ungodliness and worldly

---

[186] Romans 6:1–4

passions, and to live self-controlled, upright and godly lives in this present age.[187]

Kingdom Thinking: Is it enough to just accept God's grace and live "free in Christ?" If so, what does that mean? Free to do what?

Just Over the Horizon

This time, we look not at an attraction or a land, but for a hidden detail. You could even call it a "hidden treasure."

When walking through New Orleans Square, have you ever noticed the masts of the ships in the harbor? No? That's OK, most people haven't. But if you're walking from Frontierland toward Pirates of the Caribbean, just after you pass the River Belle Terrace, start looking up behind the buildings. You'll see masts of ships back behind them. They seem so obvious…if you know where and when to look.

Why are they there? For story, of course. When you are in this area, think about your exact location. You're in "New Orleans," with the "Mississippi River" behind you. What would be on the other side of the city (simplifying the geography just a bit)? The Gulf of Mexico. Here you see ships docked in the city's port, ready to set sail into the Gulf of Mexico, and eventually the Atlantic Ocean.

Imagineers did not have to put these sails there. I've heard any number of utilitarian reasons for their presence—possibly hiding spotlights, or disguising rooftop air conditioning equipment, for example. Whatever the practical reasons may be (if any), even if

---

[187] Titus 2:11–12

most people never see them, they subliminally set the scene. They remind you of the bigger context for where you are so that it feels more realistic. And yet as the masts sit behind the buildings, just over the horizon (so to speak), they remain hidden from many, as do many of the special, intricate details.

Sometimes God's provision is the same way. He may start to answer our prayers long before we ever see the answer—maybe even before we ask. But we must continue to follow and obey until we're in the just-right place for Him to reveal an answer— and for us to receive it. Think about when God told Abraham to sacrifice his only son, Isaac.

Here is the main part of the story:

Then God said, "Take your son, your only son, Isaac, whom you love, and go to the region of Moriah. Sacrifice him there as a burnt offering on one of the mountains I will tell you about."

Early the next morning Abraham got up and saddled his donkey. He took with him two of his servants and his son Isaac. When he had cut enough wood for the burnt offering, he set out for the place God had told him about. On the third day Abraham looked up and saw the place in the distance. He said to his servants, "Stay here with the donkey while I and the boy go over there. We will worship and then we will come back to you."

Abraham took the wood for the burnt offering and placed it on his son Isaac, and he himself carried the fire and the knife. As the two of them went on together, Isaac spoke up and said to his father Abraham, "Father?"

"Yes, my son?" Abraham replied.

"The fire and wood are here," Isaac said, "but where is the lamb for the burnt offering?"

Abraham answered, "God Himself will provide the lamb for the burnt offering, my son." And the two of them went on together.

When they reached the place God had told him about, Abraham built an altar there and arranged the wood on it. He bound his son Isaac and laid him on the altar, on top of the wood. Then he reached out his hand and took the knife to slay his son. But the angel of the LORD called out to him from heaven, "Abraham! Abraham!"

"Here I am," he replied.

"Do not lay a hand on the boy," he said. "Do not do anything to him. Now I know that you fear God, because you have not withheld from me your son, your only son."

Abraham looked up and there in a thicket he saw a ram caught by its horns. He went over and took the ram and sacrificed it as a burnt offering instead of his son. So Abraham called that place The LORD Will Provide. And to this day it is said, "On the mountain of the LORD it will be provided."[188]

While Abraham was obeying God's command, God was providing the answer to his prayer that somehow he wouldn't lose his only son. But Abraham could not see the answer until the moment it was needed (which I'm sure was well past the time he would have liked to have seen it). God provided, but "over the horizon," in a way and a place that Abraham couldn't see. All he could do was trust God.

---

[188] Genesis 22:2–14

Abraham did not know what was going to happen, and what he was commanded to do seemed absurdly difficult. But he did it anyway, because he trusted that God could somehow keep His promise, despite all evidence to the contrary at that moment. As the writer of Hebrews says,

> By faith Abraham, when God tested him, offered Isaac as a sacrifice. He who had received the promises was about to sacrifice his one and only son, even though God had said to him, "It is through Isaac that your offspring will be reckoned." Abraham reasoned that God could raise the dead, and figuratively speaking, he did receive Isaac back from death.[189]

Sometimes God calls believers to step out in faith, not knowing how what we're doing makes any sense at all—or any difference. We may be uncomfortable, or even afraid. But God is faithful. Or we may be caught in the middle of circumstances we don't understand. They're painful and it seems hopeless to even wish for a way out. But God is faithful. He is preparing the answer to your prayer even as you pray it, but you will not see it unless you continue in faith and obedience. Only when He is ready will you look up and see the answer to your prayer, caught in the bushes or just over the horizon.

Kingdom Thinking: When have you seen God's provision appear (in your life or someone you know) from "just over the horizon" even though you couldn't see it before it came?

---

[189] Hebrews 11:17–19

Transitions Fountain: Altars and Reminders

Just outside the entrance to the Haunted Mansion in an area surrounded by benches and trees stands a fountain. I'm sure this area has an official name, but honestly I have no idea what it is (if you know, please tell me). Unofficially, it's called "Transitions Plaza," and the fountain is called "Transitions Fountain."

The reason for this somewhat unusual name is actually quite simple. As Disneyland existed at the time—and as it continued to be for several years—this area marked a significant transition. Everything on one side of this area (up to and including Pirates of the Caribbean) was completed or largely completed while Walt Disney was still alive. Everything on the other side—the Haunted Mansion and Bear Country/Critter Country—was completed or nearly completed after Walt Disney died.

This lovely but unassuming location stands as a silent reminder of the time of Disneyland's creator's passing. It symbolically marks the place where a significant event happened.

The nation of Israel also commemorated events. As we read through the Old Testament, especially the Torah (the first five books of the Old Testament), we see individuals or the nation as a whole stopping what they are doing to commemorate something significant God had done.

> The LORD appeared to Abram and said, "To your offspring I will give this land." So he built an altar there to the LORD, who had appeared to him.[190]

> There he built an altar, and he called the place El Bethel, because it was there that God revealed Himself to him when he was fleeing from his brother.[191]

---

[190] Genesis 12:7
[191] Genesis 35:7

Moses built an altar and called it The LORD is my Banner.[192]

So Gideon built an altar to the LORD there and called it The LORD is Peace. To this day it stands in Ophrah of the Abiezrites.[193]

David built an altar to the LORD there and sacrificed burnt offerings and fellowship offerings. He called on the LORD, and the LORD answered him with fire from heaven on the altar of burnt offering.[194]

Of course, Bible readers need to be careful. A thorough reading of the Old Testament reveals the nation of Israel building altars to idols at least as often as they built them to God. Still, those reminders were important. It's akin to buying souvenirs and taking pictures when we go on vacation. Those mementos help us remember, and they take us back to those moments we enjoyed or that were significant to us.

When in the middle of a trial, humans naturally tend to forget, especially when it comes to God's care and provision for us in the past. We focus on what seems true now and forget about how He's shown Himself on our behalf in the past—even the recent past. These altars stood as a reminder of what God had done for the Israelites.

In the New Testament, though we don't see the church building altars, we do have Jesus instituting what we call The Lord's Supper, The Eucharist, or Communion.

For I received from the Lord what I also passed on to you: The Lord Jesus, on the night He was betrayed, took bread, and when He had given thanks, He broke it and said, "This is My

---

[192] Exodus 17:15
[193] Judges 6:24
[194] 1 Chronicles 21:26

body, which is for you; do this in remembrance of Me." In the same way, after supper He took the cup, saying, "This cup is the new covenant in My blood; do this, whenever you drink it, in remembrance of Me." For whenever you eat this bread and drink this cup, you proclaim the Lord's death until He comes.[195]

Believers in Christ need special reminders of God's faithfulness. Communion serves as a critical one (and, in some traditions, as a means of grace).

But some people have other reminders, too. Perhaps some have a special place they go to. Or, maybe it's something they keep on their desk (a rock, a toy, a photo, etc.) to remind them of a significant event. Some have a song. Some plant a tree.

These items are not something we worship, as an idol would be, but rather they remind us of the One we worship and what He did in a specific time and place. Then, when we feel afraid, alone, abandoned, overwhelmed, hopeless, or helpless, we can look at this object, go to that place, hear this song and remember. And when you remember, you acknowledge that the One who cared for you *then* is "the same yesterday, today, and forever."[196] He protected or provided *then*—in His time and probably in a way you didn't expect—and He will do the same *now*.

Kingdom Thinking: What special possession or place stands as a reminder of God's work in your life?

---

[195] 1 Corinthians 11:23–26
[196] Hebrews 13:8

Pirates of the Caribbean

Dead Men (Used to) Tell Tales

On July 24, 1966, New Orleans Square became the first new "land" added to Disneyland since the park opening, though Imagineers had been working on concepts for it since 1957. The first attraction to open in the new land was Pirates of the Caribbean.

Pirates of the Caribbean opened on March 18, 1967, and was the most advanced, elaborately themed attraction that had ever been built. Over sixty Audio Animatronic human characters, around fifty Audio Animatronic animals, and rich details made this sixteen-minute attraction an instant and perpetual favorite.

It's also the last attraction that Walt Disney personally supervised. New Orleans Square opened about five months before he died, and Pirates opened about three months after. Major work was completed by the time he passed away on December 15, 1966, ten days after his sixty-fifth birthday.

Pirates of the Caribbean has undergone two major changes over the years. In 1997, the ride was closed for about two months for an update that included modifying a scene where pirates were chasing women so that they would be shown chasing food instead. The dialog of one of the only pirates who speaks in this scene (sometimes unofficially known as the "Pooped Pirate") was also changed to conform to the new scene. This update led to what show writer "X" Atencio referred to as "Boy Scouts of the Caribbean."

In 2006, Captain Jack Sparrow and others from the *Pirates of the Caribbean* films (which were inspired by the attraction) were added. The storyline was also changed significantly at that time, but it seems few are aware of the magnitude of the change. Originally the story portrayed random pirates looting and pillaging a town, but now the pirates were searching for Jack Sparrow. Most importantly (to me, anyway), the last scene was completely overhauled.

Let me back up for a moment.

As the ride begins, passengers are warned that "dead men tell no tales," and then we plunge down two waterfalls into a grotto that shows the skeletons of pirates—some mid-battle, one piloting a shipwreck, and a couple having a drink (or trying to—it's tough with no insides). We float through the Captain's Quarters, where we see the captain—as a skeleton—admiring the treasure piled up around him. We again hear a disembodied warning that "These be the last friendly words you'll hear. You may not survive to pass this way again."

And with that, we pass through fog and into a battle between the pirates and occupants of a fort. Suddenly everyone is alive and shooting, or drinking, or chasing, or burning, or whatever. After passing through all of the town scenes and a final shootout, we arrive at the hill that takes us back to the dock, and it is here that the most significant story change has occurred.

Originally, and up until the addition of the movie characters, the final scenes consisted of two pirates trying to drag a huge haul of treasure up the hill, escaping from the city with their riches. A short distance farther up the hill we would see the pirates, now as skeletons and with one attacking the other, but still clutching the treasure chest as the ghostly voice again echoes, "Dead men tell no tales."

Now, however, in that same space, Jack Sparrow lounges in a room full of treasure and gloats about his success.

Think about what the story *was*, because it is there that we find our lesson. We began the boat ride at the end of the story, with pirates as skeletons, not learning from the dangers of their ways: that their path would end in death. This theme lasts all the way up to the dark grotto after the Captain's Quarters, but when we pass through the fog we, in effect, step back in time to see the pirates as they were. We travel through and see them doing what they do, and it kind of looks like fun. They sure seem to be having a good time, anyway. But as we begin to climb the hill, we literally and figuratively head back to where we started, and we are reminded of the perils of being "rascals, scoundrels, and ne'er-do-well cads" (as the song says).

Dead men have, indeed, told tales. Is there a Christian parallel?

The apostle Paul reminds us in Romans 6:23: "For the wages of sin is death, but the gift of God is eternal life in Christ Jesus our Lord." The wages of sin here (at Pirates) were, indeed, death. We may think it's different for us, but while it may not be as obvious, the end result is still the same.

Do you see how dramatically the storyline has changed?

The lesson in the attraction has spelled itself out for us (though subtly enough that most people completely miss it). But did you know it goes even farther than that? You may have heard of the "Seven Deadly Sins." It is not a biblical concept, really (though Proverbs 6:16–19 serves as a basis for the idea), but it does have roots as far back as the mid-fourth century. All seven of these "deadly sins" were illustrated in the Pirates of the Caribbean attraction, and many still are. Take a look:

Pride: Most everything the pirates do is rooted in pride in one form or another. A couple of townspeople provide examples, too: "the redhead" (who looks pretty full of herself) and Carlos, who refuses to give up the location of the treasure, but seems to be defiant (at least in part) to impress his wife.

Envy: The pirates try to get the location of the treasure out of the mayor. They want what he has. (This can also fall under greed.)

Gluttony: The pirates chase the food. Before the attraction's overhaul, and even now, there are many scenes of pirates loaded up with food and/or alcohol.

Lust: The auction scene shows women being offered as brides for sale. Also, before food was added to a woman's hands, pirates were lustfully reaching for women. (The Pooped Pirate was lust at its most obvious.)

Anger/Rage: All of the fighting scenes demonstrate this sin, especially the battle between the ship and the fort.

Greed/Avarice: The Captain's Quarters and the two pirates stealing the chest at the end are probably the best examples of this vice.

Sloth: At least two pirates on the right side of the boat just lounge around (one with a couple of pigs interested in him, the other trying to entice a couple of cats).

You may have thought of other examples as you trekked through this sin-laden fictional place. With the addition of characters from the movies, some of these vices are no longer obvious, but without much trouble you can probably find new examples to replace the ones that have been removed.

While the attraction reflects more of a movie tie-in now, Pirates of the Caribbean used to have its own story. Many remnants of that story can still be seen today. It's a fun ride, but it's also a reminder. Our actions have consequences, and whether we want to admit it or not, sin, no matter how much fun it may seem at the time, does lead to death.

Kingdom Thinking: What "seemed like fun at the time" to you, but after spiritual reflection you've since realized was destructive in your life?

Haunted Mansion

Two Views of What Comes Next

Have you noticed something of a split personality in the Haunted Mansion? The first part is pretty eerie. A hanging man, a murderous bride, dead people trying to escape coffins. Even the dancers in the ballroom are waltzing to a fairly macabre-sounding song. But then we get to the graveyard and suddenly it's a party for the 999 happy haunts! The music is upbeat and fun (and catchy!), and dead people are enjoying picnics. Only the caretaker and his dog seem to be afraid. Why the difference, and why do we care?

Let's take those questions one at a time, and we'll let Doombuggies.com help us with the first one.

Walt Disney, always a definitive leader with a heady vision, passed away on December 15, 1966. This became a crucial matter to the design team working on the Haunted Mansion for many reasons. For one, many of them were intimately involved with Walt, and had a heavy emotional response to his passing. But a more direct threat to the project was that Walt had never made up his mind about the premise of the Haunted Mansion. He had given the WED [Imagineering] designers lots of room to follow their passions while creating ideas and concepts for the attraction, but wasn't with the team in the end to decide definitively in which direction to take the project.

From the beginning, Ken Anderson had been creating various eerie storylines while Yale Gracey and Rolly Crump worked on creating a feasible method of showing guests impossible visions. Claude Coates, an accomplished art director with WED, had been working on the Mansion project and felt that the attraction could be a powerful, haunting, effects-laden spectacle—although Marc Davis, one of Disney's famed "Nine Old Men," felt that the ride would better succeed as a character-driven, silly romp. In fact, the attraction as it exists today remains split into distinct sections: a mysterious introduction, an eerie ride with an ominous tone, and a conclusion with an overwhelming cacophony of gags and silly characters.[197]

---

[197] "History of the Haunted Mansion—Chapter Four: Walt Disney's Imagineers at Work," http://www.doombuggies.com/history4.php, accessed

Thus we have two very different takes on a "haunted mansion" that together make one unique and entertaining (and a little creepy) ride. And, riders will see two very different views of death and the afterlife.

Which do you hold? Do you fear death and what might come after? Or do you look forward to a celebration? There are several different ways people may look at the afterlife:

- A party in hell
- A party in heaven
- Eternal boredom in heaven
- Eternal torture in hell
- Nothing
- Do it all again (reincarnation)

What does the Bible say?

Just as man is destined to die once, and after that to face judgment, so Christ was sacrificed once to take away the sins of many people; and He will appear a second time, not to bear sin, but to bring salvation to those who are waiting for Him.[198] (That pretty clearly rules out reincarnation.)

The Bible talks frequently about heaven and hell, and to make them figurative destinies requires a lot of stretching and twisting of the Scriptures. There is *something*, rather than *nothing*, after death. But what?

Again, the Bible is clear about what heaven and hell are like. There will be no parties in hell. Jesus called it "an eternal fire"[199] and said those who end up there were "thrown outside, into the

---

August 4, 2013.
[198] Hebrews 9:27–28
[199] Matthew 25:41

darkness, where there will be weeping and gnashing of teeth."[200] Jude 13 says hell will be "the blackest darkness forever." Paul told the Thessalonians people will be "punished with everlasting destruction and shut out from the presence of the Lord."[201]

Is some of this wording figurative language? Sure. Jesus (and the Apostles) knew that some things are just beyond human comprehension. "I have spoken to you of earthly things and you do not believe; how then will you believe if I speak of heavenly things?"[202] Jesus asked. Yet the truth of the horror of hell is still valid.

These verses do not mean God will vindictively send people to hell, or that He wants them to go there. Remember, "The Lord is not slow in keeping his promise, as some understand slowness. He is patient with you, not wanting anyone to perish, but everyone to come to repentance."[203] But He will not force heaven on anyone. If you choose to live without Him for the seventy, eighty, or however many years you have on this earth, He will not force you to live with Him for eternity. So your choice in this life will be honored in the next one. But please understand what this means.

God is the giver of all good gifts. He is love. He is light. In Him are joy, goodness, and peace. To choose to live without Him means you will live in eternity without all of these things. Such people will experience a complete absence of love of any kind; a complete absence of light (in any and all senses); a complete lack of anything that is good. This will not be a party. But it is a choice.

What about heaven? All clouds and harps, right? Wrong. So what is the reality of heaven?

Most fundamentally, the central reality of heaven is the presence of God. I read a blog article by Travis Agnew that I think describes it extremely well. He said:

---

[200] Matthew 8:12
[201] 2 Thessalonians 1:7–9
[202] John 3:12
[203] 2 Peter 3:9

If that isn't enough for you, then you really don't grasp what this means. It's the return to Eden. It's the way things were meant to be before mankind sinned and messed up everything good God created. In the Garden of Eden, God walked side by side with Adam and Eve in perfect harmony. God dwelled with His people face to face. They could hear the sounds of His footsteps as majesty approached (Gen. 3:8). When sin entered, God banished them from the garden, and ever since, humanity has only experienced a fraction of the life that God offered us.

Heaven is Eden's return. It is a chance to live in a place with no more hurt or suffering. You not only hear the sound of God walking towards you, but you are able to dwell with Him. No sin can separate you any longer.[204]

There will be no more suffering or pain. No more evil. And believers won't just be sitting around. We will worship and serve fully and completely. We will rest, not idly, but truly experiencing all that has been accomplished. It won't be laziness, nor will it be working to get by and struggling. It will be perfect work and perfect rest in perfect balance.

What else, you may ask, awaits God's children (as if all this isn't enough)? Again from Travis Agnew:

We will obtain heavenly knowledge. All the questions and misunderstandings about God and His work will be clarified when we encounter God Himself (1 Cor. 13:9-12; 1 John 3:2)....Heaven will be filled with unspeakable glory. As Millard J. Erikson writes, "It is likely that while John's vision employs as metaphors those items which we think of as being most valuable and beautiful, the actual splendor of heaven far

---

[204] Travis Agnew, "Heaven: More Than Clouds, Harps, and St. Peter at the Gate," http://www.travisagnew.org/?p=3338, accessed August 4, 2013.

exceeds anything that we have yet experienced. There will be no need of sun or moon to illumine the new Jerusalem, for 'The city does not need the sun or the moon to shine on it, for the glory of God gives it light, and the Lamb is its lamp' (Rev. 21:23; 22:5)" [Taken from *Christian Theology*, p. 1236].[205]

Heaven is filled with God's presence, His love, and His peace forever. Hell is the complete absence of those features. Which do you think the early part of the Haunted Mansion resembles? Does "Get me out of here!" ring any bells?

Heaven is the *real* party (though not in a graveyard)—far beyond anything we can imagine.

Kingdom Thinking: When you think of heaven, what do you picture? Do you know without a doubt that you will be there?

Coming Out of the Shadows

Before boarding your "Doom Buggy," Imagineers have done a great job in setting the scene at the Haunted Mansion. The frightful attraction starts from the creepy (but well-maintained) exterior, proceeds through the pet cemetery, and then the hillside headstones and crypt in what the Imagineers call "Act I" of the show, then into the stretching room, and past "revealing" paintings in the hallway.

It's here, at these portraits, that I'd like to stop for now. Most guests walk right by them to get on the ride, and only when the line backs up do they glance at the paintings. As lightning flashes

---

[205] ibid.

outside, these seemingly lovely portraits are illuminated by brief flashes.

As long as they are viewed only in the dim light of the corridor, the images in these paintings appear to be elegant, graceful, and beautiful. When the lightning flashes, though, the true images are revealed: ugly, decrepit, and decaying. When the lightning vanishes, the portraits return to the shadows—and their illusion of beauty. But we have seen the truth.

> This is the verdict: Light has come into the world, but men loved darkness instead of light because their deeds were evil. Everyone who does evil hates the light, and will not come into the light for fear that his deeds will be exposed. But whoever lives by the truth comes into the light, so that it may be seen plainly that what he has done has been done through God.[206]

From a distance and in the shadows we can fool ourselves into thinking we "look" good. But in the light of Christ we are revealed for what we truly are: ugly sinners. Our deeds are exposed. Our motives are exposed. Our hearts are exposed—perhaps to the world, perhaps just to God and ourselves. The audience doesn't matter. The fact is, we are laid bare. The light of Truth and Love shines in your life and you see yourself for who you really are. It can be haunting.

Then you have a choice: stay in the light and be made clean or return to the shadows. It's easier to return to the shadows and pretend that what you saw was just an illusion. It was just you at your worst moments with all kinds of reasons why it's not who you really are. You're better than that. And you tell yourself the same thing the next time it happens, and the next, and the next.

There's nothing required to stay in darkness. But no real positive change is possible in darkness, either. Especially if you would name yourself a follower of Christ, you must not remain in

---

[206] John 3:19–21

the shadows. As painful, or frightening, or difficult as it may be at times, you must come into the light of Christ's love, forgiveness, and healing. Do not be afraid.

> This is the message we have heard from Him and declare to you: God is light; in Him there is no darkness at all. If we claim to have fellowship with Him yet walk in the darkness, we lie and do not live by the truth. But if we walk in the light, as He is in the light, we have fellowship with one another, and the blood of Jesus, His Son, purifies us from all sin.[207]

Kingdom Thinking: That's His promise to you. Now, are you willing to step into the light, or will you go back to the shadows?

---

[207] 1 John 1:5–7

Chapter 7: Critter Country

Davy Crockett's Explorer Canoes

Making an Effort

*D*avy Crockett's Explorer Canoes opened as the Indian War Canoes on July 4, 1956 (I'm sure there's some irony in that date—probably unintentional) as part of the Indian Village Expansion.

This attraction has the fun distinction of being the only "guest-powered" attraction in the park. (Though, with the Cars Land expansion over at Disney California Adventure, that park has its own guest-powered attraction—Luigi's Flying Tires.) If all the guests in a canoe decide not to paddle, they're not going anywhere.

I've actually heard complaints from people who have said that they want to go to Disneyland just to enjoy the attractions passively and *not* exert any effort. They didn't use those exact words, but that was the message.

That's fine. If you want to make that your park experience, enjoy it that way. But you're missing out on some fun and unique attractions if you do.

Some people think the Christian life should be lived the same way. God accepts us as we are, and that's good enough. Grace means we don't have to try to improve. In fact, we can't improve. So we should just be how we are and if other people don't like it, that's their problem.

Doesn't that sound nice? It takes all the pressure off and we can avoid the lure of legalism. God does all the work, and we just sit back and bask in it, living a life free of rules and obligations. People who believe life coaching has no role in Christianity generally take this view. They assert that learning about who God made us to be, how we are uniquely shaped, and how to live and serve in a way that brings glory to Him by being true to how He made us, is opposed to how God says we should be.

That view is problematic. Yes, we are saved by grace. True, we don't have to—and we can't—earn God's love and favor. But that does not absolve us from trying to improve and grow.

The Christian life requires effort. God expects us to grow, and to put in the time and discipline to bring about maturity. We do it through the strength and power God has given us, but we do play a role. Scripture makes it clear.

Let us therefore make every effort to do what leads to peace and to mutual edification.[208]

Let us, therefore, make every effort to enter that rest, so that no one will fall by following their example of disobedience.[209]

For this very reason, make every effort to add to your faith goodness; and to goodness, knowledge; and to knowledge,

---

[208] Romans 14:19
[209] Hebrews 4:11

self-control; and to self-control, perseverance; and to perseverance, godliness; and to godliness, brotherly kindness; and to brotherly kindness, love.[210]

So then, dear friends, since you are looking forward to this, make every effort to be found spotless, blameless and at peace with Him.[211]

The funny thing about all these places in Scripture where we're told to "make every effort to" do something, is that the word translated "make every effort" means exactly that. Believers are to diligently and persistently apply our efforts to accomplishing this task at hand. There is no room for spiritual laziness or for trying to live "by grace" that we forget we have an obligation to the God who saved us.

Can you be a guest at Disneyland and not experience Davy Crockett's Explorer Canoes? Sure. Are you missing out on something that would give you the full experience? Absolutely.

Can you be a Christian and never change, never put in the intentional effort required to grow and become more like Christ? Probably, but why would you want to? His grace is enough to redeem you, but His grace is not all He gave you. You also have His power at work within you to enable you to grow and change and make every effort to accomplish certain goals He has given you. What are you doing with that power?

Kingdom Thinking: Do you "make every effort" to grow in Christ, or do you believe that being expected to do that is just legalism and "religion"?

---

[210] 2 Peter 1:5–7
[211] 2 Peter 3:14

All in the Same Boat

I consider Davy Crockett's Explorer Canoes one of the most overlooked attractions at Disneyland. Given their low capacity, that's probably a good thing (shorter lines), but I still think people tend to forget what makes the time worthwhile.

It's a fun, unique attraction because it is—as mentioned previously—the only guest-powered attraction in the park. In theory, if the guests did nothing and the Cast Members in the canoe did not have to keep things going, everyone would just sit there. Also, the canoes are not on a track, so within the limits of what the Cast Members allow (for safety reasons, generally) the canoe can go anywhere on the Rivers of America.

Several guests in each canoe is a good thing because one of the unique features of this kind of watercraft is the type of paddle it uses. Paddles are short, with a blade (the wide part) on only one end, and you only get one. That means if you want to go in a straight line you have two choices: half the people in the canoe place their paddles on one side and half on the other, or constantly switch sides—first paddle on the left, then lift it across and paddle on the right, then switch back and continue. If you are by yourself, that's your only choice.

Is it possible to maneuver a canoe that way? Sure. But it's exhausting, and you're guaranteed to get very wet while you do it. That's part of the value of having multiple people in the canoe. By sharing the work and each person having his own task (while "all in the same boat"), it is much easier, more efficient, and drier.

I have written elsewhere about how important it is to have other people with you in your Christian walk. This attraction provides another example of that very truth. You may be able to paddle alone, but it's hard—certainly harder than it needs to be. You need others to serve with you and to help you up when you fall. You need others so *you* can be there when *they* fall. And you need others to teach you grace and truth through community with imperfect people—including you.

> Two are better than one,
> because they have a good return for their work:
> If one falls down,
> his friend can help him up.
> But pity the man who falls
> and has no one to help him up!
> Also, if two lie down together, they will keep warm.
> But how can one keep warm alone?
> Though one may be overpowered,
> two can defend themselves.
> A cord of three strands is not quickly broken.[212]

Kingdom Thinking: What is one lesson that being in community with others has taught you, or one way that it has helped you?

Splash Mountain

Where is Your Laughing Place?

Splash Mountain occupies a particularly special place in my heart. I remember going to Disneyland with my junior high band, and we were backstage for part of that time. I don't remember a lot of the details, but I do remember being back stage and being told that Splash Mountain would be opening soon. I could hardly wait. It's

---

[212] Ecclesiastes 4:9–12

the first time I can remember feeling that way about something at Disneyland.

On July 17, 1989, this attraction officially opened to the public. With it came the transition from Bear Country to Critter Country, as the bruins in the Country Bear Jamboree across the way were no longer the only inhabitants of this area of the park. (In truth, bears had never been the only residents of Bear Country—just ask Max, Buff, and Melvin, the talking trophy heads mounted on the wall of the Playhouse (and now neatly hidden in The Many Adventures of Winnie the Pooh).

The last of the four mountains in Disneyland's "Mountain Range" (which also includes the Matterhorn, Big Thunder Mountain Railroad, and Space Mountain), it finally brought the log flume ride to the park. Along with it came fun music, entertaining Audio Animatronics (many of them from the recently defunct America Sings), and ten-plus minutes of references to a movie that now hasn't been seen for a couple of decades or more—not legally, anyway—*Song of the South*.

There is some great music in this ride, and for most of it you get to float along—with a few small drops, but nothing significant—and watch these fun characters while listening to lively songs such as *How Do You Do* and *Zip-a-Dee-Do-Dah*.

But then the ride turns darker and takes on a more ominous tone. There are hints of fear in the characters, and right before climbing a large and rather intimidating-looking hill, two buzzards sit above you, taunting. "So, you're looking for a laughing place. We've got your laughing place right here."

Halfway up the hill is a shadow of Br'er Fox lurking over Br'er Rabbit, who is tied up and blubbering: "P-p-p-p-p-please don't throw me in that there briar patch!" We crest the hill and what do we see? That very briar patch, which we get dropped into (and under)!

As it turns out, the briar patch is Br'er Rabbit's laughing place! Br'er Rabbit's "laughing place" was the place he knew best, where he was most familiar and felt the safest.

Where is your laughing place? Not the place where you *feel* the happiest, because happiness is temporary and based on circumstances. No, we're looking beyond that. As Christians, where is your "joyful place"? I propose that it can be found in only one place: the presence of God Himself.

> You have made known to me the path of life;
> You will fill me with joy in Your presence,
> with eternal pleasures at Your right hand.[213]

> How great is Your goodness,
> which You have stored up for those who fear You,
> which You bestow in the sight of men
> on those who take refuge in You.
> In the shelter of Your presence You hide them
> from the intrigues of men;
> in Your dwelling You keep them safe
> from accusing tongues.[214]

In good times and in bad, the presence of the Lord is where we find joy.

How do we spend time in His presence? There are at least two ways: reflective Bible reading and prayer. Through these disciplines we listen to what He has to say to us—sometimes about our current circumstances, or sometimes an encouragement or a reminder from the past. We talk to Him about what's going well (thankfulness) and what's going badly (confession of sin). We ask for His perspective, His wisdom, His grace, and His love. We

---

[213] Psalm 16:11
[214] Psalm 31:19–20

remember what He has done. And we remember that He has given us His Holy Spirit to dwell in us.

The reality is, we can be in His presence all the time. If His Spirit lives in us (and He does), then He is *always* with us, and we can always be in His presence. It takes intentional attention. It takes practice. It takes discipline. Some have called it "practicing the presence of God."

But isn't all that effort worth it for a more constant awareness of "the joy of the Lord," our strength, our hope, and our peace?

> **Kingdom Thinking:** Do you find it easy or difficult to be "in God's presence"? Can you think of others ways to do it?

Wickedness is a Snare

If you have ever seen *Song of the South* (and if you haven't, good luck!) or ridden Splash Mountain, you know how successful Br'er Fox and Br'er Bear are at capturing or killing Br'er Rabbit (or whatever it was they were trying to do). If you haven't, the short version is: not at all.

Every trap they set traps them instead. Every time they try to lure Br'er Rabbit or tempt him, he gets the best of them. Even when they think they finally have him, he tricks them into throwing him into the briar patch, not realizing that he's perfectly at home there.

Br'er Rabbit is confident and secure. Br'er Fox and Br'er Bear stumble at every turn.

Scripture speaks of the believer's safety when he seems surrounded by enemies:

The Lord is my light and my salvation—
whom shall I fear?
The Lord is the stronghold of my life—
of whom shall I be afraid?
When evil men advance against me
to devour my flesh,
when my enemies and my foes attack me,
they will stumble and fall.
Though an army besiege me,
my heart will not fear;
though war break out against me,
even then will I be confident.[215]

Like Br'er Rabbit, we too can be confident, only we have a much better reason for assurance than our own cleverness. The Lord is your light, your salvation, and your stronghold. When you face challenges and enemies, what more could you ask for?

At times our enemies seem to prosper and their attacks seem to succeed, but in time they will stumble and fall. No matter what comes against you, as long as you stand firm in God, you have no need to fear. "In the paths of the wicked lie thorns and snares, but he who guards his soul stays far from them."[216]

Kingdom Thinking: Have you faced an enemy (physical, emotional, or spiritual) only to see it stumble and fall?

---

[215] Psalm 27:1–3
[216] Proverbs 22:5

The Many Adventures of Winnie the Pooh

Stormy Nights

Originally a Walt Disney World attraction (it had opened in Florida in 1999), the Disneyland version of The Many Adventures of Winnie the Pooh opened in April of 2003. It replaced the much-loved but sparsely visited attraction, Country Bear Jamboree. (As a side note, I was there the last night Country Bear Jamboree was open, and was in the penultimate show. It would have been the last one, but they added one more show and I had to get up early to preach at church the next morning, so I couldn't push it much past midnight.)

The attraction was based on the 1977 animated film of the same name, which was really made up of three earlier-released shorter featurettes: *Winnie the Pooh and the Honey Tree*, *Winnie the Pooh and the Blustery Day*, and *Winnie the Pooh and Tigger Too!* The ride takes the scenes out of order—and they're different between Disneyland and Walt Disney World—but the gist of each one is clear.

One of my favorite segments of both the movie and the ride is the rain scene. In case you have not seen it or it's been a long time, this segment is part of *Winnie the Pooh and the Blustery Day*. "Happy Winds-day!" Pooh wishes everyone he meets on this blustery day. As the story progresses, Pooh meets Tigger for the first time and has his nightmare about Heffalumps and Woozles stealing his honey.

As Piglet gets caught up in the storm, he writes a note for help ("Help! P-P-P-Piglet [Me]!"), as he and Pooh float out from rising water and get caught in the middle of a severe downpour. When Owl comes to tell Piglet a rescue is coming and to be brave, Piglet replies, "It's awfully hard to be brave when you're such a small animal." After a bit more peril, Pooh and Piglet arrive safely at Christopher Robin's house. (It sounds anticlimactic, but it's really not.)

The lyrics from *The Rain Rain Rain Came Down Down Down* about Piglet's predicament really struck me.

> The rain rain rain came down down down
> In rushing, rising riv'lets,
> 'Til the river crept out of its bed
> And crept right into Piglet's!
> Poor Piglet, he was frightened,
> With quite a rightful fright.
> And so, in desperation
> A message he did write.
> He placed it in a bottle
> And it floated out of sight.
> And the rain rain rain came down down down
> So Piglet started bailing.
> He was unaware, atop his chair,
> While bailing he was sailing!

Piglet was tiny and scared (especially when he approached the waterfall!), and he was pretty helpless in the midst of the storm.

Sometimes Christians are the same way. Circumstances turn dark, storm clouds roll in, water rises and rushes, and we fear. And we have good reason to be afraid. It's hard to see anything beyond the rain.

Then we try to bail ourselves out and usually end up in worse shape than when we started. Just like Piglet, we focus on trying to fix an insurmountable problem and don't even notice it going from bad to worse—until it becomes catastrophic!

Luke 8:22–25 tells a story that may be familiar to you.

> One day Jesus said to His disciples, "Let's go over to the other side of the lake." So they got into a boat and set out. As they sailed, He fell asleep. A squall came down on the lake, so that the boat was being swamped, and they were in great danger.

The disciples went and woke him, saying, "Master, Master, we're going to drown!"

He got up and rebuked the wind and the raging waters; the storm subsided, and all was calm. "Where is your faith?" He asked His disciples.

In fear and amazement they asked one another, "Who is this? He commands even the winds and the water, and they obey Him."

In the midst of the storm Jesus was not afraid nor was He helpless. When His disciples called on Him for help, He got up and calmed the storm. But notice that He didn't stop there. He asked them a question that we don't want to hear: "Where is your faith?"

Jesus could calm the storm, and He did. But then He asks them why they needed Him to do so. Wasn't His presence enough? Didn't they trust that they would be safe, even in the midst of the storm?

God does not always calm the storm. Sometimes the rain rain rain comes down down down, and it just keeps coming. And yet He remains with us through all of it and reminds us that we can trust Him.

Thus, when the storm clouds gather and rain pours, He is especially with us in these times. Circumstances may not change. Prayers may not be answered right away the way we want them to be.

It is hard to trust in the midst of chaos, but that's exactly where we learn to do it. We rely on Him. Without dark times, we don't truly understand what it means that He is our shelter from the storm.

Christ may not calm your storm…He may want to calm *you*.

> **Kingdom Thinking:** Have you ever had a time you wanted God to calm the storm, but instead He calmed you?

Eeyore's House: Melancholy or Mindful?

Of all the Winnie the Pooh characters, Eeyore is my favorite. I never related to the others very well, though at times I may have wanted to be more like Tigger and his "bouncy" and energetic personality, or Pooh and his humility and gentleness, or Rabbit and his fastidiousness (OK, I have some of that in me, too), or Owl and his patient wisdom.

But I was drawn to Eeyore. At various times it was because I related to his apparently morose outlook on life. At other times I felt unnoticed and unappreciated, or I wanted to be known for my unselfish dedication to my friends and my deep thinking. I still fall into these three categories at various times, but I try to be in that last one more and more.

In one way, it's easy to be Eeyore—the negative one. We say things like,

"There's no point in looking for a job I love. With so many people out of work, I'll be lucky to find one that pays the bills."

"The world has never been in worse shape, and it's still getting worse by the day."

"Why should anybody love me? I have nothing of value to bring to the world."

"My family relationships will never be able to move beyond where they are now. I'm stuck, and I'd better just learn to live with it."

Have you heard statements like that? Have you made such statements?

The Bible tells us that this mindset is not only counterproductive, but also it is exactly the opposite of what God wants for you. In Philippians 4, Paul says,

> Rejoice in the Lord always. I will say it again: Rejoice! Let your gentleness be evident to all. The Lord is near. Do not be anxious about anything, but in everything, by prayer and petition, with thanksgiving, present your requests to God. And the peace of God, which transcends all understanding, will guard your hearts and your minds in Christ Jesus.[217]

"Sure, that's easy for you to say," you might respond. "You probably don't have any big problems in your life right now, maybe you never have. I'd trade problems with you in a heartbeat. What do you know?"

Well, I know that I have my own share of problems and struggles. In fact, you might be surprised and less inclined to trade if you really knew what I've faced, and what I am facing even as I write.

More to the point, I know what Paul said, and I know he said it while he was in prison. That may sound bad enough, but you need to understand that in his time, people didn't just "go to prison" for a while and then get released. Prison was where you went while you were awaiting trial. Then, if you were convicted, which you probably would be, you would be put to death. Prison was not just a bad place; it was the first step in a death sentence. That is what Paul was enduring when he wrote those words. How does your situation compare?

A reality of being human is that even when we choose to rejoice and be thankful, we are not shielded from the negative things in life. As Debra Fileta says, "But our response and perspective about those things is what leads us to the ending. God knows this to be true, and He challenges us to be thankful at all

---

[217] Philippians 4:4–7

times. He knows the influence that this kind of attitude can have in our lives."[218]

I know it's not easy, and you may not even want to hear these words, but I am not here just to commiserate with you and leave you stuck where you are. I'm here to sympathize with you, but also to encourage and challenge you to look beyond your circumstances. Look beyond what's natural to think and feel, and move forward in a healthy, productive, godly way.

This command of God (rejoicing) is not dependent on circumstances. It has nothing to do with how you feel, how things look, or what the people around you are saying or doing. It comes strictly from God and our relationship with Him. The closer we are to Him, the more His peace and joy flow into us and through us.

When we enjoy that kind of relationship with God—spending time with Him, talking to Him, and choosing to view things from His perspective—then more of the "positive Eeyore" comes through.

This is the Eeyore that I want to be like. He thinks and considers. He plans his actions and is deliberate. He's committed to his friends. He's a profound observer. He is methodical and persistent. Now, not all of these descriptions may fit exactly the kind of person you want to be (and if you're not sure exactly who you are or what kind of person you want to be, I have tools available on my website to help you[219]), but most would agree that they are admirable qualities.

So, which Eeyore are you? The fearful, gloomy, defeated one or the helpful, thoughtful, positive one? Believe it or not, it really is your choice.

---

[218] Debra Fileta, "An Eeyore Day," http://debslessonslearned.blogspot.com/2011/11/eeyore-day.html, accessed August 17, 2013.
[219] http://www.leavingconformitycoaching.com/worksheets/

Kingdom Thinking: Which Eeyore are you right now? If you're "gloomy Eeyore" what is one step you can take to begin to change your outlook?

Chapter 8: Fantasyland

Lay of the Land

The Golden Spike: Confusing the Center

One of the most common Disneyland urban legends is that of the "golden spike." Located just inside the Sleeping Beauty Castle courtyard (the other side of the castle from the drawbridge), the legend says that this spike marked the exact geographic center of Disneyland on Opening Day. Interesting, right? Makes you want to go there.

Unfortunately, it's not true. This spot was never the center of Disneyland—though since the opening of Mickey's Toontown it may be somewhat closer now than it used to be. In fact, the center of Disneyland was the Central Hub, very close to where the Partners Statue stands today. I've measured this myself using maps and photos from 1955, so I know it's accurate.

So what is this spike? What is its purpose? Simple. It's a survey marker. This marker was placed by the surveyors during construction to make sure the train station, the castle drawbridge, and the centerline of Main Street U.S.A. all lined up properly with each other. This humble tool's purpose and value have been blown out of proportion and made the center of something it was meant to be in service to, never at the heart of.

The church at Corinth made a similar error with spiritual gifts, particularly the gift of tongues. In 1 Corinthians 12–14, Paul had to remind this church that every part of the body of Christ, the church, is valuable, and each plays a role. Serving each other through whatever gifts they had been given should have been the focus and purpose, but the Corinthians placed something (gift of tongues) that was simply a tool into the center of church life.

Christians today tend to do it as well. Spiritual disciplines like prayer, Bible reading, meditation, fasting, service, etc. are all "tools." They are all incredibly valuable—imagine what Disneyland might have looked like without that spike as a reference point!—but their roles are secondary. They are not the focus and purpose. God is. And our relationship with Him, and how it expresses itself in our words, actions, and identity demonstrates that centrality. The tools have their purpose, but be sure not to confuse any one of them for the golden spike of God Himself.

Kingdom Thinking: What tool do you see most often placed in the center (often unintentionally), displacing Jesus?

Going Around in Circles

There are more rides in Fantasyland that share a specific trait in common than in any other land at Disneyland.

- The Mad Tea Party (Tea Cups)
- King Arthur Carrousel
- Dumbo
- The old Motor Boat Cruise
- Even the very briefly lived Canal Boats of the World (which became Storybook Land Canal Boats in 1956).

All have one purpose: to go in circles. There is no destination but the journey itself. There is no story, no progress, nowhere to go but the same place they started. (In an ironic twist, the Fantasyland attraction that features the song, "We're merrily on our way to nowhere in particular" actually does have a story.)

That's what happens in a life grounded in fantasy rather than the reality of faith. Vicious circles. Futile effort. The giant hamster wheel of life. Call it what you will. The truth is that a life of fantasy ultimately does not get you anywhere.

Adding a biblical component to reality makes all the difference:

Then you will know the truth, and the truth will set you free.[220]

Living in Fantasyland, not accepting and dealing with the realities of life—both good and bad, both seen and unseen—will get you nowhere. Making progress, seeing results, being successful, even being obedient to Christ, requires accepting and living with these realities.

Vice Admiral James Stockdale was one of the most highly decorated officers in the history of the United States Navy and the

---

[220] John 8:32

highest-ranking naval officer held as a prisoner of war (POW) in Vietnam. He was confined in the "Hanoi Hilton" and repeatedly tortured over eight years. In his book *Good to Great*, Jim Collins recounts going to lunch with Adm. Stockdale and trying to understand how he survived eight years as a POW while many people died after just months in captivity.[221]

Here's how Stockdale put it.

I never lost faith in the end of the story, I never doubted not only that I would get out, but also that I would prevail in the end and turn the experience into the defining event of my life, which, in retrospect, I would not trade.

When Collins asked who did not make it out, Stockdale answered:

Oh, that's easy, the optimists. Oh, they were the ones who said, "We're going to be out by Christmas." And Christmas would come, and Christmas would go. Then they'd say, "We're going to be out by Easter." And Easter would come, and Easter would go. And then Thanksgiving, and then it would be Christmas again. And they died of a broken heart.

Stockdale added:

This is a very important lesson. You must never confuse faith that you will prevail in the end—which you can never afford to lose—with the discipline to confront the most brutal facts of your current reality, whatever they might be.

---

[221] Jim Collins, "The Stockdale Paradox," http://www.jimcollins.com/media_topics/brutal-facts.html#audio=59, accessed August 5, 2013.

This is what Collins calls "The Stockdale Paradox." Accept the brutal facts, while maintaining faith that you will prevail. Doing only the former leads to despair and depression. Doing only the latter can lead to the same, for very different reasons.

A life of faith firmly grounded in truth *and* reality—including the reality of faith—will not only allow you to progress but also it will take you places you never imagined, beyond your greatest fantasy.

Kingdom Thinking: Which is harder for you: To confront the brutal facts of your current reality or to not lose faith that you will prevail in the end?

The Parable of the Wedding Banquet

When my wife and I took my parents to Disneyland for their fortieth anniversary, we had the pleasure of getting a series of Magical Moments (experiences that Cast Members create for guests). Those included riding in the front cab of the Monorail, a private ride in the Lilly Belle, parlor car of the Disneyland Railroad, and a private ride (including being taken to the front of the line) on Storybook Land Canal Boats. Of course, no Disneyland Magical Moment is complete without meeting "The Big Cheese" himself, Mickey Mouse.

Being taken to meet Mickey was a very interesting experience. We had been in Tomorrowland with Neil, the Cast Member in charge of taking care of us. But when we were to go meet Mickey, he called Mike over to take care of the rest of the time for us that day. His reasoning? "I'm not dressed properly to meet the Boss." Neil was wearing a costume from Tomorrowland, and Mickey is in

Toontown. We needed someone in a Fantasyland costume, which was acceptable attire for going in to meet Mickey Mouse.

Even at that moment the importance of this custom struck me. Would we have thought anything about it if Neil stayed with us and took us to Mickey's house? No. But Neil knew better. Proper attire is required. That's not true for guests—who are told to come as they are—but for those who are part of the Magic Kingdom, proper dress is necessary. Of course, they aren't expected to provide this outfit on their own; that is the Costuming department's territory.

In Matthew 22, Jesus tells a parable about a wedding banquet. In verses 1–14 He says:

> The kingdom of heaven is like a king who prepared a wedding banquet for his son. He sent his servants to those who had been invited to the banquet to tell them to come, but they refused to come.
>
> Then he sent some more servants and said, "Tell those who have been invited that I have prepared my dinner: My oxen and fattened cattle have been butchered, and everything is ready. Come to the wedding banquet."
>
> But they paid no attention and went off—one to his field, another to his business. The rest seized his servants, mistreated them and killed them. The king was enraged. He sent his army and destroyed those murderers and burned their city.
>
> Then he said to his servants, "The wedding banquet is ready, but those I invited did not deserve to come. Go to the street corners and invite to the banquet anyone you find." So the servants went out into the streets and gathered all the people they could find, both good and bad, and the wedding hall was filled with guests.

But when the king came in to see the guests, he noticed a man there who was not wearing wedding clothes. "Friend," he asked, "how did you get in here without wedding clothes?" The man was speechless.

Then the king told the attendants, "Tie him hand and foot, and throw him outside, into the darkness, where there will be weeping and gnashing of teeth."

For many are invited, but few are chosen.

First-century Jewish wedding customs held that the father of the groom was in charge of the event and bore all expenses associated with the wedding and reception. In the case of royalty or the very wealthy this responsibility often included providing a specially made garment to be worn over a guest's regular clothing. This wedding garment was presented to the guest upon arrival and donned immediately. Wearing it was not mandatory, but refusal was considered a great insult to the father of the groom and could get a guest ejected from the festivities. In large gatherings it also served as identification to discourage uninvited guests from crashing the party.[222]

Even without that context we can reasonably assume that—considering the fact that no one invited from the street corners would have been expected to have had a wedding garment with them—the king himself provided the garments for the guests.

There was a "dress code" for the wedding banquet, just as proper attire was expected of the escort to meet Mickey. And in both cases, the proper outfit was provided by the host. Just as Jesus was illustrating in the parable, we have "proper attire" expected of

---

[222] Jack Kelley, "The Parable of the Wedding Banquet" http://www.GraceThruFaith.com/selah/parables/the-parable-of-the-wedding-banquet/, accessed August 5, 2013.

us as part of God's Kingdom, and it is not something we provide for ourselves—it is given to us.

Isaiah 61:10 says, "I delight greatly in the LORD; my soul rejoices in my God. For He has clothed me with garments of salvation and arrayed me in a robe of righteousness, as a bridegroom adorns his head like a priest, and as a bride adorns herself with her jewels."

2 Corinthians 5:21 says, "God made Him who had no sin to be sin for us, so that in Him we might become the righteousness of God."

It is not up to us to earn such heavenly clothing but we do have to accept the gift. And when we do, our raiment will be apparent in our lives. Revelation 19:7–8 says, "Let us rejoice and be glad and give Him glory! For the wedding of the Lamb has come, and His bride has made herself ready. Fine linen, bright and clean, was given her to wear. (Fine linen stands for the righteous acts of the saints.)"

Our righteousness—which is a gift from God—expresses itself in action, in words, and in who we are. If it does not, it's worthless. "In the same way, faith by itself, if it is not accompanied by action, is dead."[223]

Think about this the next time you're at Disneyland and you see the Cast Members' costumes. They are wearing what they were given to be used for service as part of the Magic Kingdom. Are you?

Kingdom Thinking: Are you attired appropriately? Have you accepted the wedding garment provided by the King? Have you been clothed in the righteousness of God, through faith in Jesus Christ? And is that righteousness through faith expressing itself in action?

---

[223] James 2:17

Sleeping Beauty Castle

Rescued by Our Prince

Located in the southwest corner of the castle courtyard is a door that most people walk right by, even though there's a sign above it indicating what lies within: the Sleeping Beauty Castle Walkthrough. Step through that door and you enter one of the world's most photographed structures—Sleeping Beauty Castle— and step into the story of Princess Aurora herself, told through illuminated manuscripts and dioramas.

The story behind this attraction is fascinating (for example, did you know that the castle opened four years before the movie's release, and the walkthrough opened two years before the movie's release?), but for now we're going to consider the story of Aurora and hopefully see our story in that of Sleeping Beauty. We could recount much more detail—it turns out the entire Sleeping Beauty story is a fantastic allegory for the gospel story—but for now we will just look at a summary.

In the Disney version of the fairy tale, Princess Aurora is promised to Prince Phillip in a marriage arranged by their fathers (kings, of course). At her christening, she is brought gifts by the people in the kingdom, most notably by three fairies—Flora, Fauna, and Merryweather. The gifts bestowed are wondrous until the evil fairy Maleficent arrives and pronounces a curse: On her sixteenth birthday, Princess Aurora would prick her finger on the spindle of a spinning wheel and die.

Fortunately, only two of the good fairies had given their gifts, so the third one could minimize the damage caused by the curse, though not entirely undo it. Instead of dying, Aurora would only sleep, until awakened by True Love's Kiss.

After this ominous series of events, King Stefan ordered that all the spinning wheels in the kingdom be burned. Having been raised as a peasant girl they called Briar Rose, Aurora was hidden by the fairies until her sixteenth birthday. When her big day came, they returned her to the castle to reclaim her inheritance (why they didn't wait until the next day I don't know—it would have been a lot safer), and Aurora was tricked into pricking her finger anyway, and she fell into a death-like sleep. When the good fairies found out what had happened, they put a charm on the kingdom, causing everyone to sleep until the curse could be broken.

All seemed lost, but Prince Phillip came to her rescue! Captured by Maleficent, he escaped (with some help), and battled her minions and demons, eventually facing the evil fairy herself, who had transformed herself into a huge dragon. The foreign-born prince successfully slayed the dragon, though, and awakened the Sleeping Beauty to whom he had been betrothed with True Love's Kiss.

With the curse lifted and the bride (and the rest of the kingdom) awakened, the kingdom rejoiced, and the prince and princess were wed.

A lovely story, but what does this have to do with us? I'm glad you asked. Consider the crucial elements of the story:

- A princess is betrothed to a prince in an arranged marriage.
- The princess is cursed by evil, and is helpless to do anything to save herself.
- The prince arrives and battles the evil one (who ultimately takes the form of a dragon).
- The dragon is defeated.
- The princess is awakened by True Love's Kiss from the prince. (True Love's Kiss in fairy tales is the symbol of the removal of the curse and evil's influence being eliminated.)
- The prince and princess are wed.

Does it sound any more familiar now? No?

In the June 6, 2011, episode of the "Groupthink Rescue" podcast, Dan Franklin talks about the story of David and Goliath in 1 Samuel 17. He said that Bible readers tend to misread the lesson of that story. We think it's about David defeating Goliath with God's help, but David doesn't really enter the story until about one-third of the way through. It starts with Israel being afraid of this giant they are helpless to defeat, and David—the unexpected and unlikely savior—rescuing them and achieving the victory they could not attain. David wins, but then all of Israel shares in that victory. It's not a story of "I can do it with God's help," it's a story of, "I can't defeat this enemy, but Jesus Christ *can*, and when He does I can share in His victory."

Now does Sleeping Beauty sound more familiar?

The church is the Bride of Christ. We have been promised to Him, and it was an arranged marriage. "For He chose us in Him before the creation of the world to be holy and blameless in his sight."[224]

We live under a curse, though. Thanks to the sin of Adam and Eve, and our own sinful nature, we are helpless to do anything to save ourselves.

We were dead in our sins, but God sent His Son to do for us what we could not do for ourselves.[225]

Jesus is victorious over the enemy through the Resurrection. "The great dragon was hurled down—that ancient serpent called the devil, or Satan, who leads the whole world astray. He was hurled to the earth, and his angels with him."[226]

The Prince of Peace frees His bride from the curse through the Resurrection and the gift of the Holy Spirit. "No longer will there be any curse. The throne of God and of the Lamb will be in the city, and His servants will serve Him."[227]

The story of Sleeping Beauty is a graphic depiction of our helplessness before enemies that we cannot defeat—especially the

---

[224] Ephesians 1:4
[225] Colossians 2:13–15, Ephesians 2:4–5
[226] Revelation 12:9
[227] Revelation 22:3

greatest enemy: death—and of the One who gained the victory for us and brought us to Himself as His bride.

> **Kingdom Thinking:** Where do you really see yourself in the story of Sleeping Beauty—or David and Goliath? Are you still trying to fight the battle and win the victory on your own (or with "help") even though it's beyond you?

Peter Pan's Flight

Growing Up in Faith

In the story of Peter Pan, Peter brings Wendy and her brothers to Neverland, where he has a climactic showdown with Captain Hook. In the end, Wendy decides that her place is at home and she brings all the boys but Peter back to London. Peter returns briefly, and he meets Mrs. Darling, who has agreed to adopt the Lost Boys. She offers to adopt Peter as well, but Peter refuses, afraid they will "catch him and make him a man."

How many kids relate to that? For that matter, how many adults do? It can be fun to not have responsibilities and stresses and remain a kid.

Is it any surprise, then, that Peter Pan's Flight consistently has one of the longest lines of any of the rides in Fantasyland? It's common on even a moderately busy day for this ride to have a forty-five minute wait when most of the others are at twenty minutes or less (some even being walk-ons).

Granted, some of that wait time is due to hourly ride capacity. But I have no doubt that some of it has to do with the desire to become immersed again in the adventures of The Boy Who Wouldn't Grow Up.

But there are perils to "I won't grow up." Let's go back to the original story by J. M. Barrie, *Peter and Wendy*, shall we? This scene is toward the end of the book. Wendy and the boys have returned to England. Thanks to an agreement, Peter comes to visit after a year.

> [Wendy] had looked forward to thrilling talks with him about old times, but new adventures had crowded the old ones from his mind.
>
> "Who is Captain Hook?" he asked with interest when she spoke of the arch enemy.
>
> "Don't you remember," she asked, amazed, "how you killed him and saved all our lives?"
>
> "I forget them after I kill them," he replied carelessly.
>
> When she expressed a doubtful hope that Tinker Bell would be glad to see her he said, "Who is Tinker Bell?"
>
> "O Peter" she said, shocked; but even when she explained he could not remember.
>
> "There are such a lot of them," he said. "I expect she is no more."[228]

That's the danger of "I won't grow up." You see, if you don't grow up, you have no future. And with no future there is no need for a past. There is nothing to look forward to, and nothing to learn from. It's not natural. It's not healthy. And that's true not just physically, but also spiritually, as explained by the author of Hebrews.

> We have much to say about this, but it is hard to explain because you are slow to learn. In fact, though by this time you ought to be teachers, you need someone to teach you the

---

[228] J. M. Barrie, *Peter and Wendy* (UK: Hodder & Stoughton, 1911), 255–56.

elementary truths of God's word all over again. You need milk, not solid food! Anyone who lives on milk, being still an infant, is not acquainted with the teaching about righteousness. But solid food is for the mature, who by constant use have trained themselves to distinguish good from evil.[229]

Do you see the expectation here? Believers must grow. They must mature. There's a bumper sticker that says, "I may get older, but I refuse to grow up." Getting older is easy. Maturity requires intentional effort.

The issue is not whether you are saved, it's whether you "grow in the grace and knowledge of our Lord and Savior Jesus Christ."[230] Without that growth you'll remain a spiritual infant, at risk of falling prey to teaching that sounds good, but is empty at best and dangerous at worst. You'll forget where you came from, and so lose your perspective on both where other people are and where you're heading.

If all you are doing to grow in your faith is going to church out of obligation—and you might not even be doing that—you won't get very far. If you are not reading the Bible (seeing what God has to say), praying (talking to God), and putting what you're learning into practice, you will remain a "mischievous little boy" and won't grow up in your faith.

Kingdom Thinking: Are you putting intentional effort into your spiritual growth? Or are you a spiritual Peter Pan, not wanting to grow up?

---

[229] Hebrews 5:11–14
[230] 2 Peter 3:18

Mr. Toad's Wild Ride

Counting the Cost

Mr. Toad's Wild Ride holds some interesting distinctions.

- It is an Opening Day attraction.
- It has a scene that doesn't appear (or is even hinted at) in its source material.
- It is the only true "ride" at Disneyland. All of Disneyland's rides, shows, parades, etc. are known as "attractions," so when you're looking for rides, "Mr. Toad's Wild Ride" is the only such one.

As with the rest of Fantasyland's dark rides, Mr. Toad was based on an animated feature, in this case, "The Wind in the Willows" segment of *The Adventures of Ichabod and Mr. Toad.* (Ichabod Crane gets his story represented in Liberty Square and the Halloween parade in the Magic Kingdom at Walt Disney World). Released in 1949, it was the last of the "package films"—animated features consisting of two or more shorter "featurettes" but released as a single movie.

In it, Basil Rathbone narrates the story of J. Thaddeus Toad, Esq. ("Mr. Toad"), the happy-go-lucky, wealthy owner of Toad Hall. Mr. Toad believed in fun, adventure, and traveling to "Nowhere in Particular." He had a fascination with fads and manias, and chased one after the other. Of course, that landed him in trouble.

I won't spoil the rest of the story for you. For now, let's focus on that initial description of Mr. Toad.

"Toad was the one disturbing element. Incurable adventurer, mad, reckless, tried everything. A positive mania for fads, and he never counted the cost," says the narrator in his opening description. "He never counted the cost." Interesting phrase. Luke 14 recounts Jesus telling two parables with the same idea.

> Large crowds were traveling with Jesus, and turning to them He said: "If anyone comes to me and does not hate his father and mother, his wife and children, his brothers and sisters— yes, even his own life—he cannot be My disciple. And anyone who does not carry his cross and follow Me cannot be My disciple.

> "Suppose one of you wants to build a tower. Will he not first sit down and estimate the cost to see if he has enough money to complete it? For if he lays the foundation and is not able to finish it, everyone who sees it will ridicule him, saying, 'This fellow began to build and was not able to finish.'

> "Or suppose a king is about to go to war against another king. Will he not first sit down and consider whether he is able with ten thousand men to oppose the one coming against him with twenty thousand? If he is not able, he will send a delegation while the other is still a long way off and will ask for terms of peace. In the same way, any of you who does not give up everything he has cannot be My disciple."[231]

There is a cost to being a disciple, and anyone who tells you differently is selling something.

This passage is not easy to fully grasp, and digging in to examine every detail and getting a full understanding of this passage is not our purpose here. Even without that, there are some clear truths. There is a cost to following Jesus, and that cost could be everything we value.

But how valuable is what we may have to surrender? How valuable is our:

---

[231] Luke 14:25–33

- status
- position
- relationships
- wealth
- security
- good deeds (that come from ourselves)?

It's easy to look at that list and balk. I'll be honest; I do. We don't want to give up those things. We wonder how a good God could even ask us to give them up. But I think that kind of thinking may have to do with how little we truly know and understand Christ. As long as we have those valuables, we can keep Him at a "safe" distance. It's only when we lose them and have nothing or nobody to turn to but Him that we understand. The apostle Paul certainly did.

> But whatever was to my profit I now consider loss for the sake of Christ. What is more, I consider everything a loss compared to the surpassing greatness of knowing Christ Jesus my Lord, for whose sake I have lost all things. I consider them rubbish, that I may gain Christ and be found in Him, not having a righteousness of my own that comes from the law, but that which is through faith in Christ—the righteousness that comes from God and is by faith.[232]

(By the way, the word "rubbish" is a bit of a euphemism. It's much stronger than that—closer to "refuse" or "dung," and...in the vernacular, well, you know.) Paul was in a prison cell when he wrote that, with the full knowledge that he was probably going to be executed. He really had lost everything. But losing everything was nothing compared with knowing Jesus Christ.

---

[232] Philippians 3:7–9

Mr. Toad never counted the cost, and he barreled recklessly through life. On a surface level, he had fun (most of the time—prison wasn't so fun for him), but how much did he miss out on? What did he sacrifice?

When you first become a Christian, you won't know everything. All you know is that you will be called to surrender, and that God is good. You may have no concept of what you may have to give up, but you also have no real grasp of how much you will gain—until you gain it!

> **Kingdom Thinking:** Have you been called to give up something (physical or otherwise) as you have followed Jesus? Was it worth it?

Dumbo the Flying Elephant

Embracing Our Uniqueness

Dumbo the Flying Elephant was not quite an Opening Day attraction, but it was close, opening just about a month later (August 16, 1955). The attraction is, of course, based on the 1941 animated feature, *Dumbo*. The movie is based on a children's story that was prepared to demonstrate the prototype of a toy storytelling display device called a Roll-a-Book. It had only eight drawings and just a few lines of text, so the Disney storytellers were free to develop the story as they desired.

When the attraction was being created for Disneyland, it was going to carry on a storytelling technique that was also being used in the Fantasyland dark rides—one which most guests never seemed to grasp. None of the title characters appeared in their attractions (Peter Pan, Snow White, etc.), with the idea being that the guests themselves took on the role of the title character. This was never clearly explained, though, and guests frequently went to Guest Relations to ask why (for example) Snow White was not in her attraction. As part of the New Fantasyland in 1983, the characters were added to their respective attractions.

Dumbo had them all beat, though. The working title of the attraction originally was "10 Pink Elephants On Parade," themed to the Pink Elephants sequence from the movie. Walt Disney objected, not wanting his guests to ride in vehicles themed to a drunken hallucination and ordered them to be painted gray. And so, when the ride debuted, guests rode in ten representations of Dumbo himself. (In 1990 the attraction was updated and expanded to include sixteen ride vehicles rather than the original ten.)

When we think of what we can draw from Dumbo, we go back to the movie. One of the shortest of the animated features (it clocked in at sixty-three minutes and was the shortest until 2011's *Winnie the Pooh* beat it by one minute), it's still packed with reminders and lessons. We could talk about letting go of our "security blankets" (or magic feathers) and trusting in what God has already given us, or the value of having someone who believes in us, and more. For now, though, let's look at one of the most obvious and valuable lessons.

God made you uniquely, and only when you embrace your God-given uniqueness will you really be able to live as He has designed you. Dumbo's ears made him unique, but for quite a while, he tried to hide or ignore them. But that didn't work. They kept coming up, getting in his way, almost demanding attention. When he was finally able to use them and be the way he was designed, he flew! Before then, his ears made him unhappy and frustrated. They made him the object of ridicule, but sometimes that's what happens. That which makes us different also makes us subject to criticism by those who think we should be just like them.

But we answer to God, not to people, and He has something different to say:

> For by the grace given me I say to every one of you: Do not think of yourself more highly than you ought, but rather think of yourself with sober judgment, in accordance with the measure of faith God has given you. Just as each of us has one body with many members, and these members do not all have the same function, so in Christ we who are many form one body, and each member belongs to all the others. We have different gifts, according to the grace given us.[233]

Our uniqueness results not from anything we've done, or earned, or deserve. It is "according to the grace given us." And that also means that to reject our uniqueness and try to "fit in" is to reject a measure of His grace.

Kingdom Thinking: What uniqueness has God given you, and are you embracing it?

Up a Tree

In every story ever told—at least every good story—the protagonist has a defining moment. It is the time when, if it's going to have a happy ending, he realizes that he can be more than what he has been.

Dumbo is a short and simple animated feature, but even here, we get to see Dumbo's defining moment. He has just visited his mom (and we hear "Baby Mine"—a song that still gets me), and is

---

[233] Romans 12:3–6a

now outside the clowns' tent. Meanwhile, a bottle of alcohol the clowns have been drinking from falls into a bucket of water—unbeknownst to Dumbo and Timothy Mouse. As he drinks from the pale, Dumbo gets a little tipsy. The famous "Pink Elephants on Parade" song is Dumbo's hallucination after he's had too much to drink.

When he wakes up the next morning, Dumbo finds himself in a most unusual place for an elephant: up in a tree. As he is stuck up there, afraid and confused, Timothy Mouse suddenly realizes what's happened: Dumbo flew! Those huge ears that had been a source of ridicule are actually good for something. As Timothy Mouse tells him, "The very things that held ya down are gonna carry ya up, and up, and up!"

Our natural inclination as humans is to avoid "getting stuck up a tree." We do everything we can to be strong, to be safe, and to have a backup plan. That works—for a while—but eventually we all come to a place where our strength is used up, our security is gone, and we've exhausted Plan B, Plan C, Plan D…and Plan Z. Then what?

Then we get to the place where we should have started. It is those very things we try to avoid because we think they're going to hold us down that will truly carry us up.

The following passage describes the plight and the hope for a great outcome:

> But we have this treasure in jars of clay to show that this all-surpassing power is from God and not from us. We are hard pressed on every side, but not crushed; perplexed, but not in despair; persecuted, but not abandoned; struck down, but not destroyed. We always carry around in our body the death of Jesus, so that the life of Jesus may also be revealed in our body. For we who are alive are always being given over to death for Jesus' sake, so that His life may be revealed in our mortal body. So then, death is at work in us, but life is at work in you.

It is written: "I believed; therefore I have spoken." With that same spirit of faith we also believe and therefore speak, because we know that the One who raised the Lord Jesus from the dead will also raise us with Jesus and present us with you in His presence. All this is for your benefit, so that the grace that is reaching more and more people may cause thanksgiving to overflow to the glory of God.

Therefore we do not lose heart. Though outwardly we are wasting away, yet inwardly we are being renewed day by day. For our light and momentary troubles are achieving for us an eternal glory that far outweighs them all. So we fix our eyes not on what is seen, but on what is unseen. For what is seen is temporary, but what is unseen is eternal.[234]

If you never experience those times of trial, of fear, or of significant change, then you miss out on some tremendous blessings. If you rely on your strength to do what you need to do, then you miss out on God's strength in you. If you stay safe and secure, then you have no need to rely on God. If what is seen is enough for you, then you will never look for what is unseen.

Sometimes finding yourself up a tree is the best place you can be—where else will you discover you can fly?

Kingdom Thinking: When have you found yourself "up a tree" and later discovered that this time and experience was exactly what you needed?

---

[234] 2 Corinthians 4:7–18

The Meanness of People

Dumbo is one of the most heart-tugging of Disney's animated features. Maybe it's because I'm an only child. Maybe it's because I never really fit in with most of my peers. Maybe it's because I have a soft spot for animals—even animated ones. But whatever the reason, *Dumbo* touches me.

Some of the scenes that get to me the most are the ones in which either Dumbo or Mrs. Jumbo (his mother) are being mocked, taunted, or ridiculed by other members of the circus. The other elephants and the clowns are merciless to these two. It's only when Dumbo proves to them, and to the ringmaster, that his "weirdness" is actually valuable that they respect them.

This does not surprise me. We see it all the time in the real world. I know several people—some of whom I highly respect—who believe that people are basically good and will do what's right. The bad ones are an anomaly and we can generally expect the best from people. I think they're wrong.

Of course, what I think doesn't really matter. What does the Bible say?

The heart is deceitful above all things and beyond cure. Who can understand it?[235]

The hearts of men, moreover, are full of evil and there is madness in their hearts while they live, and afterward they join the dead.[236]

There are other passages, but hopefully these make the point. In our natural state, we are not good people. We are deceitful, cruel, selfish, arrogant, envious, and more. I do not expect the best from people as a whole, because people as a whole are not capable

---

[235] Jeremiah 17:9
[236] Ecclesiastes 9:3

of the best. Sure, we have our few shining moments, but they stand out as remarkable because they are so rare.

Not very uplifting, is it? Unfortunately, it's the way humanity is apart from Christ. But it's not how everyone has to be.

> Do you not know that the wicked will not inherit the kingdom of God? Do not be deceived: Neither the sexually immoral nor idolaters nor adulterers nor male prostitutes nor homosexual offenders nor thieves nor the greedy nor drunkards nor slanderers nor swindlers will inherit the kingdom of God. *And that is what some of you were.* But you were washed, you were sanctified, you were justified in the name of the Lord Jesus Christ and by the Spirit of our God.[237]

As Christians, we have the power, through the Holy Spirit, to choose not to remain that way. It's not easy, and we won't be successful 100 percent of the time this side of heaven, but we can grow from such a darkened state. We're expected and even commanded to grow.

We see the elephants and the clowns in Dumbo and we're outraged at their attitudes and behavior. Our hearts hurt for Dumbo and Mrs. Jumbo. Why? Because we see ourselves on both sides. You've been the one who is scornful, hurtful, and malicious. You're reminded of who you were, and who you still have a tendency to be. And you've been the one who was the object of ridicule, spite, and even hatred.

There is always someone on your side, strengthening you against the attacks of others and reminding you that you now have the power not to attack (actively or passively) others but to help them. Sometimes that person is a friend who stands with you like Timothy Mouse stood by Dumbo. Sometimes that Person is God Himself, as the Holy Spirit living within you.

---

[237] 1 Corinthians 6:9–11, emphasis added

Dumbo is a reminder that the world is a cruel place, filled with people who are more interested in their own interests than in helping others—and that you used to be one of them, and so did I. But you don't have to stay that way. You can choose to rise above the spitefulness, through the power of God and by claiming your new Supernatural Kingdom Identity in Him.

Kingdom Thinking: As you look back over the last few months or years, do you see that you've grown in how you treat others? You may not be who you want to be, but thank God you're also not who you used to be!

Casey Jr. Circus Train

Is Thinking You Can Enough?

Casey Jr. Circus Train was almost an Opening Day attraction, but it didn't quite make it. Originally it was slated to be more of a roller coaster style attraction, but there were some safety concerns, so it was retooled and actually debuted on July 31, 1955, two weeks after Disneyland opened.

At the time Casey Jr. premiered, there wasn't much to see. Storybook Land was still the Canal Boats of the World, which is to say the banks of the canal were pretty much just dirt. Once that ride became Storybook Land, with all of its intricately detailed miniatures, there was much more to see.

Casey Jr. also has the distinction of being one-half of one of only two pairs of attractions that come from the same movie—excluding Storybook Land, which has miniature scenes from several movies. (Dumbo and Casey Jr. both come from *Dumbo*.

Can you guess the other pair? Here's a hint: you'll find the other pair in Fantasyland as well.[238]) It's a fun, whimsical attraction that's almost as enjoyable to watch as it is to ride. Who can dislike an attraction that has a passenger car with bars on it labeled "Monkeys"?

When I think of the Casey Jr. Circus Train—both the attraction and the character in the movie, one phrase comes to mind right away: "I think I can, I think I can."

That's a great message, right? Confidence. Looking forward. Accomplishing goals. That's exactly what God wants for us, isn't it?

I don't think so. We may *appear* to accomplish a lot, but it takes more than just the positive attitude of Casey Jr. In fact, when I hear, "I think I can, I think I can," my mind recalls the Shel Silverstein poem "The Little Blue Engine." It goes like this:

> The little blue engine looked up at the hill.
> His light was weak, his whistle was shrill.
> He was tired and small, and the hill was tall,
> And his face blushed red as he softly said,
> "I think I can, I think I can, I think I can."
>
> So he started up with a chug and a strain,
> And he puffed and pulled with might and main.
> And slowly he climbed, a foot at a time,
> And his engine coughed as he whispered soft,
> "I think I can, I think I can, I think I can."
>
> With a squeak and a creak and a toot and a sigh,
> With an extra hope and an extra try,
> He would not stop—now he neared the top—
> And strong and proud he cried out loud,
> "I think I can, I think I can, I think I can!"

---

[238] Still not coming to mind? OK, it's Alice in Wonderland and the Mad Tea Party, which both come from *Alice in Wonderland*.

He was almost there, when—CRASH! SMASH! BASH!
He slid down and mashed into engine hash
On the rocks below…which goes to show
If the track is tough and the hill is rough,
THINKING you can just ain't enough![239]

Sometimes thinking you can just ain't enough. Bad grammar aside, that's the lesson of Scripture, too.

> Therefore, my dear friends, as you have always obeyed—not only in my presence, but now much more in my absence—continue to work out your salvation with fear and trembling, for it is God who works in you to will and to act according to His good purpose.[240]

> I can do everything through Him who gives me strength.[241]

> Remain in Me, and I will remain in you. No branch can bear fruit by itself; it must remain in the vine. Neither can you bear fruit unless you remain in Me. I am the vine; you are the branches. If a man remains in Me and I in him, he will bear much fruit; apart from Me you can do nothing.[242]

I have actually heard people say that in this last passage, "nothing" does not really mean "nothing." They downplay it. But the text seems pretty clear to me, especially when I went back to the Greek, the original language of the New Testament. The good news is, there is an implied promise as we look at the rest of John 15 and the other passages I quoted (along with others). Without

---

[239] Shel Silverstein, *Where the Sidewalk Ends* (New York: HarperCollins Publishers, 1974), 158.
[240] Philippians 2:12–13
[241] Philippians 4:13
[242] John 15:4–5

Him we can do nothing, but He promises His presence, and because of that we can "bear much fruit."

Sometimes thinking we can just isn't enough. Those times are much-needed reminders of our dependence on Him—and of His promise to be with us as we "abide in Him." The closer we are to Christ, the more fruit we can bear and the stronger we become. But it is *His* strength that bears fruit, the strength that comes from the Vine, not what little we can squeeze out as branches until we wither away.

Only in Him does "I think I can" mean anything. We might better say, "I think I can. I know I can as Christ gives me strength to do His will."

Kingdom Thinking: When have you had to rely on God's strength, when "I think I can" just wasn't enough?

Transition Between Lands

From Fantasy to a New Frontier: Getting Past the Gate

When you are at Disneyland, it is usually pretty easy to tell when you are moving from one land to another. With one exception, there's some kind of clear indicator that you've left one land and entered another.

Most of those signs are welcoming, even inviting. But one is intimidating, even formidable. It consists of a giant wood and iron gate that can clearly be opened…and closed.

You could argue that the passage from Main Street U.S.A. to Frontierland fits this description, but for now, we're talking about the gates as you pass from Fantasyland to Frontierland. I had never noticed until just recently how large—and kind of intimidating—this gate is. There's no hopping over this fence (not that you should anyway). There's no mistaking that here you leave one place and enter another. If the gate is closed, even partially, it's almost enough to make you change your mind and decide it's better to just stay where you are.

I have found the same to be true in my life, and it is probably true in yours, too, especially when making this particular transition.

We like to live in a type of Fantasyland, a negative one, where we have rules, beliefs, and patterns that are safe, comfortable, and yet often untrue and damaging. We tell ourselves:

- Things will never get better.
- I'll be just like my dad (or mom).
- I'll never be a good parent.
- This is all there is.
- I could never get a better job.
- It's ridiculous to even consider finding work that I love.
- I have nothing to contribute to the world.
- My dreams are just that, dreams, and they're foolish.
- My value comes from what I do, and the only way to be more valuable or significant is to do more, achieve more, have more.
- God could never love me.

These are lies. Every single one of them. But to leave them behind and move into truth we must be willing to face the barriers that block us from new frontiers, from pressing forward into unexplored territory.

What is that barrier for you? What's holding you back?

What's the first word that came to mind when you read those questions? The odds are very good that your first inkling is true.

For just a moment, before your filters and safeguards had a chance to engage, you were honest with yourself. That's the only way to begin breaking through these gates.

Here is further encouragement:

> I call upon you, therefore, brethren, through the compassions of God, to present your bodies a sacrifice—living, sanctified, acceptable to God—your intelligent service; and be not conformed to this age, but be transformed by the renewing of your mind, for your proving what [is] the will of God—the good, and acceptable, and perfect.[243]

It's not easy to "present your bodies as a sacrifice" or to "be transformed by the renewing of your mind." But that's exactly what we are each called to do. That is how we move out of those lies and fantasies and into the new frontiers God has prepared for us. The question is, how?

We already considered the first step. Identify what's keeping you in Fantasyland. But don't stop there. It does no good to break down the walls if you don't cross through. So answer these two questions:

1. What am I not doing because of one or more of these fatal fantasies?
2. What am I willing to do to address one of those lies I've believed, to move out of my comfort zone, even if just slightly?

Do not try to do twenty things. Start with one, maybe two. If you're not sure where or how to start, get help. Sometimes it takes another person in our lives to encourage us, push us, challenge us, or give us tools—or even just a different perspective. But don't make excuses. Resist the temptation to accept "good enough."

---

[243] Romans 12:1–2 (YLT)

The enemy of "best" is not "bad." The enemy of "best" is "good enough." Don't let that enemy win!

Kingdom Thinking: When you look over the gate into Frontierland in your life, what do you see?

King Arthur Carrousel

Unique, Individual, and Equal

Carousels have always occupied an important place in Disneyland history. As Walt Disney told the story, he conceived of the idea for Disneyland while sitting on a bench in Griffith Park (Los Angeles) watching his daughters ride the merry-go-round.

He felt that every park needed a carousel, and for his park he had some very specific ideas about what he wanted. Disneyland's carousel was built in 1875 by William Dentzel and had operated since 1922 at Sunnyside Amusement Park in Toronto, Ontario, before being moved to Disneyland in 1954. During those months leading up to Opening Day it was refurbished. Technicians replaced some of the animals to make them all horses and added some more, making all seventy-two of them "jumpers." On Opening Day, the carousel sat right in the middle of the Sleeping Beauty Castle courtyard and served as the "wienie" (a visual icon in the park that draws guests forward) to draw people through the castle and into Fantasyland.

The single white horse became so popular that in 1976 all the horses were repainted white. Other significant changes included a relocation about twenty yards north (away from the castle) in 1983 and the removal of four horses, replacing them with two benches so all guests can now ride.

King Arthur Carrousel (spelled with two "r's" to reflect an older, British variant of the spelling) is made up of several dozen horses that are all going in the same direction. They are unique, each decorated differently and having its own name, but their individuality is less important than their equality. Every guest (except those who choose the bench) gets to ride a leaping white horse. All get an equal experience.

As Christians, we too are individuals, but when it comes to our value and identity, individuality is less important than our equality. That may sound like heresy to American Christians especially, but Scripture bears it out.

> So in Christ Jesus you are all children of God through faith, for all of you who were baptized into Christ have clothed yourselves with Christ. There is neither Jew nor Gentile, neither slave nor free, nor is there male and female, for you are all one in Christ Jesus. If you belong to Christ, then you are Abraham's seed, and heirs according to the promise.[244]

Your identity as a child of God does not come from your ancestry, your social status, your gender, or anything other than the answer to this question: "Do you belong to Christ?" If so, then you are a child of God.

That means you do not have to earn His favor—or your salvation. You do not have to jockey for a better role or a more important position. You need not concern yourself with "getting ahead." Do what you were designed to do—as part of the team, the community—in service of the overall mission. You have been created uniquely, but you are not better or worse, more or less important than anyone else.

---

[244] Galatians 3:26–29

Now, among the sixty-eight leaping white horses of King Arthur Carrousel, there is still a "lead horse," the first among its "brothers and sisters." The lead horse is considered horse #1 by the manufacturer and the maintenance crew, and it is usually the most decorated one on the outside row. In this case, its name is Jingles, and you can identify it by gold leaf horseshoes, the flowers and references to Mary Poppins, and a few more distinctive features on the golden saddle.

In the same way, among the children of God, there is a "lead horse" if you will, the first among His brothers and sisters: Jesus Christ.

For those God foreknew He also predestined to be conformed to the image of his Son, that He might be the firstborn among many brothers and sisters. And those He predestined, He also called; those He called, He also justified; those He justified, He also glorified. What, then, shall we say in response to these things? If God is for us, who can be against us?[245]

You are Jesus' brother or sister. You are an heir together with Christ. But He's still the "lead horse" and all the rest of us are His followers. That means following Him in the way He connected to the Father, in the way He served and loved people, and in His suffering. That's not very popular, but it is the context for the promises in Romans 8.

Let King Arthur Carrousel stand as a reminder of (1) your identity in Christ, not having to earn it or be better than anyone else, and (2) of your equality in Christ, and that you are a coheir (with everything that entails) with Him.

---

[245] Romans 8:29–31

> **Kingdom Thinking:** Does this reminder lessen a burden on you? How can you use it or allow it to take some of the pressure off and just be who God made you to be—or maybe step up and live up to who you already are?

The Sword in the Stone

It's not What Others Say or Do

Have you noticed what effect your relationships have on how you view yourself and what you're willing and able to do? I know I have.

Good relationships contribute to feelings of confidence, security, and love, and they help me to be more willing to take risks. That's because I know people who will do everything they can to support me and catch me if I fall. I am more willing to sacrifice for others because I know I can rely on people who will sacrifice for me. I can love others (and myself) because I am loved.

On the other hand, bad relationships can lead to fear, self-doubt, and even self-loathing. In some cases, we get so caught up in these relationships that we blind ourselves to the difficulty—even abuse—we receive, maybe because we think we don't deserve any better. Or, we think we can't do any better, or lack a frame of reference that shows life can be different. Our capacity to love is squelched or smothered because what love we *have* tried to show has not been returned. Perhaps it has even been ridiculed (actively or passively) by those whose opinions matter most to us. Like a flower deprived of light and water, we wither. And when (or if) we do get out of those toxic relationships, rediscovering all those things that had been denied us can be a difficult (if also exciting) journey.

But what does that have to do with Disneyland?

Walk with me across the Sleeping Beauty Castle drawbridge and into Fantasyland. Continue straight ahead and the first thing you'll run into (unless there happens to be an outdoor vending cart in the way) is a stone and anvil right in front of King Arthur's Carrousel. It is a very special stone and anvil with a sword stuck in the top. Yes, our reminder is The Sword in the Stone, and what it serves to remind us of is the love of God.

Consider the story of Arthur Pendragon, king of all Britain. As one version of the legend goes, after the King of England, Uther Pendragon, died, the "Sword in the Stone" appeared in London with an inscription proclaiming that "Who so Pulleth Out This Sword of this Stone and Anvil, is Rightwise King Born of England." Nobody can remove the sword, which is soon forgotten, leaving England in a Dark Age.

Years later, Arthur (a.k.a. "Wart" in the Disney version), a twelve-year-old orphan training to be a squire, accompanies his older foster brother, Kay, on a hunting trip. Through a series of events, he meets Merlin, who becomes his tutor and mentor. Kay treats Arthur very badly, though. He is mean, rude, and abusive to Arthur. In fact, the only one who seems to care about Arthur at all is Merlin—because Merlin can see something in Wart that the others cannot, or will not. Eventually (spoiler alert), Arthur pulls the sword from the stone, fulfilling the prophecy and becoming king.

The Sword in the Stone that sits here in Fantasyland gave guests a chance to live that event for themselves, more or less. Merlin the Magician appeared several times a day to announce that the Realm was having a (temporary) leadership crisis, and needed a new (temporary) Ruler. But can someone be found who has the requisite courage and strength to be the new Ruler? Merlin selected several volunteers who attempted to pull the sword from the stone. (Typically a rather burly man was the first selected, and failed miserably, only to be shown up by a five-year-old.)

Arthur was destined to become king, but no one saw his worth except Merlin, and Merlin refused to give up on him. God does the same for us because He loves us.

Consider God's attributes. Here are a few: self-sufficiency, goodness, graciousness, and holiness. Now consider that very few places in the Bible does it say that "God is" something, and one of those is that "God is love." This is one trait that more identifies and defines who God is than anything else. God gives grace. He gives peace. He creates. He administers justice. But He *is* love.

Scripture speaks of His love abundantly:

For God so loved the world that He gave his one and only Son, that whoever believes in Him shall not perish but have eternal life.[246]

The LORD your God is with you,
He is mighty to save.
He will take great delight in you,
He will quiet you with His love,
He will rejoice over you with singing.[247]

But God demonstrates His own love for us in this: While we were still sinners, Christ died for us.[248]

For I am convinced that neither death nor life, neither angels nor demons, neither the present nor the future, nor any powers, neither height nor depth, nor anything else in all creation, will be able to separate us from the love of God that is in Christ Jesus our Lord.[249]

---

[246] John 3:16
[247] Zephaniah 3:17
[248] Romans 5:8
[249] Romans 8:38–39

How great is the love the Father has lavished on us, that we should be called children of God! And that is what we are![250]

God loves you so much that He sent His Son Jesus to die for you, so that you can have eternal life if only you will believe in Him. He takes great delight in you. Nothing can separate you from His love. You are called a child of God. He knows how valuable you are, and it is simply because you are His child. It is not because of anything you've done to earn it. And there is nothing you can do that will make Him love you less.

Still, He won't force His love on unwilling people. If you choose to accept Him, all of the foregoing describes you and you have eternal life with Him. If you choose not to accept or believe in Him, He loves you so much that He will not force you to spend eternity with Him, and only one place has been reserved where He is not found in His loving presence. It is your choice.

Arthur was to be King of England whether anyone knew it or not. Before his true identity was revealed, some people treated him very badly. Even he did not see his potential, because he thought he was limited by his station in life and that what others said about him was true. Then he learned otherwise when he pulled a sword from a stone (which was sitting in a churchyard, incidentally).

You are a child of God and He loves you. Others may treat you poorly, they may abuse you, put you down, and try to extinguish the love you have for others and for yourself. You may believe that you deserve it, but you don't. After all, who knows your value more than the One who made you? And He says you are worth more than you can imagine.

Let the Sword in the Stone stand as a monument of God's love for you. Just as the sword revealed Arthur's true identity, let it remind you that you are a Prince or Princess—because you are a child of the King of Kings! Nothing anyone can say or do can ever

---

[250] 1 John 3:1a

take that away from you, and it remains true no matter what others say about you or how they treat you.

Kingdom Thinking: Who defines your identity? If it's not God, how might your life be different if you started listening to what He says about you instead of what other people say?

Pinocchio's Daring Journey

What Are Your Strings?

Pinocchio's Daring Journey opened in Disneyland's Fantasyland in 1983 as part of the "New Fantasyland" overhaul and expansion, led by Imagineer Tony Baxter and his team. It replaced the Fantasyland Theater (originally called the Mickey Mouse Club Theater). This classic-style dark ride retells the story of the little wooden boy who dreamed of one day being a "real boy."

As the ride begins, we first see Pinocchio singing "Hi Diddle Dee Dee (An Actor's Life for Me)," but not in the original context from the film. The setting here is basically the scene in the movie where he sings "I've Got No Strings."

That scene in the movie is telling. Of course, woodcarver Geppetto made Pinocchio without physical strings, but the only way for the wish they share to be granted by the Blue Fairy is for the little wooden boy to prove himself to be "brave, truthful, and unselfish" and able to tell right from wrong by listening to his conscience. So his life still comes "with strings."

Pinocchio starts out with the best intentions, but gets sidetracked by Honest John and Gideon, and joins a puppet show led by Stromboli. It is here that he sings "I've Got No Strings." He revels in his supposed freedom, celebrating that he has no strings and is not subject to anyone's control and can do whatever he wants. That lasts right up until he tries to leave and Stromboli will not let him go. Pinocchio thought he was free to do as he pleased, but it turned out he was trapped in an enslavement far worse than having physical strings like the other puppets.

Of course, Pinocchio does get to become a real boy, but only because he submits to the Blue Fairy's requirements that she laid out at the beginning. He was still subject to someone other than himself, but this time it was for benevolent reasons and it turned out for his best. By accepting those "strings" he was able to become what he most desired and what his father (his maker), wanted for him.

Don't we as human beings do the same thing? The heart of our separation from God is our claim that "we've got no strings"; we want to live the way we choose, and we may even flaunt our supposed independence. But the reality is that we are all servants of something, either of our own sinful natures or of God. We will serve one or the other. As it says in Romans 6:16–23:

> Don't you know that when you offer yourselves to someone to obey him as slaves, you are slaves to the one whom you obey—whether you are slaves to sin, which leads to death, or to obedience, which leads to righteousness? But thanks be to God that, though you used to be slaves to sin, you wholeheartedly obeyed the form of teaching to which you were entrusted. You have been set free from sin and have become slaves to righteousness.
>
> I put this in human terms because you are weak in your natural selves. Just as you used to offer the parts of your body in slavery to impurity and to ever-increasing wickedness, so now offer them in slavery to righteousness leading to holiness. When you were slaves to sin, you were free from the control

of righteousness. What benefit did you reap at that time from the things you are now ashamed of? Those things result in death! But now that you have been set free from sin and have become slaves to God, the benefit you reap leads to holiness, and the result is eternal life. For the wages of sin is death, but the gift of God is eternal life in Christ Jesus our Lord.

We all have strings—something we serve, someone we seek to please, or even desires we "just can't seem to control." What we can choose is what those strings are.

Pinocchio sees strings as things that would "...hold me down / To make me fret, or make me frown / I had strings / But now I'm free / There are no strings on me.... / I've got no strings / So I have fun / I'm not tied up to anyone." (Interestingly, as soon as he starts singing this song, the first thing that happens is that he trips and falls on his face. Symbolism?) His claim isn't necessarily the case, though. Many of the other marionettes in this scene can do things that Pinocchio cannot, precisely because they are connected by the strings. It all depends on what the strings are, and who holds them.

Kingdom Thinking: Who do you serve? Are you a slave to sin or to righteousness? What do you think the "strings" are that connect someone to God? Is Pinocchio's view of strings as negative accurate?

Let Your Conscience Be Your Guide?

Several rides at Disneyland have a recurring character throughout (for example, the raven in the Haunted Mansion, Jack Sparrow in

Pirates of the Caribbean, and of course, the title characters in each of the Fantasyland dark rides). One of these rides has a second character that is also featured in multiple scenes.

Jiminy Cricket appears throughout Pinocchio's Daring Journey, acting—as he does in the movie—as Pinocchio's conscience. The little wooden boy is encouraged early on to let his conscience be his guide. If he had heeded that advice, he would have avoided nearly all of the problems he encountered.

During the ride, Jiminy Cricket gives Pinocchio at least four specific types of guidance. He tries to direct him:

- out of danger
- away from temptation
- toward restoration
- home

Clearly, Pinocchio would have been better off to let his conscience be his guide. Just as clearly, this is one of the main lessons we as viewers/riders are supposed to learn from this story. We should always let our hearts/that little voice inside/whatever you want to call it be our guide. And that's great advice.

Isn't it? Close, but maybe not the best advice. Why?

The heart is hopelessly dark and deceitful, a puzzle that no one can figure out.[251]

There is a way that seems right to a man, but in the end it leads to death.[252]

I care very little if I am judged by you or by any human court; indeed, I do not even judge myself. My conscience is clear, but that does not make me innocent. It is the Lord who judges me.

---

[251] Jeremiah 17:9 (MSG)
[252] Proverbs 14:12

Therefore judge nothing before the appointed time; wait till the Lord comes. He will bring to light what is hidden in darkness and will expose the motives of men's hearts. At that time each will receive his praise from God.[253]

Maybe, just maybe, our own conscience is not the best source of guidance. But we are not without help.

And I will ask the Father, and He will give you another Counselor to be with you forever—the Spirit of truth. The world cannot accept Him, because it neither sees Him nor knows Him. But you know Him, for He lives with you and will be in you.[254]

Because those who are led by the Spirit of God are sons of God. For you did not receive a spirit that makes you a slave again to fear, but you received the Spirit of sonship. And by Him we cry, "Abba, Father." The Spirit Himself testifies with our spirit that we are God's children.[255]

Doesn't the Holy Spirit do all the same things Jiminy Cricket did for Pinocchio, and more? If we'll listen, He leads us:

- out of danger
- away from sin/temptation
- toward restoration
- home

Just as with Jiminy, the Holy Spirit will not force anything on you. He won't shout. You must listen. But if you do, He'll guide you in the paths of righteousness. The Holy Spirit and your

---

[253] 1 Corinthians 4:3–5
[254] John 14:16–17
[255] Romans 8:14–16

conscience are not necessarily mutually exclusive, but when there's a conflict between them, be sure the Spirit wins.

> **Kingdom Thinking:** How do you know when you're listening to your own conscience vs. when you're listening to the Holy Spirit?

Snow White's Scary Adventures

Fearing God

Snow White's Adventures was an Opening Day attraction, and for the most part the ride remains very similar to when it opened in 1955. According to Mouseplanet.com, "The big change is in perspective. The original conception of the attraction was that the rider was Snow White, and therefore she was never actually seen in the ride. As part of the New Fantasyland in 1983 this was changed so that Snow White is now seen in several locations during the ride. The name was also changed at that time from Snow White's Adventures to Snow White's Scary Adventures to emphasize that the ride would be scary to young riders."[256]

I watched *Snow White and the Seven Dwarfs* recently and one line in particular jumped out at me. At one point Snow White says, "But you don't know what I've been through. And all because I was afraid. I'm so ashamed of the fuss I made."

"All because I was afraid." How telling. Fear is such a prevalent part of our lives. We spend so much time and effort trying to avoid

---

[256] Mouse Planet, "Snow White's Scary Adventure," http://www.mouseplanet.com/guide/799/Disneyland-Resort/Disneyland-Park/Fantasyland/Snow-Whites-Scary-Adventure, accessed August 6, 2013.

or overcome things we're afraid of, yet there is some fear that's good.

> The fear of the LORD is the beginning of knowledge, but fools despise wisdom and discipline.[257]

In his *BasicSeries*, Francis Chan talks about the fear of God. In it, he says, "As people would say certain things are unpopular, the church would almost get embarrassed of those things, like embarrassed of certain doctrines, maybe even embarrassed at the way God described Himself....One of the biggest issues that you see in Scripture is this idea of the fear of God."[258]

Often, Christians tend to downplay the word "fear" in this context. I have done it, too. We say things like, "Well, 'fear' doesn't really mean to be afraid. It just means 'awe and reverence.' It's the same thing as being afraid of fire. It's just having a healthy respect for the fire." The problem with that analogy is that if God is like a fire, He's not like a fire in our fireplace, or even a nice, healthy campfire. He is a raging inferno through a forest of all dry brush and trees. This is not something that commands a "healthy respect."

The word "fear" in Proverbs 1:7 and similar verses comes from Hebrew words such as *yir'ah* (Proverbs 1:7; 9:10; Psalm 2:11; 19:9; 34:11), *yare'* (Psalm 33:8; 86:11; Jeremiah 5:22; Ecclesiastes 12:13), and *pachad* (Job 23:15). These words mean "fear," "terror," or "dread." The Hebrew language is clear, and if something other than fear was intended, there are other Hebrew words with softer meanings.

The reality is, we sometimes lose sight of who God truly is or we try to minimize Him to make Him seem more approachable. But consider: He is the Creator of the universe. Everything that

---

[257] Proverbs 1:7
[258] Francis Chan, "BASIC: Fear God" (DVD), David C. Cook Distribution, 2010.

exists does so because of Him. He is holy. He is omnipotent and omniscient. He is.

The fear of the LORD is the beginning of wisdom. Isn't it entirely appropriate, understandable, and even expected to fear Someone like that? Doesn't casual familiarity or even disregard become unthinkably presumptuous?

Again, Francis Chan: "In church, we started going...let's talk about the other areas of God. But if we skip the fear of God, we won't understand the other areas....when people came in contact with this God, it didn't look like just a respect or an awe...it sure appears that they are terrified....The reality is, whoever you are, the moment you see God, you are going to fear Him."[259]

Fear can be an appropriate motivator:

"Woe to me!" I cried. "I am ruined! For I am a man of unclean lips, and I live among a people of unclean lips, and my eyes have seen the King, the LORD Almighty."[260]

When I saw Him, I fell at His feet as though dead.[261]

We start with a fear of God. But we do not have to stay there. Consider what comes next in both passages above:

"Woe to me!" I cried. "I am ruined! For I am a man of unclean lips, and I live among a people of unclean lips, and my eyes have seen the King, the LORD Almighty." Then one of the seraphs flew to me with a live coal in his hand, which he had taken with tongs from the altar. With it he touched my mouth and said, "See, this has touched your lips; your guilt is taken away and your sin atoned for."[262]

---

[259] ibid.
[260] Isaiah 6:5
[261] Revelation 1:17a
[262] Isaiah 6:5–7

When I saw Him, I fell at His feet as though dead. Then He placed His right hand on me and said: "Do not be afraid. I am the First and the Last. I am the Living One; I was dead, and behold I am alive for ever and ever! And I hold the keys of death and Hades."[263]

God says, in effect, "I am the Creator of everything. I am this amazing God whom you should fear. But once you get to that point and understand it, you don't have to live in terror of Me." What does our worship look like when we understand God like that? Doesn't it become entirely reasonable to trust Him?

One of the most oft-repeated commands in Scripture is, "Don't be afraid." One last time, here is insight from Francis Chan: "Then we would see, okay, now I know why I need to fear this God. And now I don't want to just flippantly disobey His commands anymore. I want to take Him seriously, but not just that...it would change our whole mindset, 'cause we'd realize, now that I've seen Him, I realize there's nothing else to fear."

What, then, shall we say in response to this? If God is for us, who can be against us?[264]

The fear of the LORD leads to life: Then one rests content, untouched by trouble.[265]

Snow White had very good reasons to be afraid. She was being targeted for murder by the powerful Wicked Queen. Until she happened upon the Seven Dwarfs, she was lost and alone in a dark, scary place. That was her reality. But often these Fantasyland attractions remind us that what we see is not what is true. The

---

[263] Revelation 1:17–18
[264] Romans 8:31
[265] Proverbs 19:23

fantasy disguises a greater reality, and that is the case with Snow White's Scary Adventures.

Sometimes we, too, feel lost and alone. We feel like we are being unfairly and unjustly targeted or attacked. But we know something that Snow White did not: unseen but ever-present is our God. We start with fearing God and out of that comes comfort. From that place of refuge we can stand, even when the world seems completely against us, not in our own strength, but shielded and loved by The One who is bigger than all our problems, our fears, our challenges. Without the proper perspective, we remain trapped in these "scary adventures." With the proper perspective, we stand and say, "If God is for us, who can be against us?" and these truths finally become more than just words.

Kingdom Thinking: What are you most afraid of? Is it bigger or more powerful than God?

Fantasy Faire

Rapunzel: When Will Your Life Begin?

On March 12, 2013, Disneyland opened the new Fantasy Faire in place of the former Carnation Plaza Gardens. With this new area of Fantasyland, just off the Hub, a very popular character has a new home: Rapunzel.

Rapunzel now has a representation of her tower in the middle of the Faire, and a daily show in the Royal Theatre. This lesson/reminder focuses on the song from the opening of the movie (*Tangled*), called "When Will My Life Begin?" The song isn't sung in the Royal Theatre show, but the pianist does play it a couple of times.

Rapunzel has been trapped in a tower all her life. She has busied herself with things—cooking, cleaning, reading, painting, exercise—that are good for her. But she's continuing to do the same thing day after day and it is driving her crazy. She feels like there's no escape, so she just keeps on going through the motions, all the while wondering when her life will truly begin.

Do you ever feel that way? You know that you have new life in Christ and that Jesus promised abundant life, but you're wondering where it is. Let me suggest two reasons you may be missing it.

1. You've missed the "in Christ" part.

At first blush, that may sound ridiculous. "Of course I'm 'in Christ'!" you say. If you've received Christ, then yes, you are. The Bible is clear on this point. But that assertion is what we would call "positional." You have that position. You could also call it your identity. "In Christ" defines who you are.

But *having* the identity and *living* like it are two different things. You could be a prince, the daughter of a rock star, or even a famous author. But if you live like you're broke, unknown, and unable to access significant resources, what good does that do you? You still have the identity, but you're not living like it. Rapunzel had her own true identity though she did not know it for most of the story, and it kept her from living the life she was made for.

Remember, Jesus said,

I am the vine; you are the branches. If you remain in Me and I in you, you will bear much fruit; apart from Me you can do nothing. If you do not remain in Me, you are like a branch that is thrown away and withers; such branches are picked up, thrown into the fire and burned. If you remain in Me and My words remain in you, ask whatever you wish, and it will be done for you. This is to My Father's glory, that you bear much fruit, showing yourselves to be My disciples.

As the Father has loved Me, so have I loved you. Now remain in My love. If you keep My commands, you will remain in My love, just as I have kept My Father's commands and remain in His love. I have told you this so that My joy may be in you and that your joy may be complete. My command is this: Love each other as I have loved you. Greater love has no one than this: to lay down one's life for one's friends. You are My friends if you do what I command.[266]

In order to bear fruit and have the abundant life He promised, it takes a living connection to Him—which He pretty clearly says here is characterized by keeping His command to love one another as He has loved you. How well does that describe your life?

Of course, it takes regular time with Jesus, discipline, and training to develop such a life. It cannot be done through your own strength or willpower. But it can be done as long as you remain actively "in Christ."

2. You're still trapped in your tower.

Rapunzel's lack of knowledge of her identity kept her trapped in her tower. So did fear—fear of the outside world, of the anger of her "mother," and of the unknown. She longed to go "out there" but felt caged in. She believed the lie that all she could do is what she had done before (over and over). And there was no other way. It took someone else to come along and help her see that she could be free—that she could have the life for which she was made.

---

[266] John 15:5–14

Flynn Rider may not be the best role model—not at first, anyway—but he still served that purpose for her. Do you have someone in that role for you? That's what I do for my coaching clients. They have to take the step out of the tower, but I help them develop the tools, the confidence, and the new perspective needed to break free and live in their true identities.

Could you use that kind of person in your life? Maybe coaching isn't what you need right now. That's OK. Maybe you need a counselor, a mentor, or a supportive friend—or maybe a coach is exactly what you need. Each has their time and place. Whichever you need, though, find someone. They may not come through your tower window—though that is, in effect, what I'm doing right now—so seek them out if you need to.

Break free of your tower and live the life you were designed for. Become the "you" God made you to be!

Kingdom Thinking: What is keeping you imprisoned in your tower, and what step can you take today to break free of it?

Belle: Bringing a New Story

Rapunzel has her own stage show in the new Fantasy Faire area at Disneyland, but there is another princess whose story is told in the Royal Theatre as well: my favorite Disney princess, Belle.

Though she is my favorite princess, in many ways, the story of *Beauty and the Beast* is not really Belle's story, it's the Beast's. After all, the movie opens focused on the Beast (as a prince, before he was cursed), and we learn right away about his character flaws: he is "spoiled, selfish, and unkind." Because of these shortcomings, he is cursed, being transformed into this hideous beast. He knows he must learn to love, and find someone who would love him in return before his twenty-first birthday or he would be trapped in this form forever. (There's a whole aside about how unfair it is to do this to an eleven-year-old, who is also apparently an orphan, but we won't get into that.)

The Beast

For ten years the Beast waits, hidden in his castle—now more of a prison—believing no one could ever love him. "After all, who could ever love a Beast?" It's only when Belle comes and, though afraid at first, she learns to look past his exterior—both his physical exterior and the emotional walls he's erected—and see the prince inside. She does come to love him, and he loves her. Though they are almost destroyed, in the end the curse is broken by true love. And, for a change, we do not see the prince rescuing a princess, but a peasant girl rescuing a prince.

What makes the difference? What does Belle bring that is unique among all others in the village? A story. She loves books and stories, and her mind is broadened beyond the provincial world around her, so when she meets the Beast she brings not only beauty but also a new story.

He has spent almost a decade believing that what he has been is all he can be. There is no one to love him. Life is hopeless. He believes he deserves what he's getting. Any hope he had for freedom and redemption is foolish. And then Belle brings him a new story—one that says someone can and *will* love him. The curse can be broken. He can be restored, not just to what he once was, but to a better version of himself. It just took someone new coming into his story with her own story and a new way to understand his, showing him that love is possible and hope is not foolish.

The Disciples

The day of Jesus' resurrection, on the road to a town called Emmaus two of His disciples were stuck in a story. All they could see around them was darkness, broken dreams, and shattered hopes. At that point in their story, their Messiah and King was dead. When Jesus (whom they did not recognize) came alongside them on the road and asked what they were talking about, they said:

> About Jesus of Nazareth. He was a prophet, powerful in word and deed before God and all the people. The chief priests and our rulers handed Him over to be sentenced to death, and they crucified Him; but we had hoped that He was the One who was going to redeem Israel. And what is more, it is the third day since all this took place. In addition, some of our women amazed us. They went to the tomb early this morning but didn't find his body. They came and told us that they had seen a vision of angels, who said he was alive. Then some of our companions went to the tomb and found it just as the women had said, but they did not see Jesus.[267]

Did you see it there? "...*but we had hoped*." Such a small phrase, yet so telling. They knew how the story should have gone. They knew their biggest problem. They knew the Messiah was the solution—until He wasn't. And then their hopes were crushed.

But just like Belle brought the hopeless Beast a new story, so Jesus brought these deflated disciples a new story.

> He said to them, "How foolish you are, and how slow to believe all that the prophets have spoken! Did not the Messiah have to suffer these things and then enter His glory?" And

---

[267] Luke 24:19–24

beginning with Moses and all the Prophets, He explained to them what was said in all the Scriptures concerning Himself.[268]

The facts had not changed, but their understanding of them did, because they were missing one thing: the knowledge that there was one Person who could, and had changed everything. Jesus brought His remarkable story to them and helped them see theirs in a new and better way.

You

He does the same thing for you. Like the Beast, you may have been spoiled, selfish, and unkind. You may see yourself as someone that no one could possibly love. You see the monster and believe there is nothing else you can be. So you've hidden, built walls, and tried to protect yourself.

Or like the disciples, you had hoped. Maybe you had hoped for that promotion—or just to get a job. Maybe you had hoped for a spouse who would meet your needs and fulfill your expectations. Maybe you had hoped for the resolution of a financial problem. You knew what you needed, and it didn't happen.

Whichever mirror you see yourself in, perhaps in both, Jesus has come to tell you a different story, and to give you a new understanding of your own. He says to you:

You are beautiful to Me. I can change you to be the Prince (or Princess) you were made to be, not this monster or hopeless creature you see yourself as. I love you exactly as you are. You don't have to earn it. You can't earn it. Just let Me in. I will help you to become more than you have been, more than you see yourself as, because I will put My Spirit within you. I am the answer. I am what you need. Put your trust and your hope in Me. Give Me your story and allow Me to make it into something new. There can

---

268 Luke 24:25–27

*and will be a "happily ever after." It may not be in your time or in the
way you expect, but it will come.*

True love has already broken the curse of sin and death.
Whatever the facts of your story were, they have changed because
now you can be in Christ, and in Him your story is forever new.

> **Kingdom Thinking:** Where do you see yourself more today,
> as the Beast or the disciples? Will you allow Jesus to change your
> story?

Clopin's Music Box: God's Topsy-Turvy Kingdom

With the opening of Fantasy Faire, besides the two stage shows
and princess greetings, guests will notice a few interactive elements
in the area. One of the most exceptional, and my favorite of these,
is Clopin's Music Box.

Just to the left of the entrance to the Royal Hall (where the
princesses wait to greet their guests) stands a large music box with
a hand crank on the front. As guests turn the crank, the scene
inside (which not only contains Clopin and Quasimodo, but also
many characters from other Disney animated features) is set to
motion while a music-box style version of the song Topsy-Turvy
plays. It's yet another example of one of those things Imagineers
did not have to do, but because they did, the area is so much more
enjoyable and authentic.

I'll be the first to admit that there are some very dark elements
to Disney's 1996 animated feature, *The Hunchback of Notre Dame*. At
the same time, though, it has one of the best songs to come out of
a Disney movie ("God Help the Outcasts"), and some stunning

visuals. The opening song to the movie, the same one used in the music box, sets the stage exceptionally well for what's to come in the film and its message (though not the specifics) is quite informative for us today.

In case you've never heard the song, Clopin and the crowd sing about "Topsy Turvy Day," January 6th (or "the sixth of Januervy," as the song says it), a day when the norms and social conventions of Paris are turned upside down. The humble (like the common man, and the "bums and thieves and strumpets") are celebrated, and the exalted (like kings and priests) are mocked. The people indulge in laughter, merriment, and celebration. And the highlight of the day is the crowning of the "King of Fools," the ugliest person in Paris.

It's at once entertaining and disturbing. The song is infectious and fun, but when you really listen to the lyrics, what it celebrates borders on debauchery. In spite of this, though, the concept rings a bell, so to speak, with the Bible's description of the down-and-outers.

The greatest among you will be your servant. For those who exalt themselves will be humbled, and those who humble themselves will be exalted.[269]

But many who are first will be last, and many who are last will be first.[270]

Truly I tell you, unless you change and become like little children, you will never enter the kingdom of heaven. Therefore, whoever takes the lowly position of this child is the greatest in the kingdom of heaven.[271]

---

[269] Mathew 23:11–12
[270] Matthew 19:30
[271] Matthew 18:3–4

For the message of the cross is foolishness to those who are perishing, but to us who are being saved it is the power of God. For it is written: "I will destroy the wisdom of the wise; the intelligence of the intelligent I will frustrate."...Jews demand signs and Greeks look for wisdom, but we preach Christ crucified: a stumbling block to Jews and foolishness to Gentiles, but to those whom God has called, both Jews and Greeks, Christ the power of God and the wisdom of God. For the foolishness of God is wiser than human wisdom, and the weakness of God is stronger than human strength....But God chose the foolish things of the world to shame the wise; God chose the weak things of the world to shame the strong....Therefore, as it is written: "Let the one who boasts boast in the Lord."[272]

The Kingdom of God is a "topsy-turvy" kingdom:

- The greatest among us is the servant of all.
- The humble are exalted and the exalted are humbled.
- The first are last and the last are first.
- We must become like little children to enter the kingdom.
- The message of the cross—the most profound event in history—is foolishness to those who are perishing.
- The foolish things of the world shame the wise.
- The weak things shame the strong.

Consider your own life. What do you value most? Success? Achievement? Having it "all together"? Being financially secure? Prosperity? Health? Significance? There's nothing inherently wrong with any of those, but are they your top priority? Are they what you seek after the most? Or do you prioritize time with God, service, relationships, giving, and taking risks for God?

---

[272] 1 Corinthians 1:18–31

It's not easy to live contrary to the wisdom of the world, but the wisdom you follow, the truths you accept, are an important indicator of which kingdom your heart really belongs in—God's, or the world's.

Kingdom Thinking: Consider your bank account, your discretionary time (yes, you have some), and what preoccupies your thoughts most often. Which kingdom does your heart fit most comfortably in? If it's not the one it should be, what is one step you can take to change it?

Snow White's Grotto

A Change in Perspective

There is a lovely spot off to the right of Sleeping Beauty Castle's drawbridge. For a long time, it was one of the quiet, tranquil parts of Disneyland. It's still relatively quiet—though it's become busier in recent years. It also has a history that most guests who walk by it—or even spend time there—have never heard.

Snow White's Grotto and Wishing Well opened in the Spring of 1961. The white marble statues of Snow White and the Seven Dwarfs were sculpted by an unknown Italian artist and given to Walt Disney. They create a lovely scene, but there's a problem. All eight figures are about three feet tall (Snow White is a little taller, but not much). Legendary Imagineer John Hench came up with a creative solution, one which had been and continues to be used throughout the Disney parks: forced perspective.

Set decorators set the statues some distance away, and sculpted woodland creatures to go into the scene. By putting Snow White on the top with a smaller-than-it-should-be deer next to her, arranging the dwarfs' figures lower, and a few other visual tricks, she looks much taller than they are, and the visual impression is that they are all the correct proportions—but now you know better.

We all face problems and challenges. A job we hate. A decision that seems impossible. A difficult relationship. A sin we can't seem to overcome. And when that happens, we need to do the same thing John Hench did: *force a change of perspective*. We need to look at things a little differently—or maybe a lot differently. But how?

There are three primary ways we can change our perspective: seek God's perspective, seek wise counsel, and seek a change of scenery.

1. Seek God's Perspective

Most of our perspective issues arise because we look at things through our own eyes, not God's. He has a much different view of the world than we do.

One of the best parts of being a Christian is that we can ask Him to show us that perspective. But in order to get His perspective we have to make time to read His word and seek Him in prayer.

Remember the Sermon on the Mount? Five times Jesus said, "You have heard that it was said… But I tell you…."[273] A change in perspective.

Are you suffering and experiencing trials? "Consider it pure joy, my brothers, whenever you face trials of many kinds, because you know that the testing of your faith develops perseverance. Perseverance must finish its work so that you may be mature and complete, not lacking anything."[274] A change in perspective.

---

[273] Matthew 5:21, 27, 38, and 43 (and a variant of it in 33)
[274] James 1:2–4

Would telling a "little white lie" be easier than telling the truth? "Then you will know the truth, and the truth will set you free."[275] A change in perspective.

2. Seek Wise Counsel

Sometimes we're too close to a situation, we don't have enough information, or we're overwhelmed. Whatever the reason, it is important to get counsel from others. But not just anyone—some people, though well-intentioned, just give bad advice on certain topics or issues. That's why you need to seek *wise* counsel.

Listen to advice and accept instruction, and in the end you will be wise.[276]

The way of a fool seems right to him, but a wise man listens to advice.[277]

Listen to the words of the wise;
apply your heart to my instruction.
For it is good to keep these sayings in your heart
and always ready on your lips.
I am teaching you today—yes, you—
so you will trust in the Lord.[278]

Find someone who has overcome the same issue that concerns you, and seek his wisdom. He or she has probably made a similar decision to what you need to make. Ask for their advice. Then heed it!

---

[275] John 8:32
[276] Proverbs 19:20
[277] Proverbs 12:15
[278] Proverbs 22:17–19 (NLT)

3. Seek a Change of Scenery

Sometimes we need to get away for a while to clear our heads and refocus, or see things from a different angle. It could be a walk around the block (or in a nearby park), a day trip, or a full vacation. Whatever it is, take time to get away. You will likely remember and learn from such refreshing getaways.

Kingdom Thinking: What do you need a different perspective on, and what is one step you will take today to get it?

Pixie Hollow

Dwelling Among Us

One of the most important aspects of Disneyland's three-dimensional storytelling is that the guests must believably "step into the story." Most of the time the transition into the narrative is subtle and unnoticeable, but at other times it is obvious.

Pixie Hollow is one of the latter. Remember, pixies (like Tinker Bell) are tiny creatures. If we were to try to meet her or her friends all at our normal sizes, we'd hardly be able to see her, much less take a photo with her or get an autograph. So Disney Imagineers have made sure that will not be a problem.

As you walk the path—or wait in the line—for Pixie Hollow, you may notice that the landscaping around you gets larger and larger, until eventually the blades of grass are gigantic, towering over you. The landscape is getting larger and you are shrinking! Only then are you the proper size to meet Tink, Rosetta, Fawn, Silver Mist, and the others.

In order to meet them we must "shrink down" and become part of their world. In order to save fallen humanity, Jesus had to do the same.

In the beginning was the Word, and the Word was with God, and the Word was God. He was with God in the beginning....The Word became flesh and made His dwelling among us.[279]

Let this same attitude and purpose and [humble] mind be in you which was in Christ Jesus: [Let Him be your example in humility:]

Who, although being essentially one with God and in the form of God [possessing the fullness of the attributes which make God, God], did not think this equality with God was a thing to be eagerly grasped or retained,

But stripped Himself [of all privileges and rightful dignity], so as to assume the guise of a servant (slave), in that He became like men and was born a human being.

And after He had appeared in human form, He abased and humbled Himself [still further] and carried His obedience to the extreme of death, even the death of the cross![280]

Since the children have flesh and blood, He too shared in their humanity so that by His death He might destroy him who holds the power of death—that is, the devil—and free those who all their lives were held in slavery by their fear of death....For this reason He had to be made like His brothers in every way, in order that He might become a merciful and faithful high priest in service to God, and that He might make atonement for the sins of the people. Because He Himself

---

[279] John 1:1–2, 14a
[280] Philippians 2:5–8 (AMP)

suffered when He was tempted, He is able to help those who are being tempted.[281]

Just as we shrink down to the size of pixies and become part of their world, Jesus lowered Himself to share in our humanity for a much grander purpose. He did it to save us from our sins and provide the way for us to be reconciled to God. What greater purpose is there?

Kingdom Thinking: Have you ever had to "lower yourself" to help someone on their level? Is there someone who needs you to?

Matterhorn Bobsleds

Redemption

The Matterhorn's placement at Disneyland is unique, straddling two lands (Fantasyland and Tomorrowland). But the story of its origin is even more intriguing.

In 1954, when the moat for Sleeping Beauty Castle was being excavated, the dirt was piled up behind the castle. Removing the dirt from the site would have been too expensive, so Walt Disney had a fence built around it, and it was called "Holiday Hill." At first, it consisted of mostly dirt, but that would get blown around during windstorms. So Bill Evans' groundskeeping team landscaped it with some shrubs and sod to hold the dirt in place.

---

[281] Hebrews 2:14–18

When the Magic Skyway was being built, the hill became the location of a large steel support tower. It did the job, but it was something of an eyesore. So Walt talked about some possibilities with Admiral Joe Fowler (the man Fowler's Harbor at Disneyland was named after), and eventually the Matterhorn, the first tubular steel continuous track roller coaster in the world, was born.

What started as dirt in an unwanted place turned into a large mound of dirt, which became a landscaped mound of dirt—and briefly a lookout point—then part of a support system for another attraction, to finally a landmark attraction of its own—one of the very first E-ticket attractions! The dirt started with little to no value, and over time, with hard work and purposeful perspective, it became something of incredible value.

What do we call it when something that has little to no intrinsic value is given worth? Think of a coupon. A little piece of paper that by itself is worth nothing, but can become worth money— sometimes a lot of money. What is that process called? Redemption.

We redeem a coupon. We redeem wasted time to make it useful. The mound of dirt that was Holiday Hill was redeemed (through a process) to become one of the most recognizable landmarks in the park, the Matterhorn. And through Christ, our lives are also redeemed.

> For you know that it was not with perishable things such as silver or gold that you were redeemed from the empty way of life handed down to you from your forefathers, but with the precious blood of Christ, a lamb without blemish or defect.[282]

> For He has rescued us from the dominion of darkness and brought us into the kingdom of the Son He loves, in whom we have redemption, the forgiveness of sins.[283]

---

[282] 1 Peter 1:18–19
[283] Colossians 1:13–14

Everything that we are, we owe to God's unique creation. He gives us meaning, purpose, salvation, and eternal life. For one of God's creatures to truly make a difference, to live a life that matters and not just resemble rats in a maze, first requires that God redeems us. That redemption is what takes our lives and gives them real value.

You have value because you are God's child, "a chosen people, a royal priesthood, a holy nation, a people belonging to God, that you may declare the praises of Him who called you out of darkness into His wonderful light."[284] How much more valuable could you ever want to or hope to be?

Just as it was a process to go from the dirt behind the castle to Holiday Hill to the Matterhorn, so our being redeemed is a process. In 1 Corinthians 1:18, Paul says, "For the message of the cross is foolishness to those who are perishing, but to us who are being saved it is the power of God."

Did you see it? "...to us who *are being* saved." It's a process. And no matter where you are in that process, God won't quit. He won't give up on you. In fact, "He who began a good work in you will carry it on to completion until the day of Christ Jesus."[285]

You may think you are just a mound of dirt, but if you are a child of God, you have value because you have been redeemed. He is shaping you into something special. Live out that new life of value, not to earn God's favor, but because you already have it!

Kingdom Thinking: What is one way you've seen that God has redeemed something in your life?

---

[284] 1 Peter 2:9
[285] Philippians 1:6

Choosing Fantasy or the Future

When a culture's general outlook on life is positive, science fiction is popular. When that outlook is negative, fantasy is popular. Looking to the future—even a fictional one—means embracing change. Looking to fantasy means clinging to the way you perceive things to be, and being unwilling to change.

Leadership author and speaker John Maxwell has said, "People change when they hurt enough that they have to, when they learn enough that they want to, and when they receive enough that they are able to." Are you choosing to look to embrace change or hold tightly to fantasy, which provides an illusion of stability?

The Matterhorn stands at that point of decision: hope and looking to the future, or retreat into the perceived safety of fantasy. It is the only current ride that straddles two lands (there were four Autopias, but each was an entirely separate attraction, so that doesn't count). Interestingly, the only other ride (which is no longer in existence) to exist in two lands covered the same two lands: the Magic Skyway.

On the Fantasyland side of the Matterhorn, riders experience a lot of curves. The track twists and turns back on itself. But there are very few surprises: only a couple of small dips, and no real drops. Of the two tracks it is the smoother and it feels slower.

The Tomorrowland side has fewer curves, but more dips, and even a couple of respectable drops. It's the rougher of the two tracks, and it feels faster (though there is really no difference in speed on average).

In much the same way, the choices between fantasy and the future amount to choices between a perception of safety and security versus a perception of greater risk. But the truth is, both are risky in their own way. Clinging to perceived safety means not stepping out, not growing, not progressing and becoming the person God made you to be. It means a life half-lived. Moving into the future means risking change, even possible failure. But it also means growing into the person God designed you to be. A life fully lived.

Read Hebrews 11 and notice how often faith is connected with action verbs.

> By faith Abel offered God a better sacrifice.
> By faith Noah…built an ark.
> By faith Abraham…obeyed and went.

> And what more shall I say? I do not have time to tell about Gideon, Barak, Samson, Jephthah, David, Samuel and the prophets, who through faith conquered kingdoms, administered justice, and gained what was promised; who shut the mouths of lions, quenched the fury of the flames, and escaped the edge of the sword; whose weakness was turned to strength; and who became powerful in battle and routed foreign armies. Women received back their dead, raised to life again. Others were tortured and refused to be released, so that they might gain a better resurrection. Some faced jeers and flogging, while still others were chained and put in prison. They were stoned; they were sawed in two; they were put to death by the sword. They went about in sheepskins and goatskins, destitute, persecuted and mistreated—the world was not worthy of them.[286]

Of course, there are times to "wait on the Lord," but that's different from just playing it safe, clinging to the illusion of security, refusing to follow Jesus out of a fear of risk. Sometimes it means persevering. Sometimes it means sacrificing our own plans. Always it means trusting that "we know that in all things God works for the good of those who love Him, who have been called according to His purpose."[287]

---

[286] Hebrews 11:32–38
[287] Romans 8:28

> **Kingdom Thinking:** Which do you choose? Fantasy or the future? Perceived safety or risking in faith?

Alice in Wonderland

Making Sense of "Curiouser and Curiouser"

Around the corner from the main dark rides in Fantasyland is a unique one: Alice in Wonderland. It's the only attraction that has an outside as well as an inside portion. It was not an Opening Day attraction, but it came relatively soon after, in 1958. Even with the changes made in the 1983 Fantasyland refurbishment (thirty-two years after the film's release), the ride uses all new narration (not recycled from the animated feature), voiced by Kathryn Beaumont, who was also the voice of Alice in the movie.

In both the Lewis Carroll story and the Disney animated feature, Alice falls down a rabbit hole, changes size unexpectedly (and repeatedly), and attends a tea party given by a March Hare. Along the way, she meets such unusual characters as the Mad Hatter, the Caterpillar, the Cheshire Cat, the Red Queen, and others. Alice is sure this is not the real world because things get "curiouser and curiouser"—they just don't make sense.

But who ever said life would make sense all the time?

Each time Faye or I lost a job—and there have been a few times—I've tended to try to immediately look for the reason for the timing of the job loss, or why we ever landed those jobs to begin with.

"If you'd still been working at that preschool, we wouldn't have been able to move where we did, and you wouldn't be going to the school where you are."

"If I hadn't been at that company while I was, I would have never learned the basics of accounting."

You know what? I've given up on trying to figure out *why* any more. Oh sure, I still think about it, but it doesn't bother me nearly as much when I do not have a definitive answer. Sometimes it's obvious right away; most of the time it is not. And it does not have to be. Even biblical prophecy nearly always made sense only after the fulfillment.

But life does not have to make sense for me to trust that God is in control. I don't have to understand exactly what is happening to know that God is working through it all. In fact, if I only trust Him when life makes sense, what good is that?

Great is our Lord and of great power; His understanding is inexhaustible and boundless.[288]

And we know that in all things God works for the good of those who love Him, who have been called according to his purpose.[289]

When life gets "curiouser and curiouser," you really can trust that God is not surprised by anything that's happening, and even though you may never understand it fully, He will use those experiences for your good if you trust Him.

Kingdom Thinking: When have you thought you had something "all figured out," only to discover later that God had a completely different way to use that event or circumstance?

[288] Psalm 147:5 (AMP)
[289] Romans 8:28

Mad Tea Party

Where is Your Focus?

One of my favorite rides in Fantasyland is the Mad Tea Party, aka "the teacups" aka "how can you possibly ride that thing without getting nauseous?" Fantasyland has at least two attractions and one shop dedicated to the animated feature *Alice's Adventures in Wonderland*. The actual Alice in Wonderland attraction did not open until June of 1958, but the Mad Tea Party was an Opening Day attraction, though in a slightly different place than it is now. (It used to be where the carousel currently sits, and the carousel was farther forward, closer to the castle.)

The reason most people seem to dislike the attraction is that it makes them very dizzy, or they just don't like spinning. I kind of like being dizzy and I think spinning is fun (whatever that may say about me). I've also learned a secret to keep from getting dizzy. The trick is to have someone sitting across from you and staring at their left shoulder the entire ride. Keep your eyes locked there and you generally won't get dizzy (or the dizziness will be slight). You can probably look other places too, but the left shoulder has always worked for me. Of course, this requires having someone willing to ride with you. That's always the challenge for me.

How many times in life do we feel like things are spinning out of control and we're caught in the middle, whirling, getting dizzy and nauseous? What do we do in times like that? The same thing we do when riding the teacups: fix our eyes on one unchanging point that goes with us through the madness. But what point is that?

Hebrews chapter 4 says:

Let us fix our eyes on Jesus, the author and perfecter of our faith, who for the joy set before Him endured the cross, scorning its shame, and sat down at the right hand of the throne of God. Consider him who endured such opposition from sinful men so that you will not become weary and lose heart.[290]

The only way to endure the chaos is to keep our eyes fixed on Him. He is in the midst of it all, "riding with us," and has promised not to abandon us.

Something else I have noticed about the Mad Tea Party is that when you are riding in it, it feels completely random, and the movement almost senseless. All you know when you're on it is that you're spinning wildly, almost out of control. But when viewed from outside—especially from above—there is an order and a pattern to the movements. Our lives are the same way. They may feel random, directionless, confusing, and even sickening. We may search, but find no pattern. And yet, it is there. In the midst of the frenzy, we must trust Him whose ways are higher than our ways, and Whose thoughts are higher than our thoughts. He has a view we do not…yet.

We may still get a little dizzy on the ride sometimes; Jesus never promised us an easy one. But He did promise to be right there with us. If we do not consciously, intentionally, and regularly fix our eyes on Him, though, how will we ever know?

Kingdom Thinking: What is one way you can intentionally "fix your eyes on Jesus"?

---

[290] Hebrews 12:2–3

Storybook Land Canal Boats

Created to Create

Creating has been on my mind a lot lately. I just finished creating the website for my wife Faye's massage therapy business, Crane Massage Therapy. A friend of ours, Jarrod Huntington (the same person who created the original *Faith and the Magic Kingdom* logo seen at the beginning of each chapter), had started it, and I used his formatting as the basis for the layout of many of the pages. However, much of it—the backgrounds, links, text color, etc.—is my creation, and I spent many hours creating it. It was the first site I've created since about 1999 or so, and I'm quite pleased with it.

Now, when it comes to Disneyland, obviously the whole park is Walt Disney's creation. But when I think about the park, there is one attraction that really stands out in its connection to Walt Disney and his passion to create: Storybook Land Canal Boats.

Walt loved miniatures. Jim Korkis (writing as Wade Sampson), says, "Walt's mind started focusing on the magic of a perfect miniature world when he saw the famous Thorne exhibit of miniatures at the Golden Gate International Exposition in San Francisco, Calif., in 1939."[291] In 1949, he created a miniature called Granny's Cabin. It was that project, that plan, that led to Disneyland itself.

When it comes to Disneyland, much of the park is created in varying scales, creating forced perspective. However, the one attraction that features miniatures *as* miniatures is Storybook Land. Passengers take an outdoor boat ride through a winding canal featuring diminutive settings from recreated Disney animated films.

---

[291] Wade Simpson, "The Disneylandia Story Part One," http://www.mouseplanet.com/9370/The_Disneylandia_Story_Part_One, accessed August 7, 2013.

When considering God, the first thing we learn about Him as we read the Bible is that He creates. "In the beginning, God created,"[292] and later in the creation account we read that when God created humanity, He created us in His image[293]—what theologians call the *imago Dei*. The Bible is never very clear about exactly what this means, but it apparently encompasses several aspects, among them: the ability to choose to love, spiritual awareness, rationality, complex language, and creativity.

Theologian Wayne A. Grudem describes how the image of God distinguishes humans from the rest of creation:

Our likeness to God is also illustrated by our use of complex, abstract language; our awareness of the distant future; and the entire spectrum of human creative activity in such areas as art, music, literature, and science. Such aspects of human existence reveal the ways in which we differ from animals absolutely, not merely in degree. Furthermore, the degree and complexity of human emotions indicate just how vast is the difference between humankind and the rest of creation.[294]

Human ability and desire to create reflects our being made in the image of the Creator. Whether it's painting, sculpting, music, architecture, writing, dance, website design, or whatever method of creative expression there might be, it can be used as an expression of love and praise for God. Such works bring glory to Him, not only in the subject matter but also by simply reflecting His glory in the act of creating.

Storybook Land Canal Boats is a fairly small ride in Fantasyland, but it gives us one of our best glimpses into the mind

---

[292] Genesis 1:1a

[293] Genesis 1:26–27

[294] Wayne A. Grudem, *Bible Doctrine: Essential Teachings of the Christian Faith*, ed. Jeff Purswell (Grand Rapids, MI: Zondervan, 1999), 192.

and heart of Walt Disney, and it reminds us that we create because we are made in the image of our Creator.

> **Kingdom Thinking:** As you live out your life, how are you reflecting the image of God? How is the *imago Dei* evident in your life?

Three Little Pigs and Fear

After passing through Monstro the Whale (it's not as bad as it sounds), one of the first vignettes guests come to is of three little houses—one made of straw, one made of sticks, and one made of "wolf-proof bricks."

Most everyone is familiar with the story of the *Three Little Pigs*, especially as told in the 1933 Silly Symphony. Now, as is often the case, the story we see in the short film is somewhat different from the original story, but we'll just go with the Disney version.

The story begins with one little pig building his house with straw, the second pig with sticks, and the third with bricks. The first two just want to get the job done so they can play their flute and fiddle and have fun. But the third one knows the danger that's coming and keeps building his brick house.

The Big Bad Wolf comes and, of course, blows the first house down. The lone scared little pig runs to his brother's house of sticks. It takes a bit more effort, but the wolf blows that one down, too.

So the two scared (and homeless) little pigs run to the brick house of their brother. In here they are safe, but when the wolf comes after them, they cower under the bed. The wolf tries trickery, force, and an attempt to come down the chimney, but in every case the Big Bad Wolf is thwarted.

The first two pigs (in later shorts named Fiddler Pig and Fifer Pig) were traumatized and their security destroyed, but then they sought refuge in the strong house their brother (Practical Pig) built. When the wolf attacked, Practical Pig took even further steps to protect his brothers. And yet every time they felt threatened, they hid, not trusting in the more secure house or in their brother.

We do the same thing, don't we? We start out on our own, building our house with the materials we have in our own strength and resources—flimsy as that house may be. Then problems arrive with a fury and our house collapses around us.

So we turn to others, to systems, ideas, programs, or people who seem like they have it more together than we do. That goes a little better, and we find some value in them. But ultimately the wolf comes back and that house crumbles, too.

Finally we run to our Brother, Jesus, and the house He made. We take refuge in Him and His word. We hear His words and put them into practice. We live there with Him as our strength and our shield.

Then the wolf comes. Calamity strikes and what do we do? We hide in fear. We are *safe* in His house, and nothing can truly harm us. Sure, we still face pain and suffering, challenges and setbacks, but our hope and our future is secure. We have His strength and do not have to trust in our own. We have His wisdom and guidance and do not have to be in control of everything and have a backup plan for the backup plan.

Yet still we hide. Still we fear. We fear that the house will once again crumble.

Who shall separate us from the love of Christ? Shall trouble or hardship or persecution or famine or nakedness or danger or sword? As it is written:

"For your sake we face death all day long; we are considered as sheep to be slaughtered."

No, in all these things we are more than conquerors through Him who loved us. For I am convinced that neither death nor life, neither angels nor demons, neither the present nor the future, nor any powers, neither height nor depth, nor anything else in all creation, will be able to separate us from the love of God that is in Christ Jesus our Lord.[295]

Nothing can separate us from His love. Nothing can separate us from *Him*. He is our strong tower, our fortress, our house of bricks.

Kingdom Thinking: What do you still fear that now holds no real threat to you because you are in Christ?

Diamond in the Rough

One of the most striking scenes in Storybook Land is the city of Agrabah and the Sultan's Palace from *Aladdin*. Obviously not available when the attraction first had its miniatures installed (since they debuted on June 16, 1956, and the movie premiered in 1992), this scene was one of several added in 1994. It replaced Toad Hall, which moved to another location about a year later.

The principal lesson of Aladdin is basically "Don't judge a book by its cover." By all appearances, Aladdin is worthless in the eyes of his society: an orphan, vagrant, and a thief. He is clever, but that only gets him in trouble. He has a good heart, but does not have an opportunity to show it until he meets Jasmine.

---

[295] Romans 8:35–39

In the city of Agrabah below, he is merely a street rat. In the palace above he pretends to be Prince Ali, a show to impress others, but not true to who he is. He loses his way, as most of us do at one time or another, but the truth of his character is first revealed when he passes the test at the Cave of Wonders. Here its depth is shown when he risks his life to save Jasmine and the Sultan and then uses his last wish to grant the Genie his freedom.

It is easy to judge by appearances or actions. In both cases, we can easily be wrong. Appearances can be deceiving. Actions can have roots, causes, and circumstances surrounding them that we don't see or understand.

Before God selected David as king over Israel, Jesse paraded his taller, stronger sons before the prophet Samuel.

Do not consider his appearance or his height, for I have rejected him. The Lord does not look at the things man looks at. Man looks at the outward appearance, but the Lord looks at the heart.[296]

Judging by the heart and not by appearances does not mean we can never have an opinion, or even call a brother or sister in Christ on sin when we see it, though that should be done carefully and with grace and love. What it does mean is that it is usually wiser to give people the benefit of the doubt. Give people the chance to surprise you in a good way.

And don't assume that someone is worthless. Everyone has value to God, including you.

Kingdom Thinking: Have you ever been surprised by someone who turned out to be "a diamond in the rough"?

---

[296] 1 Samuel 16:7

Do You Trust Me?

On Storybook Land Canal Boats, after floating past the city of Agrabah, we float under some archways. These represent the "A Whole New World" scene in the movie. These two vignettes together remind us of one all-important question: "Do you trust me?"

Aladdin asks Jasmine this question twice, once in the marketplace and once in his guise as Prince Ali. In the first, they are fleeing the guards and he asks her to risk a jump that seems insane and impossible. He reaches out his hand, looks her in the eye, and asks that fateful question. She says she does, then proves it as she takes his hand and they jump to safety—a safety she could not see but he knew was there.

The second time, Jasmine has become frustrated one too many times and yells at him in frustration to jump off the balcony. He does, onto his flying carpet. Of course, she's captivated and wishes she could fly on it. He offers and she hesitates, so once again he reaches out his hand, looks her in the eye, and asks that fateful question. She says she does, takes his hand, and steps onto that wondrous carpet.

The instant he asks that question the second time, she recognizes him.

Jesus asks us that same question every day, often many times a day. It's easy to say yes in times of ease. It may even be easy to say yes when it seems we have no other choice. We're backed into a corner and His way appears to be the only way out.

But when we have a choice, He still holds out His hand and asks, "Do you trust Me?" And then we must decide—play it safe or jump? Try our own way or choose His way? Be confident in His presence or panic and doubt?

The Lord is a refuge for the oppressed,
a stronghold in times of trouble.

Those who know Your name will trust in You,
for You, Lord, have never forsaken those who seek You.[297]

How do we answer when Christ asks:

In times of trouble, do you trust Me?

Trust in the Lord with all your heart
and lean not on your own understanding;
in all your ways acknowledge Him,
and He will make your paths straight.[298]

When it's easier to take matters into your own hands, do you trust Me?

Some trust in chariots and some in horses,
but we trust in the name of the Lord our God.[299]

Do you rely on your own strength and resources, or do you trust Me?

When I am afraid,
I will trust in You.
In God, whose word I praise,
in God I trust; I will not be afraid.
What can mortal man do to me?[300]

When you are afraid, do you trust Me?

May the God of hope fill you with all joy and peace as you trust
in Him, so that you may overflow with hope by the power of
the Holy Spirit.[301]

---

[297] Psalm 9:9–10
[298] Proverbs 3:5–6
[299] Psalm 20:7
[300] Psalm 56:3–4
[301] Romans 15:13

When you're lacking joy and peace, do you try to find them with temporary pleasures and happiness, or do you trust Me?

These archways are a reminder that we can discover "A Whole New World" with Jesus, a life we always wanted but never dreamed was possible. Let us answer that fateful question with an enthusiastic "Yes," every time He asks.

> **Kingdom Thinking:** Like almost everything else in the Christian life, this mindset is a process, a journey. So, how can you choose to say "Yes" one more time today than you did yesterday?

Cinderella's Choices

The village and castle from Cinderella dominates its section of Storybook Land Canal Boats. And that's as it should be. After all, Cinderella has her own castle as the centerpiece of the Magic Kingdom in Walt Disney World. At least she gets something permanent here in the Original Magic Kingdom.

Often considered "just another one of the princesses," Cinderella has some special character qualities that make her stand out as a role model.

Her Choice of Attitude

Cinderella is treated cruelly by her stepmother and stepsisters. They are unfair to her, unkind to her, even mean to her (vile may be a more apt description). She could become sullen or respond hatefully. But she doesn't. Instead, Cinderella chooses to be kind and polite. She serves—not always entirely by choice, but still, she does even though she has other options. At the very least, she could have tried to run away or harm those who were treating her so terribly.

> Do not repay anyone evil for evil. Be careful to do what is right in the eyes of everybody. If it is possible, as far as it depends on you, live at peace with everyone.[302]

Her Choice of Work Ethic

Cinderella has every reason to complain about her circumstances and to refuse to do anything. Her tasks are dirty and demeaning. You may not be aware, but in the original Brothers Grimm fairy tale, her given name is not mentioned. Her stepsisters gave her the name "Cinderella" ("Ashputtel" in the original language). As the story goes, "Besides this, the sisters did her every imaginable injury—they mocked her and emptied her peas and lentils into the ashes, so that she was forced to sit and pick them out again. In the evening when she had worked till she was weary she had no bed to go to, but had to sleep by the fireside in the ashes. And as on that account she always looked dusty and dirty, they called her Cinderella."[303]

Instead of refusing to do work that was "beneath her" or not wanting to work for people who were unkind to her, she did her work constructively and often even cheerfully.

> Whatever you do, work at it with all your heart, as working for the Lord, not for men, since you know that you will receive an

---

[302] Romans 12:17–18

[303] Jacob Grimm, Wilhelm Grimm, *The Harvard Classics*, vol. 17 ed. Charles W. Eliot (New York: P.F. Collier & Sons, 1909), 98.

inheritance from the Lord as a reward. It is the Lord Christ you are serving.[304]

Her Choice of "Destiny"

With all the odds that were against her, Cinderella could easily have given up hope. When the announcement was made that a ball was being held so the prince could choose his princess, she wanted to go, just as every other eligible lady in the kingdom did. But she had every reason to ignore her dream. Her family would never let her go. She had no dress (especially after they destroyed it). She had no time. Why would he choose a scullery maid anyway?

But she chose hope and stepped up to pursue her dream. She tried to dress for the ball. When she was shoved down she got some help from a new friend—her Fairy Godmother. Even then she could have declined the Fairy Godmother's offer, but she didn't. She accepted—not knowing how it was possible or what would happen—and went to the ball. When the prince came looking for the woman whose foot fit the glass slipper, she stepped forward and claimed what she had dreamed of.

There's no Bible verse I know of that describes this explicitly, but Nehemiah is a great example of an underdog looking to God for help. After an extended time of prayer seeking God's will and his own role in it, this is the last line of his prayer before going to the king:

O Lord, let Your ear be attentive to the prayer of this Your servant and to the prayer of your servants who delight in revering Your Name. Give Your servant success today by granting him favor in the presence of this man.[305]

---

[304] Colossians 3:23–24
[305] Nehemiah 1:11

Then he went to the king, made his requests, and when they were granted (which was by no means a sure thing), he acted!

Kingdom Thinking: In which of these three ways—attitude, work ethic, or destiny—do you need to be more like Cinderella?

The Old Mill

The Old Mill, a 1937 animated short film produced by Walt Disney, is one of the last scenes in Storybook Land. In case you've never seen it, the film shows a community of animals living in and around an old abandoned windmill in the country, and how they deal with a violent thunderstorm.

This Silly Symphony was, among other things, a way for the animators to experiment with new techniques and technology. *The Old Mill* is most notable for employing the first use of the multiplane camera. (According to Wikipedia, "The multiplane camera is a special motion picture camera used in the traditional animation process that moves a number of pieces of artwork past the camera at various speeds and at various distances from one another. This creates a three-dimensional effect.")

The most striking thing (to me) in this short is the way the animals count on the cartoon's namesake. When the weather is calm, they rest at the Old Mill. When it turns violent they take refuge there. Sure, the mill gets battered, but ultimately it serves well as protection for these creatures.

As the Old Mill was for the animals, God is for us. He is much sturdier (if one can use that term for God) than the windmill, of course, but still, He is where we rest in the calm times and seek refuge in times of trouble.

Find rest, O my soul, in God alone;
my hope comes from Him.
He alone is my rock and my salvation;
He is my fortress, I will not be shaken.
My salvation and my honor depend on God;
He is my mighty rock, my refuge.
Trust in Him at all times, O people;
pour out your hearts to Him,
for God is our refuge.[306]

Just imagine how much trouble the animals would have been in had they not stayed close to the Old Mill. When times were good and the weather was calm, they could have wandered off. But what would have become of them when the storm struck? Would they have made it back in time? Would they have been able to find shelter elsewhere? Perhaps, but then again, perhaps not.

What do you do and where do you go when times are good? Do you stay and find your rest in God, rejoicing in what He has provided and drawing comfort and strength from His presence? Or do you wander off, only to get caught in one of life's storms and then running to try to find your way back to Him in the darkness?

Kingdom Thinking: The Old Mill stands as a reminder of our place of peace, security, strength, and faith. Which of those do you most need today? Are you seeking to find it in God, or somewhere else?

---

[306] Psalm 62:5–8

"it's a small world"

The Need for Unity and a Prayer for Peace

"it's a small world" (stylized in quotes and lowercased by The Walt Disney Company) was originally conceived of and introduced as one of four attractions Walt Disney (or his Imagineers) designed for the 1964–65 New York World's Fair—this one for the Pepsi pavilion.

The ride was originally titled "Children of the World." When Uncle Walt demonstrated it to songwriters Robert and Richard Sherman, the ride's soundtrack featured numerous national anthems all playing at once, which resulted in a cacophony. Walt said, "I need one song." In response, the Sherman Brothers wrote "it's a small world," a single theme song for the ride that could be easily translated into many different languages.

The Sherman Brothers' first version of the song was played as a ballad. Walt requested something more cheerful, so the song was sped up and sung as a round. At the first presentation to Walt, the brothers performed the song while walking through a scale model of the attraction, singing and clapping their hands. Walt was delighted, and that song became the famous "it's a small world (after all)" tune.

At the D23 "Destination D: Disneyland '55" event in September 2010, event attendees had the privilege of hearing Richard Sherman tell us about writing the story, and even playing and singing a portion of it in that balladic form in which it was originally conceived. He also shared with us that when he and his brother wrote it, they had in mind "a prayer for peace for the children of the world." It may be an earworm as is, but as a ballad it is a beautiful song. Consider the lyrics:

It's a world of laughter,
A world or tears
It's a world of hopes,
And a world of fears.
There's so much that we share
That it's time we're aware
It's a small world after all.

CHORUS:
It's a small world after all
It's a small world after all
It's a small world after all
It's a small, small world

There is just one moon and one golden sun
And a smile means friendship to everyone.
Though the mountains divide
And the oceans are wide
It's a small, small world.

(chorus)

Let's consider the context again. The song idea for this attraction had been every country's children singing their own national anthem, which resulted in a cacophony. Walt wanted "one song" to unify them. That song was a prayer for peace. Does this remind you of anything?

You are all sons of God through faith in Christ Jesus, for all of you who were baptized into Christ have clothed yourselves with Christ. There is neither Jew nor Greek, slave nor free, male nor female, for you are all one in Christ Jesus. If you belong to Christ, then you are Abraham's seed, and heirs according to the promise.[307]

May they be brought to complete unity to let the world know that You sent Me and have loved them even as You have loved Me.[308]

Blessed are the peacemakers, for they will be called sons of God.[309]

Glory to God in the highest, and on earth peace to men on whom His favor rests.[310]

His purpose was to create in Himself one new man out of the two, thus making peace, and in this one body to reconcile both of them to God through the cross, by which He put to death their hostility. He came and preached peace to you who were far away and peace to those who were near. For through Him we both have access to the Father by one Spirit.[311]

There is one body and one Spirit—just as you were called to one hope when you were called—one Lord, one faith, one baptism; one God and Father of all, Who is over all and through all and in all.[312]

One of the consistent and powerful messages of the gospel is our unity in Christ. Not just unity for its own sake, but unity in Jesus and through Him to draw and point people to the Father.

---

[307] Galatians 3:27–29
[308] John 17:23b
[309] Matthew 5:9
[310] Luke 2:14
[311] Ephesians 2:15b–18
[312] Ephesians 4:4–6

Much of "it's a small world" highlights diversity between cultures and nations. But if the song they sang had been their own national anthems, all hope for unity within the attraction would be gone. It is only when the children all sing the same song—even at the times when it is uniquely their own, because they sing it in their own language part of the time—that the attraction can work.

Sure, human beings have obvious differences, and that's OK. But those differences must never be allowed to divide us. We can sing the "same song" with our own unique variations, as long as it is the same song! Or, "In essentials unity; in nonessentials liberty; in all things love [or charity]."[313]

"it's a small world" is a song that prays for peace for the children of the world. Our unity in Christ allows us to do the same, and we know the prayer will one day be answered fully. Next time this song is stuck in your head, consider it in its original form, and make it a prayer.

Kingdom Thinking: When it comes to fellow Christians, do you focus more on what divides us or what unites us?

---

[313] Though it has been used in other places and times and has been historically attributed to a seventeenth-century theologian, this saying is perhaps most famous as a motto for the Restoration (Stone-Campbell) Movement.

Fantasyland Theatre

Mickey and the Magical Map: Too Determined to Ask the Right Questions?

"Mickey and the Magical Map," a new show that debuted May 25, 2013, features a return of two Disney traditions—one admittedly older than the other.

The newer of the two involves the venue. The Fantasyland Theater originally opened in 1985, and in a strange way owes its existence to *Captain EO*, the 3D sci-fi film starring Michael Jackson. When the Magic Eye Theater where *Captain EO* was to be shown was being built, it took the place of the Space Stage, and that left Disneyland without a venue for hosting large open-air concerts. To solve this problem, Imagineers built Videopolis (which has absolutely nothing to do with the Fantasyland theme, but that's where they put it anyway).

Videopolis offered loud and rambunctious nighttime concerts, and was extremely popular at first, especially with teenage guests. Over the next several years, though, its popularity waned, and in the early 1990s Disney used the venue to try out a new-but-old form of in-park entertainment: the stage show. That show was even more well-received, and in 1995 it sported a new name: the Fantasyland Theater. (Even that name was a nod to the past; the Mickey Mouse Club Theater—which sat where Pinocchio's Daring Journey is now—held that moniker from 1964–81.)

In 2006, the Fantasyland Theater closed and was replaced by the Princess Fantasy Faire, but now that the Fantasy Faire has a new home (sans the "Princess" part of the name) to the west of the Central Hub, near Sleeping Beauty Castle, the Fantasyland Theatre, now with a slightly different spelling to the latter word, made its triumphant return in May of 2013.

The other returning Disney tradition is much older. When Mickey Mouse debuted in *Steamboat Willie* back in 1928, he was a mischievous little character, and that continued for years. But with his increasing popularity, he was recharacterized as an "everyman," and today is often seen more as a corporate icon than a relatable character. In "Mickey and the Magical Map," Mickey returns to his adventurous and mischievous roots, but still with the same heart and dreams that made fans root for him for more than eight decades.

In case you have not yet seen the show, I'll keep this section mostly spoiler-free. The basic premise of the show is that Mickey Mouse is back as the Sorcerer's Apprentice, and Sorcerer Yen Sid has created a magical map (hence the show's title) that can "transport dreamers to any place imaginable." The map is incomplete, though. Because Mickey is only an apprentice, he takes this as his golden opportunity. If he can just paint the unfinished spot on the map, he's sure Yen Sid will make him a Map Maker.

He tries his best, chasing the spot all over the map—and into the map, through scenes and songs from Disney animated features. Mickey is persistent, determined, even conniving at times—sneaking up on the spot, trying to overpower it or trick it. [As a side note, anywhere other than in a Disney production, everything I just said in describing this plot would make no sense at all. Here, it is completely logical.]

Eventually, he manages to trap the spot so he can paint it—I'm sure this will come as no surprise or spoiler to you—and declares, "Gotcha! I'm gonna paint you, like it or not! I've just gotta be a Map Maker!"

There's more to the story, of course, but that line jumped out at me. Have you ever been that way? There's something you want to do, something you think you should do—you may even imagine how great things would be if only you could do this one thing. All the doors it could open! All the problems it could solve! All the ways you could serve!

The apostle Paul had something similar happen to him on one of his missionary journeys. We read of it in Acts 16.

Paul and his companions traveled throughout the region of Phrygia and Galatia, having been kept by the Holy Spirit from preaching the word in the province of Asia. When they came to the border of Mysia, they tried to enter Bithynia, but the Spirit of Jesus would not allow them to. So they passed by Mysia and went down to Troas. During the night Paul had a vision of a man of Macedonia standing and begging him, "Come over to Macedonia and help us." After Paul had seen the vision, we got ready at once to leave for Macedonia, concluding that God had called us to preach the gospel to them.[314]

Paul knew where he wanted to go, what he wanted to do, and who he wanted to help. But God kept putting obstacles in his way, things to slow him down and redirect him. Finally, God sent him a vision of where He actually wanted Paul to go next. I don't know why He didn't tell him right away. Maybe Paul wasn't ready to listen, being so fixated on his plan that God had to get his attention first. Whatever the reason, when Paul was ready, God said, "OK, Paul. Here's what I want you to do," and Paul and his companions immediately changed their plans.

Later in life, Paul was more open to that kind of redirection and interruption. In Romans 15,[315] Paul tells the church in Rome that he really wants to come visit them, and he plans to do just that. It will be wonderful when he can finally make it to Rome, but he has been given another assignment first. In spite of what he wants to do, he's going to go where God has directed him. He has learned to listen for that voice and obey the direction he's been given.

What about you? I'm sure you have dreams and plans, goals and ideas. I do, too. But are you open to being interrupted? Do you continue to fight so hard for that thing you've just "gotta be (or do, or see)" that God cannot redirect you? He keeps trying to

---

[314] Acts 16:6–10
[315] Romans 15:22–32

get your attention, but are you so focused on the spot that you can't see it?

Maybe you're moving full-speed ahead now. If so, that's great. But if you are encountering obstacles, how are you assessing them? One error is to assume that every obstacle is a sign from God you should change course. The other is to assume that they are all just challenges to overcome and fight through without any reflection or consideration. If doing so is causing harm to those around you or making you compromise your core values (even in small ways)—and both of these were true of Mickey Mouse as he struggled to paint the spot—take those as warning signs.

Mickey needed to take his eye off the spot for a while and focus on the bigger picture of what was happening to him and around him. So did Paul. Do you?

Kingdom Thinking: Is there an obstacle (or two) in your life that may be an indication that you need to change your approach, goal, or direction? If so, prayerfully ask God to show you if this is a challenge to be overcome or a roadblock to be heeded.

Chapter 9: Mickey's Toontown

Character Houses

The Message of Your "Home's" Décor

*M*ickey's Toontown offers guests a unique opportunity not found anywhere else: to visit and explore the homes of some of the most popular Disney characters (except for Minnie's house, which for some reason we can't go inside anymore).

When I interviewed Noah (from Noah Fine Art[316]), an independently licensed Disney artist, one of the things he told me is, "What you have in your home is your museum about your life....If I've never met you, I can walk through your home and figure out what kind of person you are based on what you have in there. What you have in your life, your little museums, is your life

---

[316] http://www.noahfineart.com

story." That's why it's such an honor for him when people choose to buy his art; they are making him part of their life story.

As you walk through Mickey's house, Goofy's house, and Donald's boat, there is no doubt whose home you are visiting. The décor tells you not only the identity of the owner, but also a lot about their "character" (so to speak) and personality.

Goofy is a sports fanatic, but is not very good at playing them. He values music and his friends. He also enjoys the outdoors, especially gardening. And he's not a very good driver.

Donald has very few photos in his boat, but those few are telling. They show him with his friends Jose and Panchito, his nephews, Daisy, and there's one with Walt Disney. Donald may put on a feisty exterior, but these are his friends and family. He really cares about them. And he has a special place in his heart for Daisy (he even named his boat after her).

Mickey cares about his friends, loves Minnie and Pluto, is something of a sports fan, and is pretty organized. He makes movies and values learning, since he has so many books and has written at least one himself.

Now, this train of thought may not come as any new revelation to you. You may not have thought about it before, but on some level it probably seems obvious now that you think about it.

So let me ask you, what about God's house? Not the church (at least not for our purposes), but the other "place" the New Testament says that He lives?

Do you not know that your body is a temple of the Holy Spirit, who is in you, whom you have received from God? You are not your own; you were bought at a price. Therefore honor God with your body.[317]

---

[317] 1 Corinthians 6:19–20

Guard the good deposit that was entrusted to you—guard it with the help of the Holy Spirit who lives in us.[318]

I have been crucified with Christ and I no longer live, but Christ lives in me. The life I live in the body, I live by faith in the Son of God, who loved me and gave Himself for me.[319]

You are the dwelling place of the Living God. You *are* His house.

As Artist Noah observed, "If I've never met you, I can walk through your home and figure out what kind of person you are based on what you have in there. What you have in your life, your little museums, is your life story."

We can learn a lot about the inhabitant of a house by what is displayed there. What do people learn about God when they look at what is on display in His house? When people see you, what does that tell them about God?

Kingdom Thinking: If the message people get when they look at your life is not the one you want them to know, what is one thing you can do to "redecorate His house"?

Roger Rabbit's Cartoon Spin

Out of Control

Roger Rabbit's Cartoon Spin is one of only two rides in Mickey's Toontown (the other being Gadget's Go Coaster). It was also the

---

[318] 1 Timothy 1:14
[319] Galatians 2:20

first "dark ride" to open since Pinocchio's Daring Journey eleven years earlier.

This ride is unique in that it combines elements of two other types of attractions into a single ride:

1. It has the vehicle on a track going through show scenes like a typical dark ride.
2. It has a wheel that guests can use to control the motion and spin the vehicle a full 360°, much like the Mad Tea Party.

That's the theory, anyway. Now, don't get me wrong; I really enjoy this attraction, but let me tell you, the spinning is a lot of work! The entire ride is a high-energy, fast-paced, often frenetic ride through the story. There's so much to see and take in and it all goes by so rapidly that it can feel overwhelming. The car spins somewhat on its own, but seemingly at random.

If you want to spin it yourself, there's the "natural" direction, where the wheel turns fairly easily, and the opposite direction where it's very difficult to turn the wheel. If you try to keep the car pointed in a specific direction (forward, for example) so you can see something specific, forget it. In fact, the last couple of times I've ridden Roger Rabbit's Cartoon Spin I was so tired after getting off that I wanted to go into Mickey's house and take a nap. [DISCLAIMER: You can't really take a nap in Mickey's house.]

It required so much effort to turn the wheel and yet it accomplished virtually nothing. The ride was still chaotic. I was still whipped this way and that, and the wheel ultimately provided only an *illusion* of control. If I had not touched it at all for the duration of the ride, I would have had essentially the same experience, but without wearing myself out trying to fight for a little bit of control that really made no difference.

What do we call it when we do the same thing in our lives? The truth is, we usually don't call it anything, but in those rare moments of honesty, it comes down to one word: worry.

- We worry about money, so we hold onto it tightly. We fear unexpected expenses, a job loss, or even generosity. After all, if we don't keep as much as we possibly can, how will we ever have enough?

- We worry about our careers, so we keep jobs we hate, take the first one that comes along when we've been unemployed, and never take a risk.

- We worry about our health, so we obsessively read articles about nutrition, watch videos about exercise, and study up on every new malady that comes on the scene. (Of course, we do all these things while sitting on the couch eating fast food, and wondering why we're in the shape we're in.)

- We worry about our country, so we shout from the rooftops our political positions, insult and vilify those who disagree with us, and complain when "our" candidate doesn't win the election. Or worse, we gloat when he does. As long as we can convince others that we're right and they're wrong, everything will be fine.

I could go on and on. I'm sure you worry about things not on this list. To be honest, so do I. When we worry, we preoccupy our minds with the problem and often concentrate our efforts on minimizing the possibility that what we worry about will happen. We make sure we fix it so it can't possibly break.

There are three problems with that approach. First, most of what we worry about won't happen anyway, so we're wasting our time and effort. Second, we don't have the skills, resources, and abilities to fix every possible problem and prevent them all from happening. At least one is going to slip through, and then all of our efforts will have gone for naught—just like trying to control the wheel in the ride.

Finally, and most importantly, it's all about us. Worry focuses your attention on *you*. What can I do to fix my problem? How can

I make sure this thing I'm worrying about doesn't happen? Look at how many things there are to worry me!

What's missing in this picture? God is.

> Therefore I tell you, do not worry about your life, what you will eat or drink; or about your body, what you will wear. Is not life more important than food, and the body more important than clothes? Look at the birds of the air; they do not sow or reap or store away in barns, and yet your Heavenly Father feeds them. Are you not much more valuable than they? Who of you by worrying can add a single hour to his life?
>
> And why do you worry about clothes? See how the lilies of the field grow. They do not labor or spin. Yet I tell you that not even Solomon in all his splendor was dressed like one of these. If that is how God clothes the grass of the field, which is here today and tomorrow is thrown into the fire, will He not much more clothe you, O you of little faith? So do not worry, saying, "What shall we eat?" or "What shall we drink?" or "What shall we wear?" For the pagans run after all these things, and your Heavenly Father knows that you need them. But seek first His kingdom and His righteousness, and all these things will be given to you as well.[320]

Is there something you can do that will make a difference for the stressor you worry about? For example, if you worry about your health, can you improve your eating habits or go for a brisk walk every evening? If so, do it. (Notice Jesus doesn't say don't act when you have the ability, don't plan, prepare, or be wise. He says "don't worry.")

If not, and if that anxiety is effectively out of the area of control God has entrusted to you, let go of the wheel. Stop fighting. "Do not be anxious about anything, but in everything, by prayer and

---

[320] Matthew 6:25–33

petition, with thanksgiving, present your requests to God. And the peace of God, which transcends all understanding, will guard your hearts and your minds in Christ Jesus."[321]

Kingdom Thinking: What do you worry about (the first thing that pops into your mind)? Now, what would be different in your life if you sought first God's kingdom and His righteousness in that area of concern?

Gadget's Go Coaster

Put Your Pieces Together

Gadget's Go Coaster is the final remaining attraction based on the "Disney Afternoon" cartoon block (which included *Chip 'n Dale Rescue Rangers*, *Goof Troop*, *DuckTales*, *Gummi Bears*, and others, depending on the season) from the 1990s. The attraction also has something in common with Sleeping Beauty Castle—sort of. The castle "premiered" at the park in 1955, four years *before* the movie was released. Conversely, Gadget's Go Coaster opened with the rest of Mickey's Toontown on January 23, 1993, more than two years *after* the final new episode of the Disney Afternoon series aired (November 19, 1990), though reruns of episodes did continue to air until about eight months after the ride opened.

This roller coaster is named for Gadget Hackwrench, a popular character from *Chip 'n Dale Rescue Rangers*, and according to the "official" Toontown backstory, she built it. Gadget is a pilot, mechanic, and inventor, the daughter of a deceased aviator and

---

[321] Philippians 4:6

inventor—and a mouse. Adventurous, energetic, and eager to help, she's also a bit high-strung—almost always moving, thinking, and acting quickly—but highly intelligent. What makes her particularly special, though, is her ability to take discarded and unrelated items and build nearly anything with them. Of course, her inventions don't always work out exactly the way she'd planned.

This ingenuity and inventiveness can be seen throughout the coaster she built. As guests take this extremely short (fifty-one second) ride, they pass unusual items that she used to make this new invention of hers: popsicle sticks, a salvaged comb, a soup can, a pencil, a thread spool, and more. Guests ride in vehicles made of acorns, and wooden stacking blocks support the track pieces. Naturally, everything is oversized so we feel "mouse size," like Gadget herself.

Gadget took her skills and abilities, combined them with her character and available resources, and built this kid-friendly coaster. It seems to me, though, that there is one part of the ride that does not fit this "built from random stuff" motif: the track itself. It's too smooth and too uniform. Gadget did all she could, but then the Imagineers must have stepped in and helped out a bit. They took the best she could do and made it better.

God does the same with His children. Think about the two times in the Gospels where Jesus feeds the hungry crowds.[322] The disciples did not have much to work with (five loaves of bread and two fish), but they gave Jesus what they had, and He multiplied it far beyond anything they could imagine to feed more than five thousand people.

God is in the business of doing more with, in, and through us than we could ever do on our own. As we are connected to Him, "rooted and established in love," He is "able to do immeasurably more than all we ask or imagine, according to His power that is at work within us."[323]

---

[322] Mark 6 and Mark 8
[323] Ephesians 3:14–21

Just as Gadget employed her talents, you too are called to build. Take what you have, however humble (or impressive) it might seem, and use those gifts, talents, skills, abilities, values, dreams, and passions all in service to God. I don't know what that looks like in your life specifically—though we could find out together.[324] It may be something you've always wanted or something you never imagined. It may involve success as the world defines it or it may center on suffering. It may feel polished and put together, or not quite what you'd had in mind. Whatever it is, though, being the best possible steward of what He's given you will be the best possible way you could live your life.

Your individual mix may feel cobbled together at times, and may not always work out exactly as you'd planned. But as long as you're being obedient and building on the foundation of Jesus Christ, you can trust the Master Builder to come alongside you, working in and through you. Then, just as the Imagineers made Gadget's invention work better than she could have planned on her own, God will make of your life something you could never be without Him.

> **Kingdom Thinking:** Have you felt like you didn't have much to offer, so you've held back and done little or nothing? How can Gadget inspire you to piece together whatever gifts you do have and then trust Him to multiply them for His service?

---

[324] See my website (http://www.leavingconformitycoaching.com) to find out how.

Chapter 10: Tomorrowland

Lay of the Land

Looking Ahead to a New Year

*W*alt Disney said in 1966, "Now, when we opened Disneyland, outer space was Buck Rogers. I did put in a trip to the moon, and I got Wernher von Braun to help me plan the thing....And since then has come Sputnik and then has come our great program in outer space. So I had to tear down my Tomorrowland that I built eleven years ago and rebuild it to keep pace."[325] That reconstruction was completed in 1967, almost seven months after Walt's death.

---

[325] Pat Williams with Jim Denney, *How to Be Like Walt: Capturing the Disney Magic Every Day of Your Life*, (Deerfield Beach, FL: Health Communications, Inc., 2004), 239.

The land began to change gradually again in 1973, then got another complete makeover in 1998 (arguably much less successfully than the 1967 remake). Another gradual change has only recently been completed.

When it came to Tomorrowland, Walt had to keep looking ahead. He had to keep reimagining it. He also said, "We keep moving forward, opening new doors, and doing new things, because we're curious and curiosity keeps leading us down new paths." Tomorrowland was designed to embody the spirit of "keep moving forward."

Every time a new year comes around it gives us a chance to remember to keep moving forward, but so does every day, if we choose to think about it. After all, the whole year isn't promised to us. In fact, not even tomorrow is guaranteed.

> Now listen, you who say, "Today or tomorrow we will go to this or that city, spend a year there, carry on business and make money." Why, you do not even know what will happen tomorrow. What is your life? You are a mist that appears for a little while and then vanishes. Instead, you ought to say, "If it is the Lord's will, we will live and do this or that." As it is, you boast and brag. All such boasting is evil.[326]

This passage is not a reason to fail to plan for the future. But it is a reminder that our days are a gift from God, so we take nothing for granted. Keep moving forward (intentionally). Plan ahead. That is not ungodly. Maybe the clearest scriptural reminder of the idea is this proverb:

> Go to the ant, you sluggard;
> consider its ways and be wise!
> It has no commander,
> no overseer or ruler,

---

[326] James 4:13–16

yet it stores its provisions in summer
and gathers its food at harvest.[327]

Tomorrowland, a world on the move. The Imagineers have
continued to update it as we move into the future. They keep
moving forward. And so do we. But at the same time, we
remember that each day is a gift.

As you close out one year and begin the next, or even one *day*
and begin the next (if it is the Lord's will), keep moving forward.
Perhaps you will follow a new path, or you may move farther along
the current one. Live each day to its fullest, because it may be the
last one you have. If it is, it will be a day well-lived, loving God and
serving others. If you live beyond today, then continue to grow and
live intentionally for God. In this way you honor Him, and grow
into the person He made you—and is making you—to be.

Kingdom Thinking: What is one way that you can move
forward today?

Agrifuture: Sowing and Reaping

The "Agrifuture" billboard, along the Disneyland Railroad track in
Tomorrowland, refers to a frequently overlooked detail. As part of
Tomorrowland's theming, Imagineers theorize that in the future
large populations will make open space and food scarce
commodities. Accordingly, ornamental landscaping will be
replaced with functional gardens that are also beautifully
manicured. A closer look at the greenery reveals that vegetables,
herbs, and fruit trees are being grown throughout

---

[327] Prov. 6:6–8

Tomorrowland.[328] For more on what kinds of plants are seen around Tomorrowland, see Plants of Disneyland.[329]

The Imagineers knew that there may be a need in the future for more spaces to be used for food and less for decoration, and so in their vision for Tomorrowland they planned accordingly. Even back when Disneyland was being built, Walt knew the importance of planning ahead when it came to the plants he would need. One of the very first things done during construction of Disneyland was to plant the trees around the waterway for the Jungle Cruise. Why? Because he knew he would need time for these plants to grow enough so that when the park opened, the flora around the Jungle Cruise would actually look like a jungle.

Sowing and reaping. It's one of the most basic principles of life. We get out what we put in. It's also a scriptural principle.

> Do not be deceived: God cannot be mocked. A man reaps what he sows. The one who sows to please his sinful nature, from that nature will reap destruction; the one who sows to please the Spirit, from the Spirit will reap eternal life.[330]

Consider how many of the most common New Year's Resolutions directly correlate to our behavior during the immediately preceding Christmas (and Thanksgiving) holiday season?

About.com features an article about the most common New Year's Resolutions.[331] Of the ten resolutions listed in the article, I see that nine of the ten can be associated with what we do (both

---

[328] "Agrifuture," http://findingmickey.squarespace.com/disneyland-facts/tomorrowland/2866166, accessed August 24, 2013.
[329] http://www.plantsofdisneyland.com/
[330] Galatians 6:7–8
[331] Albrecht Powell, "Top 10 New Year's Resolutions," http://pittsburgh.about.com/od/holidays/tp/resolutions.htm, accessed August 7, 2013.

good and bad) during the preceding months of sowing. For example, consider how these behaviors lead to popular resolutions:

- Eating too much at holiday dinners and parties, eating cookies, candy, fudge, etc. → Resolution to lose weight.
- Letting the stress of the holidays overwhelm us, and coping in unhealthy ways. → Resolution to quit smoking and/or quit drinking.
- Spending way too much on gifts—probably putting it on credit. → Resolution to get out of debt/get control of finances.
- Hectic house cleanings right before party or dinner guests arrive, or even finding gifts purchased and forgotten/lost until too late. → Resolution to get organized.
- Spending too little time with friends and family, only getting together for the holiday events. → Resolution to spend more time with friends and family.

We make the resolutions in January and insist that this year we are going to stick to them. And then we don't. Somehow, we fail to realize that we're coming off the most concentrated expression of the bad habits, and the strongest reminder of what is missing from our lives. What we have sown throughout the year, we reap at the holidays. What we have sown throughout the season, we continue to reap in the new year.

And yet we're surprised. Rather than sow different actions, attitudes, and behaviors, we do the same thing every year and then wonder on January 1 why we're pretty much where we were last year. Now I'll be the first to admit that sometimes the situations and circumstances we find ourselves in are not our fault. But more often than we would like to admit, they are. The huge financial hole you are in may be due to an unexpected and severe medical crisis, but it may be due to irresponsible borrowing on credit cards, home equity loans, student loans, etc. The disorganized mess that is your house may be due to having a new baby, but it may be due to a lack of discipline and an excess of laziness.

Think about the last few weeks of last year. What did you not enjoy? What are you dreading that may repeat itself for that time this year? How much of that concern is just a more obvious expression of behaviors and attitudes that are present throughout the rest of the year as well? Don't blame Thanksgiving and Christmas. The stress, frustrations, and excesses are simply reaping what we have sown the other eleven or so months of the year. We reap in the new year, especially at the start, what we sowed in November and December.

The Imagineers looked to the needs and restrictions of a possible future, and sowed accordingly. Walt Disney looked ahead to what he wanted the Jungle Cruise to be on opening day, and sowed accordingly. And I encourage you, look at what your life has been, especially during the most recent holidays. What do you want next year's (and even the following year's) Thanksgiving and Christmas to look like?

Kingdom Thinking: What do you need to sow now to reap the results you want at the proper time?

Astro Orbitor

Trusting Our Dad

My best friend and cater-cousin, Andy, had an interesting Tomorrowland experience on the Rocket Jets that he told me about.

Now, this was back when the jets were positioned above the PeopleMover track, where that odd sculpture—the Observatron—is now. He used to ride the Rocket Jets with his dad. Andy always enjoyed the ride. They got in and put the belt on. All he could see was the sky, and he knew the stick would make the rocket go up or down, which was fun. So he really enjoyed it. His dad never seemed fond of it, though, and he didn't know why.

As an adult, he rode it again, and found out why his dad was not a fan. As a child, the edge of the rocket came up to just above his head, so all he could see was the sky. As an adult, the edge of the rocket came to just about his waist. Suddenly, what had been fun was frightening. The ride took you more than three stories above the ground. Andy was tilted at an angle that feels pretty steep and the lap belt and vehicle lip came only to his waist. He knew a lot more, he could see a lot more, and there was no one else in the rocket to help secure him or make him feel safer.

Is that really so different from the way we live our lives? We go through tough times, and because we're trusting in God, we get through them. Sometimes things go smoothly, but not always. But that doesn't matter. As long as we're fully devoted to Him, we know that ultimately we will be OK. Paul describes our common struggle:

We've been surrounded and battered by troubles, but we're not demoralized; we're not sure what to do, but we know that God knows what to do; we've been spiritually terrorized, but God hasn't left our side; we've been thrown down, but we haven't broken. What they did to Jesus, they do to us—trial and torture, mockery and murder; what Jesus did among them, He does in us—He lives! Our lives are at constant risk for Jesus' sake, which makes Jesus' life all the more evident in us. [332]

---

[332] 2 Corinthians 4:8–12 (MSG)

A contemporary expression comes from singer Scott Krippayne. The chorus to his song *Sometimes He Calms the Storm* goes like this:

Sometimes He calms the storm
With a whispered "Peace, be still."
He can settle any sea,
But it doesn't mean He will.
Sometimes He holds us close
And lets the wind and waves go wild.
Sometimes He calms the storm,
And other times He calms His child.[333]

As long as you and I cling to Him and trust Him, as long as He's "in the rocket" with us, we can know we will be safe. That's not to say that life will be easy, painless, or easily worked out this side of heaven.

Believers do not have the promise of an easy life, but we do have the promise of a safe arrival.

> **Kingdom Thinking:** Is there a storm in your life that the Father hasn't calmed? Are you still willing to trust Him and let Him calm you?

[333] Scott Krippayne, "Sometimes He Calms the Storm," *Wild Imagination* (Nashville, TN: Word Records, 1995).

PeopleMover/Rocket Rods Track

Serving Outside Our S.H.A.P.E.

The PeopleMover opened at Disneyland July 2, 1967, as part of the "New Tomorrowland"; a leisurely, elevated sixteen-minute ride through Tomorrowland. Unfortunately, the attraction closed permanently August 21, 1995, and today remains one of the most-missed former attractions (the Skyway is also up there—so to speak). It was replaced less than three years later by the Rocket Rods.

The new attraction covered the same track in three minutes, so obviously it was intended to be more of a thrill ride than a sightseeing ride. Even more unfortunately, though, the Rocket Rods (which resemble "hot rods" on a raised track) used the PeopleMover track basically unmodified. That means it sped up on the straightaway portions and slowed down on the turns, since the turns were not banked. That pattern could not be sustained.

In writing about the Rocket Rods, Werner Weiss, curator of Yesterland.com, says of the Rocket Rod's issues:

> The constant speeding up and slowing down took its toll on the vehicles and infrastructure. Almost immediately, the ride became better known for breakdowns and limited operating hours than for entertainment and thrills. In fact, the ride was closed most of its first summer.[334]

The Rocket Rods closed permanently in September of 2000 (less than two-and-a-half years after opening), and the track sits vacant to this day.

---

[334] Werner Weiss, "Rocket Rods: Long Wait. Short Ride," http://www.yesterland.com/rocketrods.html, accessed August 8, 2013.

These raised racers were not necessarily a bad ride, but they suffered from one serious flaw: they attempted to use a ride track for something other than the purpose for which it was designed.

For we are God's workmanship, created in Christ Jesus to do good works, which God prepared in advance for us to do.[335]

Sometimes Christ-followers do the very same thing. In *The Purpose Driven Life*, Rick Warren talks about us being "SHAPEd for serving God." As Rick describes it, SHAPE is an acronym that stands for:

Spiritual Gifts
Heart
Abilities
Personality
Experiences

You were shaped to serve God.... God deliberately shaped and formed you to serve Him in a way that makes your ministry [service] unique.[336]

There are two lessons here.

First, we all have a unique way of serving God. Trying to fit into someone else's mold of how you should serve doesn't work very well. Sure, there are variations, but the closer you are to serving in a way that fits your SHAPE, the more effective you'll be.

When I say "variations," I'm talking in the degree of Superspeed Tunnel (where high-speed footage of race cars was projected on the wrap-around walls, giving the illusion of speed)

---

[335] Ephesians 2:10
[336] Rick Warren, *The Purpose Driven Life* (Grand Rapids, MI: Zondervan, 2002), 234–35.

vs. Tron Lightcycles (Game Grid) for the PeopleMover, not PeopleMover vs. Rocket Rods degree. The former consisted of two different applications that still made use of the track layout that it was designed for; the latter worked against it. Don't work against your SHAPE. Sure, there may be times when you have to do something you do not like to do or are not "gifted" to do because it just needs to get done. But spend as much time as you can doing what you were designed to do.

> We have different gifts, according to the grace given us. If a man's gift is prophesying, let him use it in proportion to his faith. If it is serving, let him serve; if it is teaching, let him teach; if it is encouraging, let him encourage; if it is contributing to the needs of others, let him give generously; if it is leadership, let him govern diligently; if it is showing mercy, let him do it cheerfully.[337]

Second, your SHAPE is for the benefit of others, not yourself. "We serve God by serving others."[338] God designed me to do certain things well, to be passionate about certain topics, to use a specific set of experiences, etc. so that I can serve others. Keeping that unique SHAPE to myself is both selfish and sinful.

> Each one should use whatever gift he has received to serve others, faithfully administering God's grace in its various forms.[339]

Next time you see the empty PeopleMover track, remember what was there, and the disaster that ensued when they tried to replace it with something the track was not designed to accommodate.

---

[337] Romans 12:6–8
[338] Warren, 257.
[339] 1 Peter 4:10

> **Kingdom Thinking:** Are you serving God in a way that's consistent with how you were designed, and serving in a way that's for the benefit of others, not yourself?

Star Tours

When Something Goes Terribly Wrong

Star Tours' planning began in the early to mid-80s (circa 1985). Executive Vice President and Senior Creative Executive Tom Fitzgerald described it as "a dark time for the company, and for live action films in particular." This was the time immediately following such films as *The Black Hole* and *The Apple Dumpling Gang*, both of which were box-office successes but received mixed reviews and were the last live-action Disney films for years to do even marginally well in theaters. As the Imagineers and executives looked for a new attraction to add to the park, they didn't have much to draw from when it came to their current films. But there was something they did have: a new partnership with George Lucas.

Disney approached Lucas with the idea for Star Tours, and with Lucas' approval, the Imagineers purchased four military-grade flight simulators at a cost of $500,000 (each!) and designed the ride structure. Meanwhile, Lucas and his special effects team at Industrial Light & Magic (ILM) produced the first-person perspective film that would be projected inside the simulators. This was completely new territory for the ILM team, because they were used to movie techniques like cutaways. That technique will not work in a first-person simulator film, so they employed other tricks to allow for the visual jumps that they needed. When both simulator and film were completed, a programmer sat inside and, using a joystick, manually synchronized the movement of the simulator with the apparent movement on screen.

On January 9, 1987, at a cost of $32 million (nearly double the cost of building the entire park in 1955), the ride opened to huge crowds. In celebration, Disneyland remained open for a special sixty-hour marathon from January 9, 1987, at 10 A.M. to January 11, 1987, at 10 P.M.

Star Tours was the first simulator-based attraction to ever appear in a theme park. But there was something else unique about it as well. As Kevin Yee explains:

> In Walt's day, most rides were slow journeys through atmospheres and environments. There didn't have to be drama, tension, or conflict. The list is long of such rides that promoted tranquility and transportation (including, perhaps, metaphorical transportation through time).
>
> The first crack in that long-standing armor of such rides came in 1979, when Big Thunder Mountain Railroad, which is not just a roller coaster through an environment (the way Space Mountain is), but features a subtle moment when "things go terribly wrong." In this case, it's the earthquake at the end of the ride. It's so subtle that most visitors pay it no mind.
>
> But at [Captain] EO (the first show to do it) and then Star Tours (the first ride to do it), the "things go terribly wrong" concept moves to center stage. The whole ride is not an adventure; it's a misadventure. And this would be a pattern to reassert itself for decades to come....Only some of the most recent attractions (Toy Story Mania, for example) do away with the need for misadventure to provide the impetus/excuse for the attraction's existence. That mold which has lasted so long was set by Star Tours.[340]

---

[340] Kevin Yee, "Time Warp,"

Star Tours is informative because it breaks the mold and introduces us to a concept never seen before in Disney parks, but seen all the time in real life: something goes terribly wrong. Tragedy strikes. Everything is moving along like it should—or at least like we think it should—and then suddenly it goes off track. (If you watched carefully in the ride film, or have seen photos of the model being worked on, you can even see the literal tracks that the Star Speeder is supposed to have gone off). Does that sound familiar? Life is humming along nicely, and then it suddenly goes off the rails?

Even the nature of the problems we encountered in Star Tours are reminiscent of what we face. After missing our destination (we must not have been properly focused on getting there), we find ourselves in a comet field. No sooner do we break free of that than we're caught in the tractor beam of an Imperial Star Destroyer. We're released from that (with some help), and what do we do? We participate in the battle to destroy the Death Star—complete with trench run!

Consider these three dangers: comets, Imperial forces, and a space battle we're not equipped to fight. They encapsulate every kind of trouble we face.

Sometimes problems "just happen." We live in a fallen world, and at times the environment itself can bring on catastrophe (natural disasters). Other times it's simply an accident—no one intends harm, but it comes anyway. We innocently fly into a field of comets.

And still other times we face problems, pain, and suffering intentionally caused by others. We "get caught in their tractor beam" as they try to harm us.

And sometimes we step into places we shouldn't be, fight battles that are not ours or that others (including God) are better

---

http://miceage.micechat.com/kevinyee/ky091410a.htm, accessed August 7, 2013.

equipped to fight, and we stick our noses in anyway. "Oh, boy! I've always wanted to do this!" Really?

Should we be surprised? No. As Westley says in the movie *The Princess Bride*, "Life is pain, Highness! Anyone who says differently is selling something." That may overstate things a bit, but the point remains.

The apostle Peter told us what to expect:

Dear friends, do not be surprised at the painful trial you are suffering, as though something strange were happening to you. But rejoice that you participate in the sufferings of Christ, so that you may be overjoyed when his glory is revealed. If you are insulted because of the name of Christ, you are blessed, for the Spirit of glory and of God rests on you. If you suffer, it should not be as a murderer or thief or any other kind of criminal, or even as a meddler. However, if you suffer as a Christian, do not be ashamed, but praise God that you bear that name. For it is time for judgment to begin with the family of God; and if it begins with us, what will the outcome be for those who do not obey the gospel of God? And, if it is hard for the righteous to be saved,
what will become of the ungodly and the sinner?
So then, those who suffer according to God's will should commit themselves to their faithful Creator and continue to do good.[341]

Trouble will follow us in this life. So what do we do about it?

Well, if it has been brought on by something we've done and are doing, we need to identify and stop doing it. Jesus said that in this world we will have trouble, but He did not say we need to bring it on ourselves. We will have plenty without doing that! But what about the perils that come to us uninvited?

---

[341] 1 Peter 4:12–19

In a sense, there is no easy answer to this question. We hurt. That is the way things are. We grieve. We get angry. We fear. We cry. And we pray.

Prayer must be a continual part of our lives, even more so when we are hurting. It's not easy to pray when problems hem us in, but that is when it is most needed. Everything in us screams to turn away, to retreat inward. But Jesus calls us to Himself, and to continue doing good. He offers peace, comfort, hope, and strength. He offers grace. And He offers us an eternal perspective.

> Therefore we do not lose heart. Though outwardly we are wasting away, yet inwardly we are being renewed day by day. For our light and momentary troubles are achieving for us an eternal glory that far outweighs them all. So we fix our eyes not on what is seen, but on what is unseen. For what is seen is temporary, but what is unseen is eternal.[342]

And so we can say with David:

> You turned my wailing into dancing;
> You removed my sackcloth and clothed me with joy,
> that my heart may sing to You and not be silent.
> O LORD my God, I will give You thanks forever.[343]

Adopting a proper attitude is not easy, and there are no simple answers. Sometimes we must simply endure the string of problems, and that's hard to accept. But when "something goes terribly wrong," remember that there is One who is not caught off guard, Who is not surprised, and He is there to work everything for your good, as you have been called according to His purpose.

---

[342] 2 Corinthians 4:16–18
[343] Psalm 30:11–12

Kingdom Thinking: How do you respond when "something goes terribly wrong"? How do you see these same categories in play in the new version, "Star Tours: The Adventures Continue"?

Captain EO

We Are Here to Change the World

Captain EO is a visually stimulating and inspiring attraction with a storied origin. It originally opened September 18, 1986, in Tomorrowland at Disneyland (though it had opened six days earlier in the Imagination Pavilion at EPCOT Center in Walt Disney World). Starring Michael Jackson and Anjelica Huston, directed by Francis Ford Coppola, and executive produced by George Lucas, at the time this seventeen-minute sci-fi film was one of the most expensive films ever made (when calculated by cost per minute) at over $1 million per minute. It also helped pioneer the "4D attraction."

This had been one of the projects (along with Star Tours, Splash Mountain, and others) being considered when Michael Eisner became CEO of the Walt Disney Company. All three were green-lit for development, but Captain EO was given a higher priority because it could be made faster and would draw crowds and help revitalize Disneyland while the other two attractions were being built.

Captain EO closed in April of 1997, but was brought back in a "tribute" form in February of 2010 for a "limited time" (which continues as of this writing).

In my opinion, this is still a fun show, "80s cheese" at its best. The songs are catchy, the effects are entertaining, and Fuzzball is one of the cutest characters ever. Even with the campiness of the show (and a theater that does the tapping to the music for you—if often out of time with the music), it's an often-overlooked but fun attraction.

There must be more to it than silliness, right? Of course there is. Have you ever listened to the lyrics of one of its main songs, *We Are Here to Change the World*? Really listened? If not, look at some of the lyrics:

We're on a mission
In the everlasting light that shines
A revelation
Of the truth in chapters of our minds
So long, bad times
We're gonna shake it up and break it up
We're sharing light brighter than the sun
Hello, good times
We're here to stimulate, eliminate
And congregate, illuminate
(We are here to change the world)
Gonna change the world,
(We are here to change the world)
Gonna change the world!

Do those lyrics resonate with you? Aren't we as Christians on a mission to change the world?

All this is from God, who reconciled us to Himself through Christ and gave us the ministry of reconciliation: that God was reconciling the world to Himself in Christ, not counting men's sins against them. And He has committed to us the message of reconciliation. We are therefore Christ's ambassadors, as though God were making His appeal through us. We implore you on Christ's behalf: Be reconciled to God.[344]

---

[344] 2 Corinthians 5:18–20

We are made in the image of God. We are His children. But many have turned away from Him, or do not realize their identity in Him. They are beautiful within but need a key to unlock their radiance. We have been charged with the mission of bringing His light to this dark world. We bring the key that unlocks the beauty within people as they come into the light of His love and grace.

Kingdom Thinking: How are you changing the world? What are you doing—or what can you do—to connect people to God and show them His love?

Space Mountain

Trust for the Journey

Space Mountain, a thrilling, imaginary journey though outer space, is not for the skittish. After the second lift you are in almost complete darkness for the rest of the ride until coming back into the station. Especially for those who don't ride often, this is an almost completely unpredictable ride.

As Christians—even just as humans—we can't always see where the future will take us. In fact, it's usually at the most significant times that we can least see what is coming next and how it will affect us. But as Christians, we have an advantage. We know the One who designed the journey.

David says in Psalm 139:16, "Like an open book, you watched me grow from conception to birth; all the stages of my life were spread out before you. The days of my life all prepared before I'd even lived one day."[345]

As Christian author Max Lucado says, when we look to the future and see where our lives are now, we can say to God, "I don't know where I am. I don't know how I'll get home. But you do and that's enough."[346] That's not to say that we don't make free choices throughout our lives, but time poses no challenges for God. He exists outside of time and already knows what we think of as "the future." Because of that, He has prepared the journey (though it's up to us to choose to take it)—one we could not have predicted or designed for ourselves, yet nonetheless amazing.

Once on Space Mountain, you are in the hands of the Imagineers who designed the ride to take you on a journey you could not take on your own. Sometimes that's not easy to do. I used to fear roller coasters. I'm still not a big fan of the steel behemoths that stand 200 feet tall, suspend you from the track, and have six loops, a flat spin, and an inline rollover. But I can at least ride California Screamin'. This coaster is only 120 feet tall, you sit in a seat, and it does only one loop. And the zero-to-55-mph-in-no-time-at-all launch is fun!

But it wasn't all that long ago that I would not have gone anywhere near this breathtaking ride, let alone to Space Mountain itself.

Back in the mid-1990s, my friend Andy (who I've mentioned several times), and I would go to Disneyland together all the time. At that time, the most I could handle was Thunder Mountain—and I even got nervous standing in line waiting for that one! Andy wanted to go on *all* the rides but he waited patiently.

Apparently, we opted for "exposure therapy," because he and I rode Thunder Mountain almost every time we went to the park. Over time—about a year, actually—I was willing to try the

---

[345] Psalm 139:16 (MSG)
[346] Max Lucado, *And the Angels Were Silent* (Colorado Springs, CO: Multnomah Books, 1992), 41.

Matterhorn. It took getting in line and chickening out two or three times before I finally rode that one the first time, but eventually I did. And it took another year or so before I was finally willing to try Space Mountain. Now I love them all, though, I have to admit I still get a bit nervous in line.

I was able to overcome my fear and enjoy the rides because I knew Andy would not take me on something that was going to hurt me. And I knew the Imagineers were experts who knew exactly what they were doing. They would not build a ride that they knew would endanger riders.

Sometimes the ride is scary. Sometimes it's exciting. But, when faced with uncertainty, we put ourselves into the hands of people who know exactly what they're doing. Of course, there's more than one "track" to the roller coaster of our lives, but God knows exactly what He's doing. He has seen, knows, and will guide the whole journey, and He's working all things together for the good of those who love Him (Romans 8:28).

Sometimes the Christian life is scary. Sometimes it's exciting. Sometimes it's unpredictable. Sometimes the journey's difficulty and our weakness and fear in the face of it is almost overwhelming. Our troubles can seem all-consuming, and our minds imagine the worst things possible.

> Therefore we do not lose heart. Though outwardly we are wasting away, yet inwardly we are being renewed day by day. For our light and momentary troubles are achieving for us an eternal glory that far outweighs them all. So we fix our eyes not on what is seen, but on what is unseen. For what is seen is temporary, but what is unseen is eternal.[347]

And so we can trust God, and enjoy the ride.

---

[347] 2 Corinthians 4:16–18

> **Kingdom Thinking:** What overwhelming, frightening, or uncertain circumstance in your life today do you need to trust God with?

Innoventions

Making Dreams Come True

(For those reading who have fond memories of the Carousel of Progress or America Sings, yes, I wish we still had one of them, too. OK, now that we have that out of the way...)

This attraction opened in 1998 and provides guests with a "high-tech, high-touch" opportunity to experience technology in an entertaining, low-risk environment. Its particular location has logged an interesting history. During Disneyland's first summer, in 1955, a restaurant called the Space Bar opened at the eastern edge of Tomorrowland. The Space Bar took up a huge area there, serving basic counter-service food. They had so much room available that in 1961 the Space Bar Dance Area opened in front of it.

The Space Bar's days were numbered, though—in that location, anyway. In 1964, Walt Disney and his Imagineers had four attractions at the New York World's Fair. One of those was a rotating theater attraction called Progressland. After the Fair ended, all of the Disney attractions were brought out to Disneyland (though not much of the Ford attraction made it), and in 1967 Progressland came to Disneyland and became the Carousel of Progress, showing four decades of American life, with thirty-two Audio Animatronic figures.

The Carousel of Progress lasted until 1973, when it was displaced by America Sings (which opened in 1974). The Carousel of Progress moved to Walt Disney World, and a six-part carousel of music took its place, with 114 Audio Animatronics celebrating America's musical heritage. That remained until 1988, and then offices occupied the theater until July of 1998, when Innoventions opened.

Much like the Carousel of Progress was moved to Walt Disney World in 1973, Innoventions was copied/duplicated from Walt Disney World and provided a place at Disneyland to showcase new technology and innovation (with varying degrees of success).

As guests prepared to enter the rotating building—which they can no longer do, as the entrance is now up the ramp on the top level—they were shown a preshow video of the host, Tom Morrow. In one of those videos, he said something that the history of this location—and Disneyland Park as a whole—proves true. "Imagining a dream and making it come true are two completely different things."

Walt Disney had a dream, and that was a good start (the dream served as the inspiration for the Sherman Brothers song "It's a Great Big Beautiful Tomorrow," which was the theme song for the Carousel of Progress and is used again today with Innoventions). But a dream was not enough. It took work, dedication, time, and sacrifice to make it a reality.

The Bible does not directly address the notion of having dreams (though it does record and explain them in redemptive history) and making them come true. But it does talk about having a purpose. Jesus said, "Did you not see and know that it is necessary [as a duty] for Me to be in My Father's house and [occupied] about My Father's business?"[348] Later He said these things:

---

[348] Luke 2:49 (AMP)

My Father is always at His work to this very day, and I, too, am working.[349]

I have testimony weightier than that of John. For the very work that the Father has given Me to finish, and which I am doing, testifies that the Father has sent Me.[350]

I have brought You [God the Father] glory on earth by completing the work You gave Me to do.[351]

Jesus knew His purpose and He fulfilled it. We, too, have a purpose to fulfill.

For we are God's workmanship, created in Christ Jesus to do good works, which God prepared in advance for us to do.[352]

God has created each of us with a unique combination of dreams and passions, gifts, skills, abilities, and interests. These combine into making you and I uniquely who we are and show the purpose we were designed to fulfill. And we have two choices:

1. Ignore or don't seek out what that purpose is. Go through life just taking things as they come and hoping for the best.
2. Take the time and effort necessary to discover your purpose. Then invest the work, dedication, time, and sacrifice necessary to develop it and live it out.

"I believe God made me for a purpose—for China. But He also made me fast! And when I run, I feel His pleasure. To give

---

[349] John 5:17
[350] John 5:36
[351] John 17:4
[352] Ephesians 2:10

that up would be to hold Him in contempt. ...to win is to honor Him" (Eric Liddell, *Chariots of Fire*).

You bring glory to God when you know who He made you to be and you live it out—not trying to be anyone else, but being the unique you.

We have different gifts, according to the grace given us. If a man's gift is prophesying, let him use it in proportion to his faith. If it is serving, let him serve; if it is teaching, let him teach; if it is encouraging, let him encourage; if it is contributing to the needs of others, let him give generously; if it is leadership, let him govern diligently; if it is showing mercy, let him do it cheerfully.[353]

It's easy to go through life without making the extra effort. Yet we want to be "good Christians." That's a great goal and perhaps a dream for some who do not think they will work hard enough. But have you moved it from a dream to becoming a reality? As the video reminds us, "Imagining a dream and making it come true are two completely different things." It takes effort on our part, not to *earn* God's favor or His love, but *because* He loves us. We do whatever we can to honor Him—including knowing who we are and living that out to the best of our ability—because He loves us.

Kingdom Thinking: Do you know what your purpose is? If not, are you taking steps to find out? If so, are you living it out?

---

[353] Romans 12:6–8

Autopia

Unhelpful Signs

The Tomorrowland Autopia, designed by Imagineering Legend Bob Gurr, is one of four Autopias that have existed at Disneyland and the only one that was an Opening Day attraction. (The other three were Junior Autopia, Midget Autopia, and Fantasyland Autopia).

When the attraction first opened, there was no guide rail for the cars, so drivers could not only bump each other (as they can now—though they're not supposed to), but also they could pass each other, swerve into each other, and possibly even go the wrong direction. The center rail was finally added in 1965, ten years after the attraction opened.

As with nearly all Disneyland attractions, the Autopia has undergone several modifications over the years, including at least eight versions of the cars themselves and multiple iterations of the track. The current version of the attraction, sponsored by Chevron, is more whimsical than the previous ones had been. Drivers will see a large video screen near the attraction's start showing cars telling jokes—usually bad ones. Also, there are several tongue-in-cheek signs throughout the attraction. One is a "Mouse Crossing" sign. Another one warns that "Pavement Ends 5 Feet" (that's not very helpful so close to where it happens!). And then there's a series of signs that shows what the track is supposedly going to do next: first a right turn, then an "S" curve, and finally a bizarre, twisting path. Some of the signs are helpful. Others…not so much.

As Christians, we often like to look for, and ask for, "signs." We are not necessarily looking for something supernatural or show-stoppingly miraculous, but something that at least gives us a clue of what we're supposed to do next. But such anticipation points to two problems: we forget that we already have a guide rail, and we look so hard for signs that what we see ultimately becomes unhelpful (even counterproductive).

I frequently hear people say—and have said myself—"I wish God would give me a sign to show me what He wants me to do!" But He has already told us a good portion of what He wants us to do. Things like:

- Love your enemies,[354]
- Pray without ceasing,[355]
- Be kind and compassionate,[356] bearing with one another in love,[357]
- Do not commit adultery, or even look lustfully at a woman,[358]
- Love your neighbor as yourself,[359]
- Be angry, but do not sin,[360]
- Submit to one another out of reverence for Christ,[361]
- And so on.

Are you heeding these signs? These serve as the guide rail for our lives, the basic path to follow. And they are important for two reasons. First, if you are not following the guide rail, any signs along the road will be useless because you won't be able to follow them. Second, if you are not already doing those things that He's made abundantly clear (or at least making every effort to do so), why should God give you any more information? If you want to know what to do, but you are not doing what He has already told you to do in the normal course of life, why should He reveal any

---

[354] Matthew 5:43–48
[355] 1 Thessalonians 5:17
[356] Ephesians 4:32
[357] Ephesians 4:2
[358] Matthew 5:27–30
[359] Romans 13:9-10
[360] Ephesians 4:26–27
[361] Ephesians 5:21

specifics? If you are not already obeying God, what reason does He have to expect that you will start doing so with an extra revelation?

What if you *are* doing those—not perfectly, of course, but growing in obedience to the Lord? It's fine to ask for a sign (I have), and to expectantly look for a response. Just be sure you are willing to accept His answer, whatever the "sign" may be. And here is where a "caution" sign might help. Why? Because we know what answer we want, or think we should get, and so we look hard for *that* sign, even if God is sending a pretty clear message saying something else.

Let's take the sign illustration a little farther down the road (so to speak). I might ask God which way to turn, but what I really want is to turn left. I get a sign that indicates I should turn right. It's not what I want, so I keep looking and see an "S-curve." If I follow that one I can go left, but I have to go right first. I really don't want to turn right, so I keep looking. The more I look, the more twisted and convoluted the signs—or at least what I perceive to be signs—become, until they are just tangled messes. And then I get frustrated that God isn't answering my prayer.

You too, huh?

Here is great direction from the Book of James:

> If any of you lacks wisdom, you should ask God, who gives generously to all without finding fault, and it will be given to you. But when you ask, you must believe and not doubt, because the one who doubts is like a wave of the sea, blown and tossed by the wind. That person should not expect to receive anything from the Lord. Such a person is double-minded and unstable in all they do.[362]

One of the main themes of this epistle is "faith without works is dead." If you ask God for wisdom in faith, that implies that when

---

[362] James 1:5–8

He gives you the wisdom you ask for, you will act on it. It means telling God, "I don't know what to do in this situation, so I'm asking You. And I commit right now, before even getting the answer, that whatever You tell me to do, whatever direction You indicate, I'll do it, no matter what it is." That is asking in faith. Continuing to look for the answer *you* want is doubting—and if that's the way you ask, don't expect an answer.

It's easy to ask for a sign, and it's easy to look for the sign we want, or that we think is best. It's harder to yield to God's signs that we don't like. It is difficult to do what we already know to do, and harder still to accept an answer to a prayer for guidance that isn't the one we want. But if you want to receive a helpful sign and not a tangled mess, heed the signs in front of you.

> **Kingdom Thinking:** What are you asking God for direction on in your life right now? Are you willing to commit to Him and follow His direction, no matter what it is?

Disneyland Monorail

Growing Up or Along for the Ride?

The Disneyland-Alweg Monorail opened June 14, 1959, on part of what is unofficially called Disneyland's Second Grand Opening. The monorail-on-an-elevated track owes its unusual name to inventor Dr. Axel Lennart Wenner-Gren (whose initials spell "Alweg" [almost]). Walt Disney saw it on a test track in Germany and partnered with Alweg to create a more "futuristic" version of it for Disneyland.

Imagineers Bob Gurr, John Hench, Roger Broggie, and Bill Martin all had a significant role in the development and construction of the Monorail for Disneyland. For all of them—Walt included—the goal was not to create simply a fun ride, but a new concept in transportation, much as the PeopleMover was later to be. However, it did not start out that way.

For the first two years the Monorail was on a closed-loop that started and ended in Tomorrowland. Only when the track was expanded to include a stop at the Disneyland Hotel did it become anything resembling actual transportation. From that point on, if you wanted to take the Monorail to actually go somewhere, you could. Of course, today that stop is in Downtown Disney, but the concept still remains true.

For regular visitors to Walt Disney World who come to Disneyland for the first time, this is one of the differences that surprises them the most. In Florida, the Monorail actually *is* transportation. It covers several miles of track, with stops at two theme parks, three hotels, and the Transportation and Ticket Center. In fact, none of the stations are inside theme parks, so guests can ride without having to pay for admission to any of the parks. The Florida property is so expansive that the Monorail is needed as transportation. When visitors come out here and see that "ours" has only two stops, one in Disneyland itself, they are usually perplexed.

It makes sense that a transportation system would actually go somewhere, doesn't it? Walt Disney World guests generally see the Monorail as a way to make progress, to go from one place to another. Disneyland guests, on the other hand, generally see it as an attraction and they board not to go somewhere, but just to go along for the ride.

Many Christians view their faith the same way. They give little thought to "going somewhere" in their Christian walk, and even less action. We go along for the ride passively—maybe going to church on Sunday morning, praying briefly before a meal, and that's about it. Our faith does not really impact our daily lives, and certainly not in a way that shows growth or forward progress.

The writer of Hebrews witnessed the same tendency in his day. He said to his readers:

> We have much to say about this, but it is hard to explain because you are slow to learn. In fact, though by this time you ought to be teachers, you need someone to teach you the elementary truths of God's word all over again. You need milk, not solid food! Anyone who lives on milk, being still an infant, is not acquainted with the teaching about righteousness. But solid food is for the mature, who by constant use have trained themselves to distinguish good from evil.[363]

There's a not-so-subtle reprimand for these believers who were stunted in their spiritual growth. They still needed the basics instead of learning the deeper truths and then teaching others. They were just along for the ride.

What about you? Are you growing in Christ, and in knowledge, understanding, and unity? Are you growing in your service? Do you plan to make that growth consistent and intentional? Or are you just riding along, wondering why your faith doesn't seem to make much of a difference in your life?

The apostle Paul points the way to a maturing faith.

> It was He who gave some to be apostles, some to be prophets, some to be evangelists, and some to be pastors and teachers, to prepare God's people for works of service, so that the body of Christ may be built up until we all reach unity in the faith and in the knowledge of the Son of God and become mature, attaining to the whole measure of the fullness of Christ.

---

[363] Hebrews 5:11–13

Then we will no longer be infants, tossed back and forth by the waves, and blown here and there by every wind of teaching and by the cunning and craftiness of men in their deceitful scheming. Instead, speaking the truth in love, we will in all things grow up into Him who is the Head, that is, Christ.[364]

Kingdom Thinking: Are you growing in your faith, or are you just along for the ride? If it's the latter, what can you do to change that?

Submarine Voyage

Do You Talk About What Happened?

"Should I enter any of this into the log?"
"No, forget it. Nobody would believe it anyway. Better take her up..."

These words, or something very close to them, have been part of the Submarine Voyage narration from its opening in 1959 through today. This unexpected adventure through "liquid space" has given passengers strange experiences. Depending on the incarnation of the attraction, it may have been an encounter with a sea serpent, mermaids, discovering the lost city of Atlantis, an active undersea volcano, a clownfish looking for his son, being swallowed by a whale, and more!

When the excitement is over, though, the captain says not to write it down. Don't bother telling anyone. No one would believe it anyway. The "crew" has seen incredible sights and discovered

---

[364] Ephesians 4:11–15

answers to age-old questions. But no one will get the benefit of these. Why? Who knows? Maybe the captain does not believe they really saw such crazy things (evidence to the contrary). Maybe he's afraid of appearing foolish, losing his rank, or some other motivation. Whatever the reason, though, the secrets stay with the submarine.

Do you do the same thing? Granted, you've never seen a mermaid or a sea serpent, but what about seeing God working in astonishing ways in your life, or in the people around you?

Have you:

- Had an answered prayer?
- Received an unexpected blessing?
- Been told you could not possibly survive something or would never walk again, but did anyway?
- Been reunited with someone you thought you had lost touch with forever, or had a relationship you had thought hopelessly broken be restored?
- Given birth to the child you thought impossible to have?
- Been there when someone you thought would never become a Christian finally surrenders to Jesus?

If you have been a Christian for any length of time, you have probably had one or more of these happen to you or seen it happen to someone around you. When these great God-caused events occur, do you talk about them? Or are you afraid people won't believe you or that you'll come across as strange? Do you wonder whether it was just coincidence—or fear others will say that?

What if the shepherds who came to see the baby Jesus had kept it to themselves? What if the women who saw the angel and the empty tomb figured no one would believe them? What if John received his Revelation from God but did not say anything for fear of seeming weird?

When God moves in our lives, we need to tell others about it. Doing so encourages them, strengthens their faith, or maybe nudges them to finally accept Jesus. We become His messengers when we tell people, "Look what God is doing!" This is what the Bible calls "the word of our testimony."[365]

Such stories also serve as reminders to ourselves when times gets hard, light grows dim, and we wonder where God is. We remember that the One who came through in amazing ways before can do so again.

Sing to the Lord a new song;
sing to the Lord, all the earth.
Sing to the Lord, praise His name;
proclaim His salvation day after day.
Declare His glory among the nations,
His marvelous deeds among all peoples.[366]

I will tell of the kindnesses of the Lord,
the deeds for which He is to be praised,
according to all the Lord has done for us—
yes, the many good things
He has done for Israel,
according to His compassion and many kindnesses.[367]

> **Kingdom Thinking:** Have you seen God answer a prayer or do something "incredible" that you know was Him at work? Tell someone about it…today!

---

[365] See Revelation 12:11
[366] Psalm 96:1-3
[367] Isaiah 63:7

Jedi Training Academy

Standing Together

One of my favorite recent additions (2007) to Tomorrowland has been the Jedi Training Academy. It's always fun to watch the little kids train and then "fight" Darth Vader or Darth Maul. (Of course, the day Darth Maul scared my wife half to death was fun too!)

If you have never experienced the Jedi Training Academy, here's the short version of what you can expect. About twenty children ("younglings" as they're called in Star Wars parlance) are selected from the audience each show to be trained as Padawans. They are brought up and given—loaned, really—a Jedi robe and a training lightsaber. The Jedi Master teaches them a simple lightsaber attack combination, and then they face off against either of the two Sith: Vader or Maul. After the encounters with the Dark Side they are congratulated and reminded of the ways of the Force by Yoda, return their robes and lightsabers, and receive a diploma.

My favorite part of the Jedi Training Academy comes near the end. After each youngling has faced a Dark Lord, he or she is gathered on the right side of the stage. When the last bout is completed, Darth Vader faces them as a group one last time and tempts them to turn to the Dark Side. As they stand defiantly against his luring, Yoda's voice comes through the air:

Wrong you are, to think these younglings will turn to the Dark Side. Skilled they are indeed, and when together they stand, very strong in the Force they are.

At the leading of the Jedi Master, they activate their lightsabers and the enemy is routed! That statement from Yoda gets me every time. And it stands as a reminder to us as believers facing dark forces.

In John 17, Jesus prayed, "I in them and You in Me. May they be brought to complete unity to let the world know that You sent me and have loved them even as You have loved Me."[368]

Also, in his letter to the Ephesians, Paul says, "As a prisoner for the Lord, then, I urge you to live a life worthy of the calling you have received. Be completely humble and gentle; be patient, bearing with one another in love. Make every effort to keep the unity of the Spirit through the bond of peace."[369]

The world knows who we are and that we are loved by God because of our unity. It is a unity that remains strong through our love for each other. As Jesus noted, "By this all men will know that you are My disciples, if you love one another."[370]

What tells the world that we are Christians, and makes them want what we have?

- It is not having the right doctrines (though truth is important).
- It is not where we stand on political or social issues.
- It is not who we disagree with—or how loudly we disagree.
- It is love and the unity that love fosters. It is humility, gentleness, patience, and bearing with each other.

The more we love, the more united we are. And the more united we are, the more the world will know that the Father sent the Son and loves Him…and us.

Love comes from God. The more connected we are to Him, the more we are able to love others. The more we love others, the more united we are. The more united we are, the more His Word and His love spreads, and the world is changed.

Or, to paraphrase Yoda, "Loving are we, and when together we stand, very strong on the world is our impact."

---

[368] John 17:23
[369] Ephesians 4:1–3
[370] John 13:35

Kingdom Thinking: What is one way you can be more united with fellow believers?

Buzz Lightyear Astro Blasters

Choose Your Targets Well

Buzz Lightyear Astro Blasters now sits where two previous attractions (well, one attraction and one attraction queue) once did. The first attraction to occupy this space was Circarama/Circle-Vision 360, an Opening Day attraction. Technically it was "Opening Day Plus One" (as *The Disneyland Encyclopedia* calls it), but that's pretty close. Circle-Vision showed various films on the unique 360° screens until the attraction ended in September of 1997.

The space was repurposed in 1998 for part of the queue for the ill-fated Rocket Rods. That lasted only until 2000, and then the space sat vacant for a few years. Finally, in March of 2005, Buzz Lightyear Astro Blasters opened!

The queue for this attraction is another feature that makes it fun. If you are a fan of the *Toy Story* movies, you'll enjoy lots of nods to them while in line—both subtle and obvious.

Buzz Lightyear Astro Blasters opened first at Walt Disney World in 1998, and proved to be so popular that it was "cloned" at Disneyland. Now it also exists in Hong Kong Disneyland, Tokyo Disneyland (which actually opened before Disneyland's), and Disneyland Paris. In 2005, Disney also debuted a home version of the ride as an Internet game that allowed users to connect with guests at the parks. The actions and scores of each affected the other.

The Disneyland version of this attraction includes a couple of major benefits/improvements over the Walt Disney World (WDW) version. At WDW the laser blasters are mounted on the vehicle, which severely limits their range of motion and makes targeting difficult. At Disneyland, they can be removed from their mounts and are tethered by a cable.

In addition, at WDW all the targets are circles and those that are farther away and those that are moving are worth more points. At Disneyland there are four shapes, and (with some rare exceptions) each is worth a specific number of points. Circles are 100 points, squares are 1,000 points, diamonds are 5,000 points, and triangles are 10,000 points. This point system makes strategy much easier. Here's mine:

There are circle targets all over and they are very easy to hit. I ignore them 99 percent of the time. Why? Consider the point values. Triangles, though rarer and harder to hit, are worth 100 times as much. So for every time I hit a triangle target, I get the same number of points as if I had hit a circle target 100 times. No matter how difficult they are to hit, I can get many more points from triangle targets (I promise you I can hit three triangle targets more easily than I can hit 300 circles).

It's definitely worth "setting your sights higher" and the same principle is true in your life. Consider these words:

> Let us fix our eyes on Jesus, the author and perfecter of our faith, who for the joy set before Him endured the cross, scorning its shame, and sat down at the right hand of the throne of God.[371]

> Not that I have already obtained all this, or have already been made perfect, but I press on to take hold of that for which Christ Jesus took hold of me. Brothers, I do not consider myself yet to have taken hold of it. But one thing I do:

---

[371] Hebrews 12:2

> Forgetting what is behind and straining toward what is ahead,
> I press on toward the goal to win the prize for which God has
> called me heavenward in Christ Jesus.[372]

When you face trials and struggles, where is your focus? Do
you focus on the problem, or on a quick-fix solution? That's the
low-point, easy-to-hit target. It's harder to look higher, and to aim
higher. But that's what Jesus did in his incredibly valuable work on
our behalf. So we fix our eyes on Him, as our example and our
strength.

When you dream of the future, are you aiming for the low-
point targets that you know you can hit, or do you press on toward
"God-size dreams"? Eternal life is about as big as dreams come,
and as believers that's what we have been promised. But on top of
that, we have also been promised abundant life here. That does not
mean an easy life, nor does it even necessarily mean "success" as
the world defines it. It means fully living out who God made you
to be.

It is easier to be average. There is more perceived safety in
being mediocre. The problem is, God did not design you for
mediocrity. You may be "average" in some respects (we are all
human), but you can use what God has given you to excel and
strive for the prize. So shoot for the high-value targets!

Kingdom Thinking: Is it easier to aim for the high-value
targets in the good times or the bad ones? How have you done it
recently?

---

[372] Philippians 3:12–14

Defining Success

In a previous section, as well as in my first book, *Once Upon YOUR Time*,[373] I wrote about my strategy for getting a high score on Buzz Lightyear Astro Blasters. One thing that makes this attraction rare is that it is both interactive and competitive in nature. Even if you ride alone, there's always the score on the display in front of you to compete against.

The highest score that will display is 999,999. It's certainly possible to get a higher score than that (I've done it), but six digits is as far as the display can go. In fact, theoretically there is no limit to the score you can get. If you are in the right places long enough, a score well into the millions is conceivable.

If that's the case, then what's the goal when riding? It can't be "to get the highest possible score," because there isn't one. So what do you consider a success when riding? Is it:

- A higher score than last time?
- Hitting a particularly difficult target for the first time?
- Hitting a certain target (or type of target) multiple times?
- Getting a higher rank?
- Scoring into the millions?
- Getting a higher score than the person you are riding with?

Your definition of success here cannot be "the highest conceivable score," because that will always be out of your reach. Instead, it must be framed in terms of progress.

Early in my Life Coaching sessions, I always talk with clients about their definition of success and suggest that they incorporate this idea into their definition: "Success is the progressive

---

[373] Randy Crane, *Once Upon YOUR Time* (CreateSpace Independent Publishing Platform, 2012).

realization of a worthy ideal."[374] It is not achieving a specific goal—although accomplishment of a goal *is* the last step in the progressive realization of that goal. It is not perfection. It is making progress on something significant, taking steps, moving forward, taking risks—and the person you are becoming while you move forward.

And what is the most worthwhile goal or ideal there is? Here's what Paul says:

So we make it our goal to please Him, whether we are at home in the body or away from it.[375]

The ultimate goal is to please God. We do that through obedience, which leads to becoming like Jesus. The obedience is not done out of obligation, nor is it to earn salvation, but it is still an important part of our growth as Christians.

To consider today a success, ask yourself if you've made progress. Were you more loving today than yesterday? Did you show more kindness? Did you spend time with God? Did you sense His leading and did you follow it rather than resisting (or did you resist less than yesterday)? Do you have a deeper understanding of God's identity, or your own Supernatural Kingdom Identity? This does not mean having achieved perfection, but rather the "progressive realization" of that most worthwhile goal.

One day your "score" will be off the charts, when "He who began a good work in you [carries] it on to completion until the day of Christ Jesus."[376] Today, seek to be better than yesterday—not for your own glory or to earn anything, but through His

---

[374] Earl Nightingale, *The Strangest Secret* (CreateSpace Independent Publishing Platform, 2012), 3.
[375] 2 Corinthians 5:9
[376] Philippians 1:6

strength, as your part of growing into the "you" God made you to be.

> **Kingdom Thinking:** What is one step you've taken, or will commit to taking today, to move yourself forward in the "progressive realization of that worthwhile goal" of becoming more like Christ?

Afterword

$\mathcal{M}$y hope is that you will continue to come back to *Faith and the Magic Kingdom* to be refreshed, challenged, and encouraged. Take it with you on your next visit to the park and reference it as you walk around. Use it as a devotional book at home. However you use it, I pray that each time you do, God blesses you through it—and from that you can, in turn, be a blessing to those around you.

Walt Disney said that Disneyland will never be complete, and that is true of the stories, the lessons, and the examples we can find in the park as well. If this book spurs your own thinking and you come up with any insights, please share them with me at randy@faithandthemagickingdom.net. I may (with your permission) use it in a future edition of *Faith and the Magic Kingdom*—and of course I'll give credit where credit is due!

That brings us to the end of this unique "tour" of Disneyland, Walt Disney's original Magic Kingdom. My prayer is that through these words you will have gained a new and deeper understanding of who God is and your Supernatural Kingdom Identity in Him, a greater sense of His presence, and a better sense of the stories, history, and lore of Disneyland.

In the alma mater of *The Mickey Mouse Club*, the Mouseketeers do not stop with saying goodbye, because the parting is not permanent. How much more true is that for us as believers? And so in that spirit and with their words, I say to you, dear reader, "See ya real soon!"

Index

G

H

I

About the Author

 Randy Crane is a nationally known speaker, author, and life coach. With the heart of a pastor and teacher, the kindness of a friend, and the willingness to challenge you to reach beyond what you think you can do and be, Randy merges his educational background, his work experience, and his unique blend of passions with a dream for helping others to realize their God-given identity and purpose.

Randy married his wonderful wife, Faye, in November of 2000, and they live in the Orange County, California area. They are active in their church and community—including walking every year in the CHOC/Disneyland Resort Walk in the Park to raise money for Children's Hospital of Orange County. They have two cats, Wall•E and Eve, who keep them almost as busy as kids will someday.

When not doing the work that he loves as a Life and Personal Development Coach, Randy can usually be found helping people with their dream vacations as a travel agent, specializing in Disney destinations & cruises, and in celebration, event, and bucket-list travel.

BOOK RANDY CRANE TO SPEAK AT YOUR NEXT EVENT

When you need to choose a speaker for your next event and you're looking for someone to inspire your audience with a new outlook, a unique perspective, and a greater connection to who they are and who God made them to be, look no further than Randy Crane.

Randy is a highly-regarded speaker, presenting engaging and thought-provoking messages on a variety of topics, mostly (but not exclusively) built around Disneyland. He has a natural rapport and connection with audiences that makes them relate well to him, engage in his presentations, and come away with a fresh understanding of the subject at hand.

Using the magic that is Disney, he is passionate about helping Christians realize and experience their God-given identity and purpose. His messages move listeners from knowledge to understanding to action, motivated not by guilt or achievement, but by a better understanding of who God is and who they are.

No matter the size of your audience, Randy can deliver a customized message of inspiration, hope, encouragement, and challenge for your meeting, retreat, or conference.

If you are looking for a memorable speaker who will leave your audience wanting more, book Randy today!

To see a video of Randy Crane and find out whether he is available for your next meeting, visit his site below. Then contact him by phone or email to schedule a complimentary pre-speech phone interview:

www.LeavingConformityCoaching.com/Speaking/Media
Randy@FaithandtheMagicKingdom.net
(714) 867-7398

TAKE A TOUR OF DISNEYLAND WITH RANDY CRANE

If you are going to Disneyland for the first time, or the 100th time, let Randy Crane be your guide. Randy will be happy to meet you, your family, or your group on the day and time of your choosing and take you on a unique journey through the Park.

You will see Disneyland in ways you've never seen it before, whether you want to experience it from a God's-eye view, a history and "Disney details" perspective, or both! Above and beyond that, Randy will enhance your magical experience by minimizing your wait times and maximizing your fun.

Contact Randy today for pricing and availability:

Randy@FaithandtheMagicKingdom.net
(714) 867-7398

Made in the USA
Coppell, TX
08 December 2020

43514974R00213